Housing and Welfare in Southern Europe

Judith Allen
Principal Lecturer in Housing, University of Westminster, London

James Barlow
Professor of Technology and Innovation Management, Imperial College, London

Jesús Leal
Professor and Director of the Department of Sociology II, Universidad Complutense de Madrid

Thomas Maloutas
Professor of Urban Social Geography, University of Thessaly, Volos and Director of the Institute of Urban and Rural Sociology, National Centre for Social Research (EKKE), Athens

Liliana Padovani
Associate Professor in Urban and Regional Policies, Iuav, University of Venice

Blackwell Publishing

Editorial offices:
Blackwell Publishing Ltd, 9600 Garsington Road, Oxford OX4 2DQ, UK
Tel: +44 (0)1865 776868
Blackwell Publishing Inc., 350 Main Street, Malden, MA 02148-5020, USA
Tel: +1 781 388 8250
Blackwell Publishing Asia Pty Ltd, 550 Swanston Street, Carlton, Victoria 3053, Australia
Tel: +61 (0)3 8359 1011

First published 2004 by Blackwell Publishing Ltd

Library of Congress Cataloging-in-Publication Data
Housing and welfare in Southern Europe/Judith Allen ... [et al.].
p. cm. – (Real estate issues)
Includes bibliographical references and index.
ISBN 1-4051-0307-8 (alk. paper)
1. Housing – Europe, Southern. 2. Public welfare – Europe, Southern. 3. Family – Europe, Southern. 4. Housing policy – Europe, Southern. 5. Housing – Europe – Cross-cultural studies. I. Allen, Judith, 1945– II. Real estate issues (Oxford, England).

HD7332.A3H677 2004
363.5′094 – dc22
2003069152

ISBN 1-4051-0307-8

A catalogue record for this title is available from the British Library

Set in 10/13 Trump Mediaeval
by DP Photosetting, Aylesbury, Bucks
Printed and bound in India
by Replika Press Pvt Ltd.,

The publisher's policy is to use permanent paper from mills that operate a sustainable forestry policy, and which has been manufactured from pulp processed using acid-free and elementary chlorine-free practices. Furthermore, the publisher ensures that the text paper and cover board used have met acceptable environmental accreditation standards.

For further information visit our website:
www.thatconstructionsite.com

RICS **FOUNDATION**

The **RICS Foundation** was established by the Royal Institution of Chartered Surveyors to promote and highlight the importance of the built and natural environment. The RICS Foundation supports and develops programmes of research to explore the key issues relevant to the way in which we manage, finance, plan and construct our built and natural environment, to make best and most effective use of the resources available to us.

Real Estate Issues

Series Managing Editors

Stephen Brown RICS Foundation

John Henneberry Department of Town & Regional Planning, University of Sheffield

David Ho School of Design & Environment, National University of Singapore

Real Estate Issues is an international book series presenting the latest thinking into how real estate markets operate. The books have a strong theoretical basis – providing the underpinning for the development of new ideas.

The books are inclusive in nature, drawing both upon established techniques for real estate market analysis and on those from other academic disciplines as appropriate. The series embraces a comparative approach, allowing theory and practice to be put forward and tested for their applicability and relevance to the understanding of new situations. It does not seek to impose solutions, but rather provides a more effective means by which solutions can be found. It will not make any presumptions as to the importance of real estate markets but will uncover and present, through the clarity of the thinking, the real significance of the operation of real estate markets.

Books in the series

Guy & Henneberry *Development and Developers*
Adams & Watkins *Greenfields, Brownfields and Housing Development*
O'Sullivan & Gibb *Housing Economics and Public Policy*
Couch, Fraser & Percy *Urban Regeneration in Southern Europe*
Leece *Economics of the Mortgage Market*
Evans *Economics and Land Use Planning*
Evans *Economics, Real Estate and the Supply of Land*
Byrne & Matysiak *Real Estate Investment*
Seabrooke, Kent & Hwee-Hong How *International Real Estate*
Ball *Markets and Institutions in Real Estate and Construction*
Dixon, McAllister, Marston & Snow *Real Estate in the New Economy*
Adams, Watkins & White *Planning, Public Policy and Property Markets*
McGough & Tsolacos *Real Estate Market Analysis and Forecasting*

Contents

Preface

This book was born from a shared interest in housing in Europe. Collectively, we have several decades' experience of housing research within our individual countries and on a comparative basis across Europe. The scale of our interests ranges from housing systems as a whole to households. Their scope embraces economic, sociological and political aspects of housing. When starting this book we were, however, frustrated that despite the now voluminous literature arising from the comparative housing research of the past two decades, little had been published on *southern* Europe, either in English (and therefore accessible to a wide audience), or adopting the cross-national research perspectives found in work on the northern countries. Indeed, there is more comparative research on housing in the transitional economies of central and eastern Europe than on the southern European countries.

Our individual experiences in our home countries made us aware that the relationships between the state, the market and civil society are rather different in the south from those in the north. This *should*, we felt, mean that the way housing is provided and consumed would be distinctive in southern Europe. We therefore embarked on a journey to explore this question, a journey that has led to this book, but one that proved far longer than any of us initially expected. This was for two reasons. First, the complexity of the relationships between possible explanatory variables led to lengthy debates, conducted with many other researchers and in many contexts. Second, this was compounded by a lack of readily available data on each country. The story we tell in this book therefore describes only part of the picture. We hope that readers will be stimulated to engage in these debates and help fill the holes. Readers from a variety of different backgrounds should find material within this book that points to new research avenues and sheds new light on the links between housing and other features of contemporary economies in general.

This book is likely to be of most direct interest to academics, policy makers and students involved in housing issues. However, the core themes, focusing on the relationships between housing and welfare policy models, will also be of interest to those interested in areas such as the convergence of welfare systems, the changing role of the family in welfare provision and comparative European politics.

From the beginning, our intention was that this book should not be an edited volume of chapters, each written by a different author and loosely bound together around a common theme. Many books purporting to undertake cross-national comparative research take this form. Many are unsatisfactory. Our aim, therefore, was to develop an argument to which we could all contribute, using our specific skills and interests, and which would unfold in the specific chapters. Nevertheless, different voices can be heard throughout, often within a single chapter. This is inevitable, given our various perspectives and our differing disciplinary backgrounds, embracing geography, sociology and economics. Still, any complex piece of work requires some division of labour. Leal was responsible for preparing Chapter 2 and part of Chapter 5. Maloutas took responsibility for Chapter 3 and Chapter 5. Allen prepared Chapter 4 and Padovani looked after Chapter 6. Allen and Barlow have written the introductory and concluding chapters, and Allen has taken responsibility for the continuity and, we hope, coherence of the final product. If our individual voices can be heard, we hope we are singing in harmony around the same tunes which run throughout this book: urbanisation, political and economic change, the nature of the labour market, family and state.

This book reflects five years of dialogue among us. Much of this involved discussions among the southern authors, Leal, Maloutas and Padovani, comparing their countries' experiences, while their northern counterparts, Allen and Barlow, listened. This proved enormously beneficial in allowing us to uncover the similarities and differences among the southern countries. We were all familiar with the comparative housing literature originating in northern Europe. The dialogue helped each of us to identify conventional wisdoms and taken-for-granted assumptions, northern and southern. It also allowed us to develop a collective southern perspective on housing which seemed different from a northern perspective.

Very early on, we discovered the need for help in producing this book. This came in a number of forms and from many people. We benefited enormously from a conference on housing in southern Europe, organised by Leal and held in Madrid. Our thanks go to the sponsors, Banco Argentaria (now BBVA) and Facultad de Ciencias Politicas y Sociologia de la Universidad Complutense de Madrid, and to all those who presented papers and engaged in the debates. Some appear in our bibliography. Early findings from our work were presented at a conference organised by Aurora Pedro and the Department d'Economia Aplicada, Universitat de Valencia, and we gained a great deal from a workshop on Reconceptualising Welfare, organised by Jim Kemeny and Tom Burns at the European University Institute in Florence. The Planning Department at the University of Thessaly in Volos generously supported our work at two workshops organised by Maloutas. Many people also helped us on an individual basis. We are indebted to them all. It is also appropriate to say that, in what has been a collective work, we are grateful to each other for stimulation and critical support throughout the project. Very special thanks go to Sue Balding for editorial support in the final stages of the project. The usual disclaimers apply. Responsibility for any misinterpretations is entirely down to us.

Finally, we began the journey with a Portuguese co-researcher, Teresa Costa-Pinto. She was unable to participate fully in this book because she started a family. We gained hugely from her contribution in the early stages of the research.

If writing this book together has been a journey, then its publication represents arriving at some sort of destination. We hope this is, somehow, an intermediate stop and not the final destination, and we hope that others will join us in continuing the journey.

The Authors

Judith Allen is Principal Lecturer in Housing at the University of Westminster in London. Her main interest is in neighbourhood dynamics, and she is currently managing two cross-national studies funded by the European Commission, one on innovations in neighbourhood management and the other on neighbourhood governance. The results of a previous project on neighbourhoods and social exclusion have been published in *Social Exclusion in European Cities* (London, The Stationery Office, 1998, with Ali Madanipour and Goran Cars) and are available at http://improving-ser.sti.jrc.it. She has worked as a consultant on housing issues in Poland, Estonia and Sweden.

James Barlow is a Professor of Technology and Innovation Management at Imperial College, London, where he co-directs the Built Environment Innovation Centre. He has been involved in research and consultancy on housing, planning and construction issues in Europe and Japan for many years. His housing-related publications include *Success and Failure in Housing Provision: European Systems Compared* (Oxford, Pergamon, 1994, with Simon Duncan), *Public Participation in Urban Development: The European Experience* (London, Policy Studies Institute, 1995) and *Property, Bureaucracy and Culture: The Middle Classes in Contemporary Britain* (London, Routledge, 1992, with Mike Savage, Peter Dickens and Tony Fielding).

Jesús Leal is a Professor and Director of the Department of Sociology II in the Faculty of Sociology and Political Sciences at the Universidad Complutense de Madrid, where he is also the Chairman. He has also been the director of the Housing Plan for Madrid and is the author of numerous books and articles about housing. He co-ordinated the *White Book on Housing* for the Spanish Government in 1992.

Thomas Maloutas is Professor of Urban Social Geography at the University of Thessaly in Volos and currently the Director of the Institute of Urban and Rural Sociology at the National Centre for Social Research (EKKE) in Athens. His work is focused on housing and changing social structures in urban areas. He is the author of several books and articles, including *Housing and Family in Athens: An Analysis of Post-War Housing Practices* (Athens, Exantas, 1990) and his recent publications include the first volume of the *Social and Economic Atlas of Greece* devoted to the cities, for which he was editor, and co-published by the University of Thessaly Press and the National Centre for Social Research in 2000, and the *Atlas de la Grèce*, which he also co-edited, published by the Documentation Française (2003a).

Liliana Padovani is Associate Professor in Urban and Regional Policies at Iuav, University of Venice, Italy. She is a member of the European Urban Research Association's Executive Committee. From 1989 to 2002 she was active as a member of the Coordination Committee of the European Network for Housing Research, ENHR. She has been involved in many housing research projects and has acted as consultant in Italy and abroad. Her publications include *Urban Change and Housing Policies: Evidence from Four European Countries* (Venice, Collana Daest, 1995), the chapter on Italy in *Housing Policy in Europe* (ed. P. Balchin, London, Routledge, 1996) and 'Le partenariat pour rénover l'action publique? L'expérience Italienne' (*Pole Sud*, no. 12 (May), pp. 27–46). She is a member of the editorial advisory board of the *Journal of Housing and the Built Environment*.

1

Introduction

Scope of this book

Since the early 1980s a literature on comparative housing research has emerged which focuses on northern European countries. This has been enormously helpful in overcoming received wisdom about alternative models of housing provision. The work has informed intellectual debates about the relationships between the state, the market and civil society. It has also informed housing policy by drawing attention to alternative practices which may be transferred across borders.

Although research has begun on welfare systems and the development of political systems in southern Europe (cf. Gunther *et al.* 1995; González *et al.* 2000), there has been little comparative research published in English on the provision of housing, where the relationships between the institutions shaping housing systems are rather different from the north (van Vliet 2000). What does exist tends to be in surveys of housing in all European countries – relatively generalised, repetitive and fitted into a framework which rests on housing *tenure* and housing *policy* – or scattered articles arising from debates internal to a specific country. Thus the Italian literature, dominated by a few authors, reflects a coherent dialogue among them. The Greek literature is dominated by economists and is concerned with the outcomes rather than the formulation of policy. The Spanish literature tends to reflect the random nature of what gets published in English-language journals, although Spain has also received some attention from British specialists. There is little on Portugal, other than a few pieces in specialist publications focusing on very specific problems. At the same time, there are vibrant debates within these countries which are not accessible to those who do not read the four languages. The bibliography at the end of this chapter sets out the existing English literature and a selection of the literature covering the most important debates within each of the southern European countries.

The aim of this book is to begin to fill this gap in knowledge. In doing so, we show how there are, indeed, differences between the southern European countries and their northern neighbours. These have not been highlighted before in comparisons of European housing systems. Our focus is on the four main countries within southern Europe: Spain, Portugal, Italy and Greece. Unless otherwise specified, we define 'northern Europe' as the remainder of the countries in the European Union. Many of the published works do not consider these four countries as a differentiated group within the European Union: Greece and Portugal seldom figure in analyses comparing housing while Spain and Italy are only infrequently considered (Oxley & Smith 1996; Ball *et al.* 1988; Kleinman *et al.* 1998). Sometimes they are considered but not as a similar group of countries (Ghékiere 1992).

This book, therefore, provides a much-needed extended treatment of housing in the four countries. As well as describing their key features in detail, we address an apparent paradox which underlies these housing systems. On the one hand, they have managed to meet housing need in a period of immense social change and do so to a quality standard in Spain and Italy which is as good as that of northern Europe. On the other hand, they have achieved this without developing strong social rented housing sectors and in the context of welfare states which are oriented mainly to cash benefits for adult male workers in the formal sector. The key to this paradox, and a fundamental reason why southern European housing systems are different from those in the north, is that their capacity to meet housing need rests on the role of the extended family as the main social institution organising access to housing for its member households. Family strategies combine a variety of housing practices: self-provision, inter-generational sharing, assisting young households with purchase and managing the family's patrimony. As a consequence, the overall configuration of housing policy in these countries can best be understood by exploring the ways in which it interacts with the role of the family in housing provision. This creates a very different kind of space for public action in housing in southern Europe.

There has been a debate on the extent to which European housing policy is converging (cf. Kemeny & Lowe 1998, and Doling 1997 for excellent summaries). We are not engaging in the convergence/divergence argument, although in our conclusions we touch on future trends that might be expected in the southern European countries. Rather, we argue that there are distinctive groups of countries whose evolution can be expected to be different. At times they can be seen to converge in some ways and diverge in others. A weakness of convergence arguments, we believe, is that they assume countries display certain basic similarities, for example 'advanced capitalism', and they tend to rest on a leaders-laggards model which can be questioned (as we do in Chapter 4).

Two comparative arguments are woven together throughout this book. The first is that the housing provision systems in southern European countries are sufficiently different from their northern counterparts to consider them as a separate group within Europe as a whole, and that, at the same time, the similarities among the four southern countries are strong enough to constitute a family resemblance. The second argument is that such a comparison cannot rest on a narrowly drawn conception of housing systems and housing policy. We suggest that housing systems are embedded in wider societal structures. If this is the case, then the *ideas* which are used to understand how housing systems function and interpret the significance of housing policies are also embedded in wider societal structures. The efficacy of ideas based on analysing *northern* European housing systems for analysing *southern* systems is therefore explored alongside the main substantive argument in this book. Thus, the comparative argument must be addressed at several levels: first, at the level of factual evidence on the nature of housing, welfare and family systems across Europe; second, as a critique of the ideas which underlie supposed pan-European comparisons; and third, by pointing out how many of the ideas in current comparative housing literature lead to a procrustean view of housing systems in southern Europe by failing to draw the scope of their analysis widely enough.

Some basic concepts

It is necessary to understand some key concepts in order to fully appreciate the arguments in this book. These are the notions of the family, patrimony, self-promotion and what has been called the 'deficit of stateness' (Ferrera 1996). All of them form the basis for the arguments in subsequent chapters. Here we provide a brief overview of these concepts and the basic reasons why they are important in explaining the specificities of southern European housing systems.

The family

In northern European countries with well-developed welfare states, the concept of family which is most commonly used is better summarised by the word 'household'. The two words, household and family, are used more or less interchangeably in housing discussions. The family-as-household concept is restricted to those persons who reside in the same dwelling, and draws on the core image of the nuclear family, parents and children. There are a number of important consequences of using this concept of family. Basic data sources are organised around it. Demographic projections assume that the nuclear family is a household structure through which individuals move at different stages in their life-cycles. Projections of housing need are based on assumptions about the relationship between dwelling unit and household. Over time, housing policies and provision systems come to be shaped on this basis. At the same time, horizontal and vertical kinship relationships embracing the head of household and/or spouse are treated under the concept of 'extended family'. Extended families living within one dwelling unit are seen as unusual, perhaps even exotic, and most importantly, of no long-run or lasting significance. They can be expected to disappear as housing need is met.

The hidden assumption, therefore, is that the dwelling unit is associated with the household and *only* with the household that resides within it. There are, of course, debates around the edges of this basic assumption. In the United Kingdom, the concept of hidden households was elaborated during the 1970s to support the allocation of social rented housing to young single people leaving home for the first time. The notion of hidden households has also informed discussion of multi-nucleated ethnic minority families, particularly in situations of overcrowding. More recently, the concept of 'homeless at home' has been developed to indicate young, newly formed households living with their parents who have a right to, but are unable to, immediately access social rented housing. Debates over the tenancy rights of gay and lesbian couples are another example of the strength of the family-as-household concept.

Nothing could be more different in southern Europe. The concept of family, first and foremost, relates to the entire set of kinship relationships extending throughout the generations and across all siblings. This meaning is captured in the Italian word, *parentela*. The synonyms for *parentela* in English are: relationship, kinship, affinity, relatives, relations. In fact, the English word for parent translates into Italian as *genitore*, meaning the specific blood relationship between two parents and their children. Similar linguistic distinctions are also made in Spanish, Portuguese and Greek. It is, however, extremely difficult to make this distinction in English. This is not a trivial linguistic excursion, but a fundamental problem in cross-national studies (cf. Allen, 1996, for further discussion).

The distinctive meaning of family is fundamentally important in thinking about housing in southern Europe. In both parts of Europe, the meaning of family carries some of the same connotations, in the sense that it is a group of related people who are responsible for the welfare of its members. The difference lies in the wider southern versus narrower northern criteria for membership of this basic group. The southern meanings are rooted in a much more recent agrarian past, in which production was the function of the family as a whole, and so also rest on a different connection with land. However, what is most crucial is that the extended grouping carries a normative responsibility for the residential living arrangements of its members. This responsibility can pass vertically, through responsibility for younger members who are entering marriage and for elder members who are no longer capable of living independently, and horizontally, taking in siblings, nieces and nephews at all generations. Furthermore, within this concept, there is the implication that property formally owned by any member of the family is, in some ways and in some circumstances, available to other members. In addition, if an extension to property is required for family residential reasons, there is an implicit call on all members of the family to provide resources, such as land, finance, labour or social connections, to acquire such property.

Patrimony

These southern family relationships are strongly associated with the concept of 'patrimony'. The Italian word *patrimonio* translates into English as patrimony, heritage, estate, total assets. (In practice, the word patrimony is seldom used in English.) The term carries implications of inherited, hereditary property, especially real and/or landed property. Thus, it refers directly to the specific stock of housing and land owned by a family. The normative assumptions associated with patrimony are strong. It is something which is not exchanged or traded on markets. Rather, patrimony is something that the family conserves and keeps. The concept thus informs inheritance legislation. There are three legal possibilities, used in different places. The first is that the patrimony will be divided among the owner's children on his death. The second is that it is kept whole and inherited by the first-born male. The third is the possibility of collective inheritance. In these latter two systems, it is not legal to divide the patrimony. Thus, patrimony, as a social institution associated with the family, is seen as being eternal, lasting, continuing much longer in time than the life of any individual within the family. It is, therefore, the specific landed and 'immobile' property which is symbolic of the family, the 'place' of the family in geographical and social space. (The phrase 'real property' in English hardly begins to capture the connotations associated with the term ' immobile property'.)

Patrimony has, thus, both a practical, material aspect and an emotional, symbolic aspect. In agrarian societies, land ownership is a basic survival strategy. Practically, agricultural landholdings have provided sustenance and economic security within the processes of rural to urban migration which have been much more recent in the southern countries. Their importance is especially marked, given the weakness and restricted scope of welfare state systems. Symbolically, keeping the family's house and land in the countryside is emotionally significant. It provides a fixed point in a changing society, and for these reasons, former rural family homes are an important component of the secondary housing stock in all four countries.

There are three implications of this strong interrelationship between patrimony and family practices. First, it affects the provision of houses for younger members of a family who are getting married. In these Catholic and Orthodox countries, cohabitation is extremely rare and the age at which children leave home is very high by European standards. Leaving home is usually associated with marriage, and marriage is associated with access to 'owned' property. Second, the symbolic importance of patrimony accounts for a significant proportion of the second and/or vacant homes found throughout these four countries. These homes in the countryside may not be used, or may only be used during a part of the year or at weekends, but they are seen as a place which must be preserved. In Madrid, for example, many households rent their housing in the city (in order to access urban facilities, jobs and education), returning to their 'own home' for the weekends. Third, patrimony as a basic social institution has far-reaching implications which limit the ways public control over land use can be organised and implemented, as well as how land and property markets function and are institutionalised. For example, it affects the rules which govern the subdivision of agricultural land to absorb urban expansion.

Consequently, land and housing ownership has a specific social significance in southern Europe. Ownership contributes to the family's patrimony. It becomes a normal expectation of family members to accede to ownership. As a consequence, only small and specific social groups are not concerned with owning their home. For example, in north-west Italy, the educated middle class make a trade-off between renting their homes and investing heavily in education. In Greece, small traders make a trade-off between owning their own home and the necessity for liquid capital. But the normal, and normative, expectation is one of home ownership. To emphasise the linkage between the social institutions of family, patrimony and home ownership, southern Europeans sometimes remark, ironically, that in northern Europe, it was necessary to invent the welfare state because of the absence of these 'southern' social institutions.

Self-promotion of housing

The third concept which underlies housing provision in southern Europe is 'self-promotion'. This concept draws out some of the housing implications of the discussion of family and patrimony. The motivation for self-promotion arises from the family's responsibility to provide for its members and conserve its patrimony. The term 'self' in self-promotion, therefore, refers more precisely to the family located within a community (Tosi 1995).

The capability for self-promotion arises from rural traditions of self-provision or self-building. These traditions have been taken into and adapted to urban situations. The necessity for self-promotion arose from the weakness of certain market mechanisms, in particular, formal credit systems. At the same time, self-promotion is supported by weak systems of public control over land development. The weakness of the control systems can also lead to illegal or irregular development, that is, housing development without the appropriate formal permissions. This is often, in turn, related to weaknesses in coordinating systems of urban infrastructure provision and land release.

The four countries vary in the extent to which self-promotion has been important and in the circumstances where it has been used. In Italy, 10 to 15% of all housing provision has been illegal, primarily concentrated in the south, but rising to 50% of the development around Rome at some points in time. The system of irregular/illegal development became so institutionalised in Italy that a system of *condono* was also institutionalised to acknowledge and deal with the consequent problems of infrastructure and property rights. In Greece, informal systems of self-promotion were supported by the use of public land, particularly around Athens, which absorbed a third of the 1.5 million Greeks who were repatriated in a period of two to three years following the collapse of the Ottoman Empire at the end of World War I. The system developed at that time provided a model for the subdivision of land by large landowners in the 1960s when 1.5 million rural migrants arrived in Athens, swelling its population from 1 million in 1951 to 3 million in 1981. Self-promotion was also a vehicle for absorbing remittances from Greeks working abroad, resulting in Greece having the highest rates of housebuilding per 1000 households anywhere in Europe (Leontidou 1990; Ambrose & Barlow 1987). In Portugal, many rural immigrants built their own homes and neighbourhoods (*clandestinos*) and more recently large-scale immigration from the former colonies supported the development of *barracas* concentrated around Lisbon and Porto. A major public programme now aims to provide new housing for 40 000 households living in *barracas* (Freitas 1998). There is now relatively little self-promotion of any kind in Spain, which is attributed to much stronger institutionalised links between large promoters and urban land release systems, as well as the strength of its mortgage lending system, which was strategically restructured in the 1980s.

The tradition of self-promotion also supports more collectivised forms of provision in urban areas. The Greek *anti-parochi* system, a cashless deal between landowners and builders for the construction of multi-family housing in which the builder is paid through the ownership of one or more flats after completion, can be seen as an urban variant of self-promotion. *Anti-parochi* is now less used, but still an important way of organising housing production. Similarly, co-operative development in Italy, which captures economies of scale in building multi-family housing while sustaining a form of private owner occupation after development, can also be seen in this light.

The 'deficit of stateness'

The pattern of political administrative capabilities in different European states can be seen as explaining some differences in housing systems. Two significant differences between northern and southern Europe tend to be highlighted. The first is the weakness of formal legal controls over land use and development, and the second is the absence of a large social rented sector. However, these differences need to be set within the social and historical contexts which have shaped southern European political and housing systems. Home ownership has been accessible to a wide range of social strata within public action systems which have delivered significant increases in the quantity and quality of housing. This process may be relevant to the changing context in northern Europe.

Of particular importance is the way rural to urban migration has occurred in the southern European countries. As well as being a more recent phenomenon, the context within which this migration has taken place is one of structural economic change not from agriculture to industry, but from an agricultural to a service-based economy. This means that the fordist industrialisation which underpinned the development of welfare states in parts of northern Europe has been largely missing in the southern countries. Of course, in each of the four southern countries, there are highly industrialised regions, in northern Spain, northern Italy, around Saloniki in Greece and Lisbon in Portugal. But developing a comprehensive, tax-based fordist-type national welfare state would have strongly intensified inter-regional conflicts. Thus, the historical geography of economic development in the four southern countries partly explains why their welfare states have been contained within corporatist, occupationally-based schemes.

These specific histories have also supported specific kinds of political relationships, based on the concentration of power within local government, the predominance of political parties as the main actors for interest aggregation and a largely non-Weberian state bureaucracy. This type of political environment accounts for a number of the specific features of the housing systems in the four countries. Thus, the weakness of the local implementation of formal central legislative controls over land development and use is not surprising in systems in which locality, community, family and self-promotion are closely intertwined (Tosi 1995).

Both Italy and Spain successfully relied on income tax relief subsidies for owner occupation in order to mobilise a mass of small private actors to address problems of housing shortage and quality. This can be seen as a very efficient strategy in societies in which self-promotion was a normal method of production. Both these undifferentiated subsidy systems overshot the mark in the late 1970s, thus accounting for a part of the current stock of second homes in both countries. Latterly, both countries have developed more differentiated subsidy systems, but the persistence of this type of subsidy as a main policy plank can be attributed both to the underlying social significance of land and housing ownership, and to the pattern of political administrative capabilities in these societies.

Similarly, the very small scale of social rented housing in the four countries is explicable in terms of broader political and social structures. To some extent, social rented housing is a problem rather than a solution in these structures. At the local level, clientelistic political systems create basic problems of managing social housing. For example, allocating it to households can become a source of political dissent which cannot be easily managed, as is currently the case in northern Italy. Here, the equally serious housing needs of recent immigrants, of those being evicted from the private rented sector and of low-paid workers are underpinning the emergence of racially-based social conflicts. In Portugal, there is serious political concern that the social rented stock (3.5% of all households) is becoming associated with issues of social exclusion, which, in turn, seems to be associated with the marginalised position of its tenants. It can also be argued that Spain rapidly developed a sophisticated mortgage finance system in the 1980s partly in response to a hard-headed assessment of the capability of the government to manage the small existing stock, owned and managed by the central government under Franco, in a context of radical devolution of government to the autonomous regions. Finally, there is a set of difficult, long-run issues of governance, managerial and financial capacity associated with reinvestment in social rented housing. The advantage of policy strategies which rely primarily on owner occupation and private renting is that political issues tend to be more manageable.

Structure of this book

The basic concepts we have just described represent core themes which appear at different levels of detail throughout the chapters in this book. There are six main chapters which move from a description of how southern European housing differs from housing in the north, through a discussion of key concepts for explaining these characteristics, to a detailed analysis of southern housing.

Chapter 2 is essentially descriptive. It serves as a general introduction to the remainder of this book and identifies four features of southern European housing systems which distinguish them from those in northern Europe: tenure mix, secondary housing, family and household cycles, housing production and promotion. It also comments on the adequacy of some of the key ideas in the general housing literature for interpreting the differences between European countries and sets the stage for the wider arguments to be developed in the remaining chapters.

Chapter 3 begins to develop the more general argument of this book. It discusses the role of housing in articulating urbanisation and economic change in southern Europe and introduces the broad demographic patterns which have an impact on housing. It concludes by showing how these broad processes can be articulated in various ways within specific systems by discussing the very different spatial patterns of urban development in Athens and Madrid.

The purpose of Chapter 4 is to set out a theoretical framework for analysing housing in southern Europe and offer reasons why it needs to be seen as fundamentally different rather than as simply a variant on a general European model. It argues that there is a distinctive southern welfare system which affects housing policy, provision and practices. This chapter uses two large-scale quantitative studies of welfare policy published during the 1990s to position the southern European welfare systems in a cross-national context. It then discusses three social institutions which shape their welfare systems: familialism, the capacity of their civil administration, and the significance of the irregular and informal sector within a strongly dualistic labour market. This enables us to clarify some of the conceptual issues associated with analysing welfare systems in southern Europe and establishes the context for a more detailed consideration of southern housing systems in Chapters 5 and 6.

Chapter 5 comprises a more detailed discussion of the relationship between family structures, housing and social cohesion. It shows how the southern European family represents a way of supporting traditional forms of social cohesion and, in doing so, provides a vehicle for creating access to housing for its members. The social meaning of owner occupation is, thus, deeply rooted in concepts of family and patrimony in the wider context of restricted welfare state mechanisms.

Chapter 6 turns to the role of public action in housing provision. We have already noted that the lack of social rented housing and high levels of owner occupation are defining features of southern European housing systems. This chapter describes why state intervention in housing has a different pattern in southern Europe. In particular, it shows why a state-centric view of housing policy cannot explain how public action mobilises a variety of actors and is oriented to provide resources which families use to improve their own welfare.

Finally, in Chapter 7 we draw conclusions on the core questions we have posed. How and why are southern European housing systems different from those in northern Europe? We also consider the way current economic, demographic and social trends may impact on the nature of southern European housing in the future, raising questions over the capacities of the welfare system and family structures to adapt to future challenges.

Bibliography

Greece

Economou, D. (1987) Housing policy in post-war Greece: basic interpretations, housing credit and policies for the rented sector. *The Greek Review of Social Research* **64**, 56–129 [in Greek].

Economou, D. (1988) Land and housing system. In: *Problems of Welfare State Development in Greece* (T. Maloutas & D. Economou, eds). Exandus, Athens, 57–114 [in Greek].

Emmanuel, D. (2002) Social segregation, polarization and inequality in the geography of Athens: The role of housing market and development mechanisms (1980–2000). *Geographies* **3**, 46–70 [in Greek].

Emmanuel, D., Velidis, S., & Strousopoulou, E. (1996) *The Housing of Low Revenue Households in Greece*. DEPOS, Athens [in Greek].

Leontidou, L. (1990) *The Mediterranean City in Transition*. Cambridge University Press, Cambridge.

Maloutas, T. (1990) *Housing and Family in Athens: An Analysis of Post-war Housing Practices*. Exantas, Athens [in Greek].

Maloutas, T. (2000) Housing tenure. In: *Social and Economic Atlas of Greece. Vol. 1: The Cities* (T. Maloutas, ed.). University of Thassaly Press, Athens and Volos: National Centre for Social Research (EKKE), pp. 66–7 [in Greek].

Maloutas, T. (2004) Segregation and residential mobility: spatially entrapped social mobility and its impact on segregation in Athens. *European Urban and Regional Studies* **11** (2), 171–187.

Italy

Cer Ministero LLPP (1996) *Rapporto sulla condizione abitativa in Italia*. Rapporto per Habitat II, Rome.

Cnel (1995) *La politica abitativa in Italia*, Documenti Cnel n. 79. Cnel, Rome.

Coppo, M. & Cremaschi, M. (eds) (1994) *Strutture territoriali e questione abitativa: evoluzione storica e dimensioni locali del problema della casa nel dopoguerra*. Angeli, Milan.

Tosi, A. (1994a) *Abitanti: le nuove strategie dell'azione abitativa*. Il Mulino, Bologne.

Tosi, A. (ed.) (1994b) *La casa: il rischio e l'esclusione: rapporto IRS sul disagio abitativo in Italia*, for Caritas italiana. Angeli, Milan.

Urbanistica (1994) n. 102, special issue 'La casa 1 nuovi termini della questione' edited by A. Tosi. See articles by M. Coppo, 'Mercato, politiche ed evoluzione del sistema abitativo', 10–15; G. Roma, 'Domanda marginale di abitazione e politiche urbane', 16–17; L. Seassaro, 'Continuità e discontinuità nelle politiche della casa – Un'interpretazione', 17–22; M. Cremaschi, 'La denazionalizzazione del problema abitativo', 23–8; A. Tosi, 'Un problema di povertà', 29–37.

Spain

Cortes, L. (1995) *La Cuestión Residencial: Bases Para una Sociología del Habitar*. Ed. Fundamentos, Madrid.

Leal, J. (1987) El boom inmobiliario madrileño: Precios altos para rentas bajas. *Alfoz* **46**, 23–84.

Leal, J. (1992) *Informe para una nueva política de vivienda*. Ministerio de Obras Públicas y Transportes, Madrid.

Leal, J. (1995) La cuestión de la vivienda o la vivienda como problema social. In: *Pensar la vivienda* (L. Cortés & J. Leal, eds). Ed. Talasa, Madrid, 17–30.

Pedro, A. & Sanchís, J. (eds) (2000) *Problemas de acceso al mercado de la vivienda en la Unión Europea*. Ed. Tirant lo Blanch, Valencia.

Rafols, J. (ed.) (1997) *Politica d'habitage en l'Estat de les autonomies*. Institut d'Estudis Autonòmics, Generalitat de Catalunya, Barcelona.

Rodriguez, J. (1990) La politica de vivienda en España: una aproximación a los principales instrumentos. *Revista Española de Financiación a la Vivienda* **12**, 11–24.

Santillana del Barrio, A. (1972) *Análisis económico del problema de la vivienda*. Ediciones Ariel, Barcelona.

Taltavull, P. (2000) La situación de la vivienda en España. In: *Vivienda y Familia* (P. Taltavull, ed.). Argentaria, Visor, Madrid.

2

Are Southern Housing Systems Different?

Introduction

The general argument in this book is that housing systems and policy in southern Europe can only be understood within their broader societal context. The most important aspect of this context is the nature of the relationship between the extended southern family and what may be characterised as a southern welfare system. The purpose of this chapter is twofold: first, to set out the key differences between housing systems in southern and northern Europe and, second, to provide a set of observations about these aspects of housing systems in southern Europe as a basis for the wider argument developed in the remaining chapters.

Four aspects of housing systems in southern Europe are distinctive. These are high rates of home ownership coupled with little social housing, the significance of secondary housing, the relationship between access to housing and household cycles, and the role of families in housing production. This chapter looks at each of these aspects in turn.

Tenure patterns in southern Europe

A home is more than a shelter satisfying a basic human need. It is also where people gain their sense of identity and establish their family relationships. The ways in which people gain access to their housing also help to define their relationship to it. An important aspect of access to housing is housing tenure, defined as the legal form or status that enables the occupant to enjoy the use value of the house. A household can be the owner of its home, residing in a rented home, or in other special conditions where its home is free because it is related to their place of work or because it belongs to another family member who allows them to live there. Understanding patterns of tenure helps us to understand better the conception of the home in different countries as well as the characteristics of households and the relationship between them and their homes.

This section of the chapter sets out the tenure patterns in southern Europe and contrasts them with patterns elsewhere in the European Union. It then discusses some of the ways of explaining the most striking characteristic of tenure patterns in southern Europe: high levels of home ownership combined with very low levels of social housing provision.

Table 2.1 shows that the four southern countries have high rates of home ownership. Three of the four countries lie above the median rate for Europe, and Portugal is the median country. Spain has the highest rate in Europe, and Greece ranks joint second with Ireland.

Higher home ownership implies a smaller rented sector. Table 2.2 shows clearly that Spain, Italy and Greece have the smallest rented sectors in the European Union while Portugal has a larger rented sector, reflecting its lower rate of home ownership.

What distinguishes the four southern countries from the other countries with high rates of home ownership is that they all have an exceptionally small social rented sector. Table 2.3 shows this clearly by setting out the

Table 2.1 Housing tenure, European Union countries, circa 2000.

Country	Owner occupied	Social rented	Private rented	Other
Spain (98)	82	1	10	7
Greece (90)	78	0	22	0
Italy (98)	69	5	11	15
Portugal (98)	64	3	25	8
Ireland (98)	78	9	16	3
Belgium (00)	74	7	16	3
Luxembourg (95)	70	3	27	0
United Kingdom (01)	69	22	9	0
Finland (97)	60	14	16	10
Austria (98)	56	21	20	3
France (96)	54	17	21	8
Netherlands (00)	53	36	11	0
Denmark (00)	51	19	26	4
Germany (98)	43	7	50	0
Sweden (90)	41	27	13	19

Source: adapted from Fribourg (2002, p. 3); for Greece, data is from Haffner (1998, p. 46). The year to which the data refer is in parentheses against the name of the country.

Table 2.2 Rented housing as a percentage of all housing, European Union countries, circa 2000.

Country	Social rented	Private rented	All rented
Spain (98)	1	10	11
Italy (98)	5	11	16
Greece (90)	0	22	22
Portugal (98)	3	25	28
Belgium (00)	7	16	23
Ireland (98)	9	16	25
Luxembourg (95)	3	27	30
Finland (97)	14	16	30
United Kingdom (01)	22	9	31
France (96)	17	21	38
Sweden (90)	27	13	40
Austria (98)	21	20	41
Denmark (00)	19	26	45
Netherlands (00)	36	11	47
Germany (98)	7	50	57

Source: adapted from Fribourg (2002, p. 3); for Greece, data is from Haffner (1998, p. 46). The year to which the data refer is in parentheses against the name of the country.

Table 2.3 Social rented housing units per 1000 inhabitants, European Union countries, circa 2000.

Country	Units per 1000 inhabitants
Greece	0
Spain	3
Portugal	12
Italy	16
Luxembourg	9
Belgium	26
Ireland	27
Germany (former FRG)	30
Finland	48
France	71
United Kingdom	92
Austria	94
Denmark	94
Sweden	105
Netherlands	149

Source: adapted from Fribourg (2002, p. 7).

number of social rented units per 1000 inhabitants. The low rates of social housing in Spain and Italy are partly a consequence of policies of selling much of what has been built as social housing. Greece has minimal social housing and the small, continuing programme in Portugal is primarily aimed at clearing squatter settlements in the two main cities. Chapter 6 discusses housing policy in all four countries in detail, but it is worth noting here that both Spain and Italy use deep subsidies to promote home ownership among low-income groups that would otherwise live in social rented housing elsewhere in Europe.

The choices facing households in southern Europe are primarily between home ownership, private renting or the tenures classified as 'other', that is, tenures which are unique to each country. However, the balance has tipped decisively towards home ownership over the past 50 years. In most European countries there has been a transition from the majority of homes being rented, to owner occupation being the main form of access to a home. There are important exceptions to this: Germany and Switzerland still have a high proportion of rented homes. Of the 12 European countries for which data are available, only Greece and Finland had more than 50% home ownership in 1950. By the year 2000, only Germany and Sweden had less than 50%. Over the whole period, Spain showed the highest rate of growth in home ownership. Its rate of growth was matched only by Italy, Belgium and the United Kingdom. The period of most rapid growth in Spain was between 1960 and 1980, and in Italy between 1950 and 1960. In contrast, growth in the United Kingdom has been concentrated in the period since 1975 and in Belgium between 1990 and 1995 (Fribourg 2002, author's data for Greece).

Thus, the distinctive tenure pattern in the four southern European countries combines high rates of home ownership and smaller rented sectors, in particular, a very small social rented sector. Two of the countries, Spain and Italy, experienced high rates of growth in owner occupation relatively early after World War II while Greece has always had a very high rate of owner occupation. (Data on the growth of owner occupation in Portugal and detailed time series for Greece since 1950 are not available.)

Countries of home owners

The distinctive tenure pattern in the southern countries raises two problems. The first is to explain why they have come to have this pattern in comparison with the other countries in Europe, and the second is to explain its social meaning in the context of the southern societies. The most general explanations tend to weave these two problems together by focusing on identifying a distinctive role for home ownership in the four southern countries.

Forrest *et al.* (1990) capture the complexity of home ownership as a tenure by distinguishing four approaches which have been used to analyse it. The first approach focuses on individual choices and preferences, and emphasises the parameters influencing individuals' decision-making processes: proximity to work place, cost of living, availability of services, and so on. The second approach sees social differentiation in home ownership as the result of generalised constraints on access and availability which affect different social groups as, for example, in Rex and Moore's (1967) concept of housing classes which rests on both bureaucratic allocation systems and market processes. The third approach suggests that home ownership and competition for housing are formed by public and private sector institutions operating within state policies. These institutions have the capacity to isolate areas within the city and mark them as unpopular. They influence the market by influencing potential owners. This approach explains discriminatory processes in housing distribution and access, especially for ethnic minority groups. The fourth approach claims that all patterns of home ownership and housing markets are ultimately determined by the capitalist economic system. Within this approach, housing is seen primarily as a commodity and decisions about housing access, production, and so on are reduced to considerations of profitability. Home ownership is preferred by the state because it generates social stability which is a precondition for maintaining the capitalist system. A variant on this perspective sees housing as a major item of consumption in all modern capitalist societies where individuals are increasingly defined by their levels and types of consumption. This view links increases in home ownership with the commodification of housing in modern societies and argues that, as a consequence, housing policy issues become framed simply in terms of consumption (Saunders 1984, but cf. the critique by King 1996).

For the purpose of comparing the meaning of home ownership among and within groups of European countries, the third and fourth approaches are the most useful because they emphasise the level and type of state intervention which, in turn, reflect different basic conceptions of the relationship between housing and welfare states (see Chapters 3, 4 and 6). However, the other approaches are more useful for looking at the linkages between households and housing (see Chapter 5).

The remainder of this section reviews four explanations for the relatively high levels of home ownership in southern Europe. The first rests on the idea of a home ownership culture. The second explains high levels of home ownership in terms of historical patterns of urbanisation. The third emphasises tenure policies and the fourth turns around the concept of housing provision systems. None of these explanations is fully adequate, but assessing their strengths and weaknesses helps to clarify the questions that are addressed in the remainder of this book.

Home ownership culture

Castles and Ferrera (1996), Morvonnais (1998) and Moreno (2000) claim there is a Mediterranean culture which explains home ownership in southern Europe, set against a general European culture found in the continental countries. In the southern countries, people prefer home ownership because it is part of their cultural heritage. Reference to a Mediterranean culture as a way of explaining the difference between northern and southern countries in Europe is also commonplace in political discourse within the four countries. Home ownership and the widespread ownership of second homes (discussed below) are considered as expressions of that cultural difference. It is true that after a long period of time some housing practices can become part of a culture but, in this case, arguing that home ownership is a cultural phenomenon hides the underlying reasons for the difference. If we consider that in 1950 home ownership was less than 50% in three of the countries, some of the problems with the cultural argument become clear. It can equally well be argued that a culture of home ownership is the result of a generalised response by households in the context of housing policies and markets which offered no alternatives. A home ownership culture in these circumstances would be a consequence rather than a cause of policy.

Historical patterns of urbanisation

The high levels of home ownership locate the cause of the differences between southern and northern Europe in broad socio-economic processes. In this form of explanation, the pattern of urbanisation is of particular significance. We develop this explanation more fully in Chapter 3, but four aspects of the process are worth noting here:

(1) With the exception of northern Italy, urban growth has taken place later in southern Europe than in northern Europe. Southern European countries are still among the countries having the lowest proportion of urban population in Europe, as Table 2.4 shows. Urban growth has primarily been related to migration from rural areas to the cities. In Spain, Italy and Greece, the highest rates of urban growth occurred between 1950 and 1980 and in Portugal, large-scale urban growth only started in 1980. Figure 2.1 sets this out graphically.

(2) Urban growth in the south has been associated with a shift in employment structure from the agricultural to service sector. In northern Europe, urban growth was associated with a shift from agriculture to manufacturing employment which was almost complete

Table 2.4 Population living in urban areas, southern and northern Europe, 1950–2000.

Country	Percentage of total population living in urban areas					
	1950	1960	1970	1980	1990	2000
Greece	37	43	53	58	59	60
Italy	54	59	64	67	67	67
Portugal	19	22	26	29	47	64
Spain	52	57	66	73	75	78
Remainder of European Union	71	75	80	82	85	84

Source: United Nations (2002).

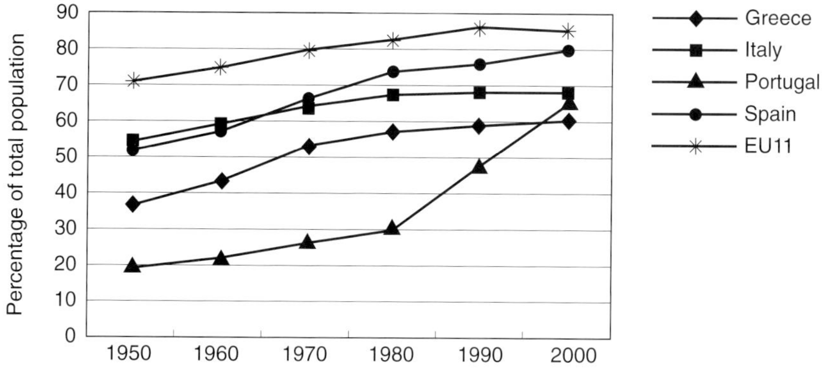

Fig. 2.1 Urbanisation in southern and northern Europe, 1950–2000. Source: United Nations (2002).

before World War II. Figure 2.2 compares the broad structure of employment in 1960 and 1993 in the southern countries with the four northern countries which were most industrialised in 1960. All four of the northern countries had started to de-industrialise by the 1960s, a process which was speeded up by the oil crisis in 1974. In contrast, the four southern countries had relatively high agricultural employment in 1960 and were still industrialising. Although they experienced some de-industrialisation after 1974, the scale was less. The most important change in the southern countries was a shift from agricultural to service sector employment. Table 2.5 gives the details of these changes. The lower level of industrialisation altogether led to a lower level of state intervention in housing to cater for the housing needs of an industrial workforce. The provision of social rented housing in northern Europe, in contrast, had its roots in pressures by industrial capital to reduce the cost of labour.

(3) Most of the southern countries did not suffer significant destruction of their housing stock during World War II. This was either because

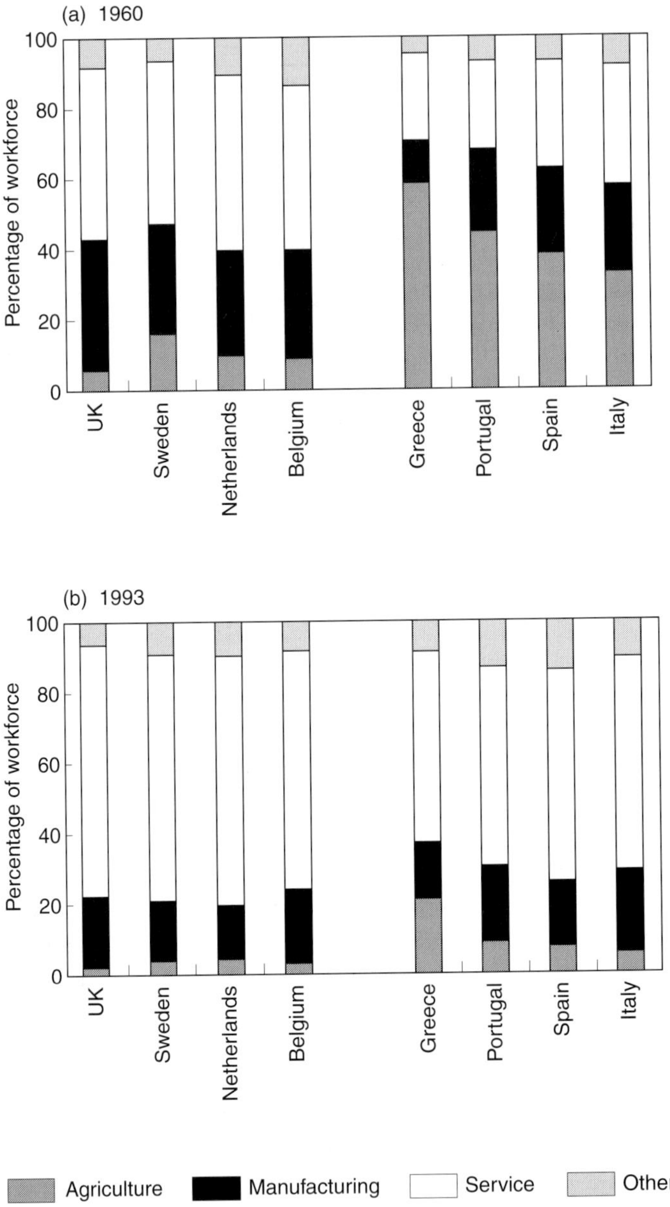

Fig. 2.2 Employment structure: industrialised versus southern countries, 1960 and 1993 (% of workforce by economic sector). Source: adapted from Castles (1998).

Table 2.5 Employment structure: industrialised versus southern countries, 1960, 1974 and 1993.

Country	Percentage of total workforce in:								
	Agriculture			Manufacturing			Service sector		
	1960	1974	1993	1960	1974	1993	1960	1974	1993
United Kingdom	4.7	2.8	2.2	38.4	34.6	20.2	47.6	55.2	71.6
Sweden	15.7	6.7	3.4	31.5	28.3	17.2	44.0	56.3	71.1
Netherlands	9.8	5.7	3.9	29.7	25.7	16.4	49.7	58.4	71.5
Belgium	8.7	3.8	2.6	30.6	31.2	21.6	46.3	55.2	67.9
Greece	57.1	36.0	21.3	11.6	18.5	15.6	25.5	36.2	54.5
Portugal	43.9	34.9	11.3	22.6	24.9	20.6	24.8	31.3	55.7
Spain	38.7	23.2	10.1	23.0	26.3	17.4	31.0	39.6	59.2
Italy	32.6	17.5	7.5	24.2	28.0	22.9	33.5	43.2	59.6

Source: adapted from Castles (1998).

they did not take part in the war, as in Spain and Portugal, or because they were rural countries where the effects of the war on housing were less pronounced, as in Greece, although Italy suffered more damage from World War II than the other countries. Their governments, therefore, did not face the same post-war housing crisis as in northern Europe.

(4) In the northern European countries, urban growth took place prior to the post-war expansion of the welfare states into the delivery of services such as health and education. In the four southern countries, urban growth has taken place at the same time as increasing levels of demand for health and education as well as, in three of the countries, major expansion of investment in transport and communications infrastructure associated with entry into the European Union. Consequently, state intervention in housing provision has had to compete with other areas of public expenditure closely related to economic change.

This argument is, effectively, simply the reverse of the most common explanations of the historical origins of social housing in northern Europe (Harloe 1995; Power 1993). Even if one assumes that rural to urban migrants bring with them a cultural predisposition to home ownership rooted in the significance of land as a productive factor in rural areas, a reasonable assumption in some places and times, this argument does not fully explain the specific mechanisms which allow these migrants to realise their aspirations. Rather, it explains the absence of social renting as an option. Nevertheless, this argument does point to the importance of the general social and historical context within which home ownership has developed in the southern countries.

Tenure policies

The variation in tenure patterns across Europe divides the European countries into groups based on their current tenure patterns and then attributes the causes of these patterns to policies to create different tenure mixes. Certainly, over the past three decades, most European countries have implemented policies in relation to housing tenure which have had the effect of increasing the proportion of home ownership. Balchin (1996) and Trilla (2001) propose three groups of countries according to the balance between rented housing and home ownership:

(1) This group includes the northern European countries: Scandinavia, Germany and the Netherlands. These countries have implemented policies based on having a high proportion of rented homes. Their approach is linked to a type of welfare state which aims to guarantee shelter for every household independent of its income and other characteristics. Housing is considered as an essential need and the state must guarantee its satisfaction. The principal way of doing this is by having a stock of housing to rent.
(2) This second group includes the central European countries, especially France and Belgium, which have a rich mixture of policy measures aimed at increasing public rented housing together with promoting private interventions which ease access to home ownership. For these countries, housing is also an important part of the welfare state, but the view is that it is better to have a higher proportion of home owners, and a number of policy measures are in place to achieve this.
(3) This group includes the southern European countries and Ireland. They are characterised by a high proportion of home ownership and low levels of public rented housing. Housing satisfaction is a shared duty within the welfare system. The state must provide shelter for the poorest households, but the family also has an important role in housing provision. Home ownership has been considered as an important objective of housing policies for both social and political reasons.

Some countries, such as the United Kingdom, illustrate the bases of this categorisation. Its decisive policies to increase home ownership were taken alongside having a high proportion of public rented housing. Increasing home ownership and selling the public housing stock to tenants have been a consequence not only of a change in welfare state arrangements, but also of a change in government.

The strength of this argument is that it directs attention to the significance of broad policy approaches in creating housing systems and it begins to link housing policy with wider welfare state policies. However, it also assumes that governments adopt explicit housing policy approaches designed to create specific tenure mixes and that these policies can be applied consistently over long periods of time. The problem with applying this argument in southern Europe is that home ownership seems to have been a side effect or unintended consequence of policies designed to meet quite different objectives, such as the promotion of economic growth, full employment, promoting social stability and minimising direct public intervention in meeting housing need. Neither does this approach explain the *absence* of a policy to support social housing. Such policies are discussed more fully in Chapter 6.

Housing provision systems

The fourth general argument, explaining the significance of home ownership in southern Europe, rests on the idea that there is a distinctive housing provision system in these four countries. Ball *et al.* (1988) argue that the dynamics of home ownership are determined by the social relations among a set of formal institutional actors comprising a housing provision system.

Within this framework, the mortgage market is of special significance in explaining high levels of owner occupation. In 1996, throughout the European Union as a whole, 24% of households held a mortgage. In contrast, in the southern European countries, only 13% held mortgages. Another way to look at these figures is that in southern Europe, two-thirds of owner occupiers had already completed payment for their homes while in the remainder of Europe, two-thirds of owner occupiers were still paying for their homes.

These figures are counter-intuitive. Relatively less use of mortgages should imply less, rather than more, owner occupation. The figures, thus, stimulate a search for explanations of this paradox. Some of the paradox can be attributed to the use of short-term mortgages with relatively low loan to price ratios (high deposits). The consequence is that less time is required between purchase and full ownership. However, this explanation raises further questions. Short-term mortgages and high deposits significantly increase the burden of repayment on households. For example, in Spain, the average household repaying a mortgage in 2002 used 45% of its income for this purpose and would do so for at least 20 years. Thus, the key question is how have such high rates of owner occupation been achieved without a well developed mortgage market?

There are other puzzles raised by the relationship between owner occupation and the mortgage markets. Although Spain is usually considered to have a highly efficient mortgage lending system, at the beginning of the 1990s, the proportion of owner occupiers with mortgages was comparable to that in Greece and Portugal, at 20%, and double that in Italy (Neves 1998). Moreover, data presented by Eurostat (2002) suggest that the increase in mortgage debt in Portugal is the most rapid in the European Union, and the total debt outstanding as a percentage of GDP is surpassed in only five other countries, none of which is in southern Europe.

This example illustrates the strengths and weaknesses of the housing provision thesis. The strength of the thesis is that it stimulates the search for other institutional arrangements which would explain this paradox. The weakness of the thesis, however, is that without an accompanying strong theoretical approach, search becomes more like mindless exploration, mapping out patterns but not explaining their significance. Furthermore, the search tends to be implicitly restricted to formal housing institutions (housing policies, land ownership, construction firms, and so on). As we argue later in Chapter 5, the paradox of high home ownership and poorly developed mortgage markets is explained by a wider social institution, the way extended southern family strategies respond to markets in providing housing for their members. The strength of the housing provision thesis is its injunction to look for patterns of institutions. Its weakness is that it does not provide, and was not intended to provide, a theoretical explanation of those patterns (Ball & Harloe 1992).

Home ownership and social position

A basic problem with these generalised comparative arguments is that they treat tenure in a naturalistic way, assuming that its meaning is fixed outside the wider social contexts within which housing is used and provided (Barlow & Duncan 1988). Differences in tenure have long been used as a way to calibrate social positions (Engels 1872 [1974]; Rex & Moore 1967; Halbwachs 1970). But the specific ways in which tenure relates to social position are not fixed in any absolute way because the social meaning of home ownership (and forms of renting) depends on the broader social context. Because tenure is a complex concept, its meaning cannot be divorced from the specific economic, legal and political frameworks and type of housing stock associated with it in different countries.

The social signification of tenure has also changed over time. At the beginning of the twentieth century, in cities such as Madrid or Barcelona, the middle classes lived in rented apartments in multi-storey buildings because ownership of the building was inextricably linked to ownership of the land. The owner of the land was the owner of the building and also often lived in one of the apartments. At the same time, parts of the working class lived in single-family owner-occupied homes on the semi-urbanised periphery of the city. Thus, when renting was the normal way of living for the middle class, many working-class people were home owners. During the twentieth century, the legal and financial frameworks surrounding multi-family housing have changed, making it possible to own a single apartment in a multi-storey building. Consequently, becoming a home owner at the beginning of the twenty-first century has a different social meaning than it had at the beginning of the twentieth century. In those countries where home ownership is now the most common means of gaining access to a home, only immigrants and people in the lowest socio-economic groups or who are changing jobs or family relationships live in rented housing. The possibility of owning one's own apartment in multi-family housing has both contributed to the growth of home ownership in southern Europe and changed the social signification of home ownership. Table 2.6 illustrates the scale of change in three of the southern European countries.

Home ownership and policy in the rental sector

The growth and high levels of home ownership in southern Europe have also been affected by changes in the rented sector. In all four countries, strong rent controls over a long period of time have inhibited investment in private rental housing, both new investment and maintenance. (In Spain, it is possible to trace the origins of rent control to royal decrees limiting rents for civil servants in Madrid in the sixteenth century.) Increasing rents in line with rising prices was difficult and sometimes impossible, so that controlled

Table 2.6 Percentage of primary residences by type of tenure, Greece, Italy and Spain, circa 1951 and 1991.

Country	Owner occupied		Rented		Other		Total
	1951	1991	1951	1991	1951	1991	
Greece	61.4	78.7**	33.1	21.3	5.5	**	100
Italy	40.0	68.0	48.7	25.3	11.3	6.7	100
Spain	45.9	77.5	51.2	14.9	2.9	7.6*	100

Source: Census for Italy and Spain; household surveys for Greece; 1951 data for Portugal are not available.

* Free dwellings and others
** Other is included in owner occupied for 1993–94.

rents dropped well below market rents. (In Lisbon in 2002, controlled rents were €5 per week in the oldest section of the city and uncontrolled rents were €80.) As a consequence, households in properties with controlled rents tended to remain in them, blocking access to the sector for younger households. It is also difficult to recover unpaid rents both because of delays in the courts and a reluctance by the courts to evict households. Thus, once economic growth began to speed up in the southern countries, alternative forms of investment also became more profitable and less risky than investing in rented housing. Much of the private rented sector is concentrated in older housing in poor repair although there is a profitable segment of the market everywhere. In Spain, a number of large companies provide luxury rented housing in the best central locations in the large cities.

Nevertheless, throughout southern Europe, the large gap between controlled rents and open market rents encourages landlords to let the housing deteriorate to the extent that it must be demolished and the site can be sold for other urban uses. In Spain, Portugal and Greece, this process of deterioration and demolition is not yet counterbalanced by processes of gentrification and conservation outside specific, historically significant areas. This is not the case in Italy where, since the mid-1970s, public policies have strongly promoted the rehabilitation of the oldest parts of the cities, including their historic centres. Consequently, private action and gentrification processes have significantly enhanced the standard of the older stock. Gentrification has also meant that much of the rehabilitated stock is now owner occupied rather than rented.

At the same time, the social rented sector is small and tends to be concentrated in the larger cities. Nevertheless, significant amounts of public rented housing have been sold to tenants. In Spain, the public rented stock was sold to tenants during the last years of the Franco regime in order to reduce urban conflicts. In Italy, half the public rented housing built since World War II has also been sold to tenants for similar reasons. In Greece, little public rented housing was ever built since easy access to land, often public, for building on served much the same purpose as social housing in the other countries. In Spain and the south of Italy, what remains of public housing is also deteriorating rapidly as a consequence of low rents, the inability of public landlords to evict tenants and poor-quality housing management. In northern Italy, much of the public stock has been rehabilitated, even though it is increasingly stigmatised as it is the only stock available to the poorest groups in the society. In Spain and Greece, there is no new investment in new social housing, while in Italy and Portugal there is still some new investment although even new developments tend to become stigmatised over time. These changes in the rental sector also encourage home ownership.

Household cycle and housing tenure

The end result is that the age of the head of household is as important as income in determining the tenure of households. Table 2.7 shows the general pattern for Spain in 1991. Young households and elderly households have a higher proportion of tenants. For young people, the reason lies in their work situation after leaving home. In Madrid, half of them rent their first home, but among households headed by a person under 30 who is also employed, only 25% are renting. The case of the elderly is different – 17% rent their homes, which is higher than average for Madrid. This is partly a legacy of rent control in the past, when rents were significantly below market prices. Among middle-aged households, the differences in tenure depend more on the type of family than on household income. In Athens, tenure also depends much more on age than on income. In 1986, the proportion of households that were renting decreased regularly from 74% in the age group of 17–25 to 22% of those over 65. Within each of the age groups, however, the proportion of those renting varies with income and/or occupation. Since the 1970s, there has also been a strong tendency towards reduced access to home ownership for households with lower incomes (Maloutas 1990, pp. 126–9 & p. 135; Emmanuel *et al.* 1996, pp. 69–75).

The deterioration of conditions in the private rented sector and the small and generally stigmatised public rented sector have gone hand in hand with changing market conditions in the owner-occupied sector. Prices have increased continuously in southern cities. During the 1990s, the market has

Table 2.7 Percentage of heads of household by age group and tenure, Spain, 1991.

Age group	Owned outright	Owned with mortgage	Total owner occupied	Free*	Renting	Other	Total
Total	55.98	19.63	77.76	4.05	16.55	1.64	100
<29	22.15	30.62	56.10	7.02	33.64	3.24	100
30–39	38.64	34.67	75.55	4.22	18.57	1.65	100
40–49	61.06	21.35	84.23	2.63	12.13	1.01	100
50–64	66.34	13.44	81.87	4.04	12.61	1.48	100
65+	64.74	8.97	75.75	4.26	18.10	1.88	100

Source: INE, Census (1991).

* Free means households living in their parents' homes or in a house which goes with a job.

seen both high levels of frontloading on mortgages, during periods of high interest rates and inflation, together with periods in which real interest rates have been negative. These conditions have enhanced the investment value of housing, inducing more households into the market at higher levels of indebtedness. But these conditions also create higher barriers to entry for lower-income households.

Thus, the longstanding trend for home ownership to increase is now facing new circumstances. Three changes are now increasing the demand for rental housing:

(1) The nature of family and household structures are changing, with an increase in the number of people without an immediate family or in a transitional position. There is an increasing proportion of smaller families, families without children, one-parent families, divorced people, and so on, although the numbers are still small compared with European averages (see Chapter 5).
(2) There is a growth in temporary work contracts, which creates the need to change homes with a change in the location of jobs. At the upper end of the income spectrum, such people may have a permanent home and rent a second home near their work. However, for younger people entering the job market and for jobs that require greater mobility, renting may be preferred to buying. Furthermore, the expansion of universities associated with the growth in high level tertiary sector jobs puts further pressure on the private rented sector if there is no additional residential provision for their students.
(3) There has been a strong growth in immigration in the last decade of the twentieth century. Immigrants commonly send savings back to their countries of origin at the beginning of their stay and these savings may be used to provide an income for their family or to buy a house in the country of origin. In these circumstances, immigrants prefer to rent in their host country. Only when it is clear that immigrants will remain for a longer period or permanently do they begin to explore the possibility of becoming home owners in their host country.

The outcome of these changes is difficult to predict. Only a small part of these changes can be diverted into demand for owner occupation. At the same time, the social infrastructure to support expansion of the supply of rental housing is weak. In the short run, the outcome is likely to be a deterioration in the conditions of those living in the rental sectors and increased pressures on families to support younger people for longer periods of time or to divert more family-based resources to providing access to owner occupation for younger people. These processes are discussed more fully in Chapter 5. Nevertheless, it is clear that the longstanding solution to satisfying housing need by expanding owner occupation is likely to be ineffective in meeting these new types of demand for rental housing.

Home ownership as the distinctive feature of southern housing

This section has necessarily presented a generalised picture of the four southern European countries. Nevertheless, there are important differences among them, some of which have been mentioned above, and there are also differences between regions within countries, and between urban and rural areas. In the countryside, home ownership has been more common than in the cities, partly as a consequence of the lower price of housing in rural areas, partly due to their joint use as a mean of production, and partly due to the importance of land ownership in the countryside. In addition, the spatial distribution of home ownership in southern European cities is quite different from cities in other countries. Most of the housing for rent is located in the centre of town and in the affluent peripheries of cities. Working-class, peripheral areas often have the highest proportion of home ownership. This pattern is most pronounced in Greece and Spain.

In conclusion, the southern European countries as a group have the highest proportion of home ownership in the European Union, as well as the lowest proportion of social rented housing. This tenure pattern reflects policies which have strongly supported the growth of home ownership while discouraging rented housing through legislation strongly favouring tenants at the expense of landlords.

In general, the strength and long historical development of this pattern leads us to think that the high level of home ownership is not a coincidence, but affirms the existence of a different kind of housing system in these countries than is found elsewhere in Europe. Attempting to explain housing tenure patterns as simply the outcome of specific housing policy mixes appears too self-referential to be adequate. Housing policies clearly have an impact in shaping the housing market faced by households, but they do not fully explain the behaviour of households within the market. The choices open to specific households are also shaped by wider family strategies. These strategies, in turn, are shaped by the nature of family solidarity, the nature and scale of both monetary and other resources which families can mobilise in order to gain access to housing and by adaptations in the family cycle, such as delay in household formation and older people living more often with their children. Housing policies, in turn, are shaped by generalised expectations about family strategies as well as by general conceptions about the relative roles of the state and the family in satisfying housing and other welfare needs. Consequently, the general argument of this book is that the differences in tenure patterns between northern and southern Europe reflect the role of housing policies within different types of welfare systems and family structures.

Tenure is only one of the characteristics which distinguish the housing systems in southern Europe from the other countries in the European Union. The remainder of this chapter looks at three other features of housing systems: the significance of secondary housing, the relationship between household cycles and access to housing, and the ways in which housing is produced.

One home in two houses: high proportion of secondary homes

The distribution of housing in the southern European countries is still afflicted by distinct contrasts. Despite considerable progress in improving housing conditions, many households still live in precarious housing. Recently, overcrowding in poor-quality housing has increased, especially in the centres of the largest cities, as a result of the need to accommodate the enormous influx of immigrants. Other deficiencies are environmental, reflecting poor urban planning and infrastructure provision. There are a large number of people who wish for and need an adequate home, including those living in substandard houses and young people who want to live independently and cannot find a home at an affordable price.

At the same time, second homes, used by their owners only for weekends and holidays, constitute 17% of the total stock of housing. This enormous stock of secondary housing is a direct expression of the unequal distribution of housing resources. Young people and immigrants have trouble finding a home while many other people live in two houses. Yet, these secondary houses cannot be used as primary homes because most of them are located in areas where the lack of employment depresses the demand for primary homes.

As Table 2.8 shows, the difference between the southern European countries and the other 11 European Union countries is considerable. Second homes constitute just over 3.5% of the housing stock in the other 11 countries compared with nearly 17% in the south. Even in the other countries, the distribution of second homes is uneven. In France the stock of secondary housing is relatively high, 10% of total stock, while in the United Kingdom, secondary housing does not even constitute 1% of the stock.

Table 2.8 Distribution of housing stock by use in Europe, circa 1991 (% of total stock).

Use	EU15	EU15 without southern Europe	Southern Europe*
Primary	85.0	90.7	73.6
Empty	5.9	4.2	9.2
Second	8.0	3.6	16.9
Others	1.1	1.5	0.3
Total	100.0	100.0	100.0

Source: Eurostat (1996).

* Portugal, Greece, Italy and Spain.

A problem with estimating the number of second homes is that a large proportion of the houses classified as empty are also used as second homes (see Table 2.9). For example, in Spain, the 2001 Census of Population and Housing estimated that second homes constituted 16% of the occupied stock and 15% of empty homes (INE 2001). However, more accurate estimates suggest that a large proportion of the empty homes counted in the census are, in fact, second homes, so that secondary housing could be as much as 20% of the total stock, equivalent to nearly 30% of the stock of primary homes. More detailed estimates are not available for the other countries, but the situation is likely to be similar.

There has been substantial growth in the secondary housing stock over the past quarter century. In the Spanish case, between 1981 and 1991, the total increase in the housing stock was nearly 2.4 million. Table 2.10 shows that only 57% of the increase in the stock was due to the growth of permanent housing, and the rest was due to an increase in the number of empty houses, and more significantly, in the number of second homes. In the 1990s, the stock of secondary housing grew more rapidly than the primary stock. The secondary stock increased by 28.6% (700 000 units) in these ten years to

Table 2.9 Distribution of housing stock by use in southern European countries, circa 1991 (% of total stock).

Use	Greece	Spain	Italy	Portugal
Primary	66.1	68.3	78.8	73.0
Vacant*	33.6	31.4	21.1	26.3
Empty	*na*	*14.4*	*7.2*	*10.5*
Second	*na*	*17.0*	*13.9*	*15.8*
Others	0.3	0.3	0.1	0.7
Total	100.0	100.0	100.0	100.0

Source: Eurostat (1996).

* Vacant includes both empty homes and second homes.

Table 2.10 Changes in the use of the housing stock, Spain, 1970 to 1991.

Use	% of total stock			% increase in stock	
	1970	1981	1991	1970–1981	1981–1991
Primary homes	79.8	70.8	68.8	22.7	13.1
Second homes	7.5	12.9	15.4	138.5	38.9
Vacant*	12.7	16.3	15.8	75.2	13.5
Total	100.0	100.0	100.0	38.2	16.5

Source: INE, *Censo de Población y Vivienda* (1970, 1981, 1991).

* A proportion of homes classified as vacant are also second homes.

become 16% of the total stock. In Italy, the increase in the secondary stock reached its peak between 1971 and 1981, when it made up almost half of the total increase in stock. What scattered data are available suggest that the changes in Greece have been similar to those in Spain. Maps of the spatial distribution of empty houses in Greece clearly show the different types of second homes (Maloutas 2003a).

The boundary between renting and owning in secondary housing is complex and changeable. The rental market has many forms. It is possible to rent a house for a very short period of time or for a long time, up to several years. Even if most second homes are privately owned by the people using them, there is a large seasonal rental market during the summer. Sometimes low-income households that live in the leisure cities leave their homes in order to rent them during the summer period, or owners use them part of the time and rent them out when they are not using them. Sometimes people rent their permanent homes and own a second home. Such residential practices make it difficult to classify these houses and households in terms of housing tenure.

There are three main ways in which secondary housing comes into the stock:

(1) Some second homes are located in places where there is not enough employment to make a living and were left empty by their owners when they migrated from the countryside to the cities. This is especially the case in agricultural villages. Later, they may have been purchased by others as second homes or the households who migrated to the cities may have retained their houses in their village of origin as their own second homes. There are other cases where homes have been inherited from parents who remained in the village while their children emigrated. This means that some of this housing belongs to low-income households that have retained them for several reasons,

primarily because they wanted to have a place of socio-geographical reference, a common phenomenon in the southern countries. The significance of a familial place of reference is especially important in those regions where the principal method of inheritance was the *mayorazgo* (the elder son inherited the agricultural land and house from the parents). There is also a more general culturally shaped desire to preserve the family home (the *casa pairal* in Catalonia) as a place of reference and identity for the family as a whole. And in some cases, there is a strong attachment to the villages of origin since property and presence gives substance to participation in localised clientelistic networks.

(2) Some secondary housing in villages arises through the investment of emigrants, who want to come back for their holidays and weekends or when they retire. Some of these are new houses, so it is not uncommon that some villages lost population during the 1960s and 1970s and now have an increasing number of houses in them alongside a stagnating or decreasing population. Some migrants living in other European countries buy a house in the south for their vacations and retirement while they live in rented homes in their host country. This practice is especially common among southern people migrating to northern countries such as France or Germany and, within Italy, among people migrating from the southern to the northern regions. They live in public rented housing and invest their savings to buy a home in their place of origin which they intend to come back to when they save enough money to start their own businesses or to retire. Such houses can be considered as second homes until the owners return since, in the meantime, they are used only for holidays by their owners.

(3) Some houses have been built explicitly for the purpose of providing second homes for households from urban areas or from other parts of Europe, especially in places of scenic beauty, for example on beaches or in the mountains, and more recently, in historical cities. The greatest increase in the secondary housing stock has been through new building in leisure areas and cities. The most dramatic increases have been along the Mediterranean and the southern coast of Portugal. All types of second homes are being built near the sea, from luxurious private villas located in secluded areas or in privileged settlements, to much cheaper small apartments. At the same time, the massive expansion of transport infrastructure, following accession to the European Union, has also played a role in the development of the secondary housing stock. Cars, trains and planes reduce the distance between primary and secondary homes. The increasing investment by northern Europeans in second homes in the southern countries is clearly related to decreasing air fares, but even within each country, the development of new train systems, roads and ferries means that second homes can be used more often.

The sources and spatial distribution of second homes show how this distinctive southern phenomenon lies at the intersection of two major social processes. The first is the substantial migration from the countryside to cities which has occurred in all the southern countries in the past quarter century, leaving empty and vacant housing in the rural villages, some of which has become second homes for migrants and others. This process also accounts for the relatively large number of low-income households that own second homes. The second is the increasing integration of the European leisure space, particularly the use of the southern countries as holiday destinations for northern Europeans. This process has also affected the villages, but has had its most pronounced effect in the growth of leisure cities throughout the southern countries.

Despite the importance of secondary housing, especially in southern Europe, the literature about it is not extensive. There is some research, but the size of the secondary housing stock and its evolution should have merited more. The problem is now beginning to be discussed in the context of recent work on rural housing policy (Gallent *et al.* 2003) and also in terms of recreational summer housing (NTUA–NCSR 1996 & 1998; Gortsos *et al.* 2000).

Secondary housing can be analysed in three ways: as an outcome of housing policy, as an important factor in the economic dynamics of these countries, or as an aspect of social behaviour related to the use of leisure time.

Housing policy and the increase in secondary housing

From this point of view, the scale of the secondary housing stock is partly a consequence of the strength of quantitative policies designed to build as many houses as possible. Such housing policies were also strongly linked with an economic policy to increase construction activity in countries with little industrial infrastructure. The Spanish and Italian cases are clear examples of this. In order to increase building activity in the second half of the 1980s, investors in second homes benefited from tax relief (Padovani & Vettoretto 2003). After completing payments on mortgages for their primary homes, many households looked for continuity in their strategy for saving money by investing in a second home. These strategies were also supported by the rapid growth in income in the southern European countries during the last decades of the twentieth century.

Economic dynamics of secondary housing

From this point of view, the growth of the leisure cities, mostly composed of second homes, was a way to promote less developed regions where there were no other resources: the southern coast of Spain, the Algarve in Portugal, some southern Italian regions and the Greek islands. The big coastal cities, where the principal economic activity was only leisure services, were developed between the mid-1960s and the 1990s. This was also seen as a way to fight unemployment because attracting foreign tourists provided an important component of the economic base in these regions. The scale of the secondary stock in some of these cities creates specific problems associated with maintaining adequate urban services when a large proportion of the population lives elsewhere for most of the year. A key problem is the scale of investment in infrastructure, such as water supply and water recycling, public transport, roads, and so on, in cities where for two months of the year the population is multiplied four- or five-fold. Nevertheless, even the holiday cities built during the 1960s and 1970s have a huge capacity to expand and attract people throughout the year. Cities such as Benidorm in Spain are a good example, now attracting a vastly increased number of elderly people during the winter. The growing proportion of retired people coming from other countries to live in southern Europe during the winter raises the vision of some regions becoming a vast retirement home for older Europeans.

Direct foreign investment in second homes by European households living in other countries must also be considered. It is difficult to measure the impact of this investment on the increase in second homes, but it is considerable. There are groups of people from central and northern Europe who own coastal homes in Greece and Spain or in historical cities in Italy. Sometimes they create whole neighbourhoods or little villages composed of people from a single country where they use their own language and customs.

From the point of view of residential practices, second homes can be considered both as an investment and as a commodity. A high proportion of second homes are owned by households. The security of investment in housing, despite increasingly attractive alternative outlets for investing savings, together with the possibility of using the second home during holidays and weekends, were the principal reasons for the demand for these homes. Investing in second homes increased the household's financial security, since the property could be sold if necessary. To some extent, investing in property also reflects the continuity of a peasant attitude towards savings in countries where agriculture has been the principal occupation until recently.

Social behaviour and leisure time

The increase in second homes also has to do with other cultural values. It is a continuation of an old method of changing living spaces with the seasons. It was normal for southern urban middle-class households to leave the urban settlements during the summer to go to the beach, the mountains, or the countryside. This practice was only for the minority who could own or rent another home and had the resources to spend the summer in this home. It was also supported by a family structure in which the only breadwinner was the man and the wife took care of the children and did the housekeeping. For middle-class families living in the big cities, the wife moved to the second home for two months or more during the summer, and the husband joined them during his holidays from work, if the home was far away, and on weekends if it was nearer. Second homes could be considered as an enlargement of the primary home for households living in apartments in the bigger southern cities. Now, the old cultural methods of changing living spaces with the seasons have been transformed and are linked with the use of leisure time and holidays. Summer homes and palaces were once exclusive goods for the aristocracy and more affluent households. They have now become available to a great number of families in a new version: little individual houses in Greece or apartments in Italy and Spain.

In summary the growth in secondary housing is the result of several factors coming together. Rooted in cultural traditions and climatic conditions, growth was supported by housing policies which emphasised increased rates of construction activity. The effects of these policies were enhanced by the considerable growth of real income in these countries, which facilitated household investment in secondary housing. Investment in secondary housing construction was also seen as another way to fight unemployment and to develop domestic and foreign tourism as an important element of the economic base in these regions. One of the most significant consequences of this combination of policies has been the development of large leisure cities.

The growth of these second homes is a characteristic of the southern countries and it is difficult to predict the limits on its growth. There is a debate about the sustainability of continuing to build second homes and continuing with an economic development model based on investment by households from other European countries.

Housing access, family cycles and residential mobility

The dominance of owner occupation, the weakness of the rental market and inequalities in the distribution of housing resources all combine to block access to housing in southern Europe. In these circumstances, the family plays a strong role in supporting access to housing and, in turn, the family is partly shaped by the strategies it adopts to secure housing for its members. While many of the elements of the social, financial and institutional frameworks which shape access to housing are similar to those in northern Europe, they interlock in a specifically southern way. The peculiarity of the situation in southern Europe should be seen primarily in relation to the high rates of unemployment, especially among young people, to the lower activity rates of women, and to problems derived from strongly dualistic labour markets, especially the increase in precariousness and job insecurity in the rapidly growing service sectors.

Housing access

Access to housing depends on the financial and economic resources which are available to households. First, there are the sources and level of household income, whether wages and the security of different positions in the job market, public allowances to households, or the level of pensions for retired people. A second important factor is the number of people within the household who have an income, which has been greatly influenced by the increasing participation of women in the labour force although this is still low by general European standards. Finally, there is the availability of other resources, including financial and non-financial aid from the wider family, the existence of a patrimony that can be used to pay for a house and especially the sale of the previous house.

The distribution of these resources among and within families shape the strategies which they can deploy in ensuring access to housing for newly forming households within the wider extended family. Familial solidarity plays an important role in solving housing problems, for young people through remaining in the parental home until they are well established in their careers or through material and non-material help provided to individuals and new households with housing problems, and for elderly people who are no longer able to live on their own. Chapter 5 discusses the role of family solidarity and housing strategies in depth, and this section is designed to introduce the topic.

In terms of the housing system, two key elements shape the problem. On the one hand, the heavy reliance on owner occupation means that the mechanisms for fixing the price of houses escapes direct control by the government and indirect controls are relatively ineffective. On the other hand, there is the virtual absence of social rented housing designed to ensure that low-income households are adequately housed and private rented housing at lower prices is scarce and of low quality. The main form of access to housing is through home ownership. The consequence is that large groups within the population experience considerable difficulty in gaining access to housing, because they cannot afford to buy a home or they must devote the majority of their income to this purpose. Thus, there is always a substantial threat of homelessness hanging over a large proportion of households. The most evident consequences, however, are the delay in leaving the parental home to create a new household and the low levels of divorce and separation, which reflect how problems of access to housing inhibit the formation of new households. These problems are discussed more fully in Chapter 5.

In terms of housing policy, state expenditure directed towards housing serves other objectives than guaranteeing access to housing for those who have less purchasing capacity. The construction sector has been used as a counter-cyclical instrument of economic policy, compensating for the decrease in economic activity and consumption during periods of economic downturn. The main instrument of housing policy expenditure is income tax relief, which means that middle- and high-income households with high income taxes find housing investment an effective way to reduce their taxes. At the same time, there is little direct monetary aid for lower-income households seeking to buy or rent a home.

The consequence is that access to finance, in particular the balance between family-based resources and mortgages, is a key resource for newly forming households to gain access to housing. The data for Spain shown in Table 2.11 indicate how the structure of mortgage lending privileges higher income groups and puts considerable strain on households with average and below-average incomes. It also shows the extent to which access to mortgage lending depends on the general state of the lending market rather than on government policy. The improvement in the situation since 1990 has been due to two factors. First, the length of time over which the loan must be repaid has been extended from 10 to 20 years, reducing annual repayments. Second, the Central European Bank reduced interest rates at the end of the 1990s. These two changes reduced monthly repayments for households, but also contributed to rapid increases in house prices and in construction activity as demand increased.

Table 2.11 Financial effort required for access to privately promoted housing in Madrid, 1990–2002.

Year	Average price of housing (€/m^2)	Average annual gross wage (€)	Total house price*/ annual wage	Average interest rate (%)	Mortgage repayment period (years)	Monthly repayment as % of average gross monthly wage
1990	878	7290	10.8	16.7	10	184.2
1993	1025	8907	10.4	11.7	13	127.3
1996	1097	9893	10.0	8.2	17	88.5
1999	1191	10963	9.8	6.7	20	61.3
2002	1868	11321	14.8	5.3	20	97.8

Source: Leal (2003).

* Calculations are based on a 'normalised house' of 90 m^2 with a mortgage covering 80% of its price.

However, the most important point about Table 2.11 is that it shows the extent to which, even in a highly developed mortgage market, other financial resources are required, through relatively high initial deposits, to access home ownership. In the less developed mortgage markets in Greece and Italy, less lending is available, higher initial deposits are required, and the term of the loans is shorter. Thus, the range of other formal and informal, financial and non-financial resources available to families becomes much more important in developing strategies to support access to home ownership by newly forming households.

Changing family strategies

The strategies available to families in ensuring access to housing have two components. The first is how they can mobilise resources to operate in the formal and semi-formal housing market structures in southern Europe. The second is how family structures are adapted to support their members.

A significant difference between southern Europe and the remainder of Europe lies in the nature of family structures. The nuclear family, composed of a couple with one or more children, is still the dominant household structure in southern Europe. Table 2.12 shows that all four of the southern countries lie well above the European average in terms of the proportion of nuclear family households. The only other country lying above the average is Ireland, at 72.9%. At the same time, the proportion of newer household forms (single persons and single-parent households) is lower than in the rest of Europe (Eurostat 1996; see also Chapter 5 of this book). Consequently, as Table 2.13 shows, average household sizes are larger in southern Europe.

Table 2.12 Family households as a percentage of all households, southern Europe and EU12, 1995.

Country	Family households as % of all households
Portugal	83.7
Spain	83.1
Greece	78.8
Italy	76.3
EU12	70.3

Source: Eurostat (1996, p. 44).

Table 2.13 Average household size, European Union countries, circa 2000.

Country	Persons per dwelling
Spain	3.1
Portugal	2.9
Italy	2.9
Greece	2.8
Ireland	3.0
Luxembourg	2.7
Belgium	2.5
France	2.4
United Kingdom	2.4
Austria	2.4
Netherlands	2.4
Finland	2.3
Germany (former FRG)	2.2
Denmark	2.1
Sweden	2.1

Source: Fribourg (2002, p. 5).

Family structures in southern Europe are changing, impelled by the increasing number of women who are working outside their homes (González *et al.* 2000). This implies convergence with patterns in the other European countries (discussed in Chapter 5), alongside an increasing trend towards single-person households throughout Europe (Eurostat 1996, p. 46). Despite the increasing diversity of household forms in southern Europe, the differences are still important and it can be argued that the strength of the family as an institution and the high stability of family relationships in southern Europe will contribute to sustaining these differences (Reher 1996; Cortes 1995; Alberdi 1994).

At present, young people's first access to their own independent housing is delayed in comparison to the European average (see Table 2.14). This is

Table 2.14 Average age when more than half of young people are living in their own homes, selected European countries, 1998.

Country	Females	Males
Italy	27.1	29.7
Spain	26.6	28.4
Greece	22.9	28.2
Portugal	25.2	28.0
France	22.2	24.1
Germany	21.6	24.8
UK	21.2	23.5
Netherlands	21.2	23.3
Ireland	25.2	26.3
Denmark	20.3	21.4

Source: European Community Housing Panel, adapted from Iacovou (2000).

especially true for young people earning low incomes or from poorer households who do not have the resources to support independent housing for their children.

The ages at which young people leave the parental home and at which they marry are rising throughout Europe. These changes are due to two things. First, increased levels of training associated with new kinds of jobs have extended the period of education for young people. Second, the difficulties for young people in the job market, the increased use of temporary work contracts and, above all, high youth unemployment rates (especially important in Spain and southern Italy) all play an important role in extending the age at which people leave home. However, the differences

Table 2.15 Percentage of young people living independently in Spain, 1987 and 1995.

Age	1987	1995
16–18	1.2	0.2
19–21	4.5	1.9
22–24	18.8	8.9
25–27	45.8	27.6
28–30	68.3	52.9
31–33	77.0	69.7
34–36	81.7	79.4
37–39	85.2	85.1

Source: INE *Encuesta de Población Activa* (1987, 1995).

between the northern and southern European countries have been maintained (see Table 2.15 for the effects of the recession in the early 1990s on the age at which young people left home in Spain), suggesting different basic social processes and institutional structures.

Throughout a large part of Europe, the period between leaving the parental home and forming one's own family has come to be considered as a normal stage in the life process, facilitated by the availability of rented housing. In southern Europe, leaving the parental home has a definitive character. More than half of those who leave their parental home in Spain start with owning their own house. These young people skip the stage of living alone or in cohabiting couples in rented housing prior to marriage and having children. This pattern holds true throughout southern Europe. Young people leave their family of origin shortly before or at the moment of marriage when they move into their own home. In purchasing a house, they are looking forward to the growth in their own family and the assumption is that they will live in their first home for an extended period of time. Consequently, housing size does not vary much in relation to the age of the inhabitants. Both young and elderly people frequently live in houses which are larger than they need. If young people move into the rental sector when they leave the parental home, then they can usually only get access to older housing in worse conditions.

Residential mobility

The houses which young people move into when they leave the parental home are usually located in proximity to the parents of one or other of the couple. The importance of familial proximity depends on social class and income. New households among the working classes are more dependent on the physical solidarity of their families, developed through direct support, such as child care and care for the elderly, or small repairs and other building works to the home. The service classes are less dependent on parental proximity because solidarity is more developed in cash terms, reflecting higher employment activity rates for women and higher cash incomes. The importance of parental proximity contributes to shaping social patterns in cities and reproduces inequalities in patterns of spatial growth.

After households buy their first home, residential mobility is considerably reduced. Mobility rates in Madrid and Barcelona during the 1990s were about 5% and Portuguese cities had about 4%, much less than the average in the other countries of the European Union. Table 2.16 compares Spain with a number of other countries. This low mobility rate also has to do with other

Table 2.16 Percentage of households moving within the previous year in several European countries and USA.

Country	%
United States	17.5
Great Britain	9.6
Sweden	9.5
France	9.4
Netherlands	7.7
Belgium	7.3
Ireland	6.1
Spain	5.3

Source: Modenes Cabrerizo (1998, p. 192). Data for Spain are for 1991, and for other countries are for 1981.

factors: a strong preference for living near to friends and strong links with specific neighbourhoods. Very high transaction taxes (typically 10–15%) associated with buying and selling houses throughout southern Europe also contribute to low residential mobility.

Problems of access to housing also limit the ability of couples to end an unsatisfactory relationship. Although they are beginning to rise, divorce and separation rates in the countries of southern Europe continue to be low in comparison to the countries of the north (see Table 2.17). The shortage of rental housing and the high cost of access to owner occupation contribute to

Table 2.17 Gross divorce rates in European Union countries, 1995.

Country	Divorces per 1000 inhabitants
Italy	0.5
Spain	0.8
Greece	1.1
Portugal	1.2
Luxembourg	1.8
France	2.0
Germany	2.1
Netherlands	2.2
Austria	2.3
Finland	2.5
Sweden	2.6
Denmark	2.7
United Kingdom	2.9
Belgium	3.5

Source: Eurostat (1997a).

lower rates of marital breakdown, especially given the reduced economic activity and independence of women.

For those outside wider family structures, especially immigrants, the main form of help that is available in accessing housing comes from a variety of non-governmental organisations. The churches in particular are pro-active with such help. Their intervention concentrates on households at risk of social exclusion and on minority groups, such as immigrants, who are not eligible for help from the state. The resources available to these institutions are scarce and come, for the most part, from the state. This method of intervention reflects the significance of the principle of subsidiarity behind the structuring of the welfare states in southern Europe (see Chapter 4) and is considered to be more efficient because these institutions are closer to the needs of the people they help.

Wider problems of high home ownership

The problems of access to housing which come about from the dominance of home ownership and the absence of social rented housing in southern Europe have wider consequences for these societies:

(1) There is a strong connection between the age at which people leave home and fertility rates. In Spain and Italy, it is not usually possible to gain access to independent housing until a young person has achieved some occupational continuity and economic self-sufficiency (Delgado 1997; Leal 1997; Garrido & Requena 1996; Iacovou 2000). Delay in forming a new household implies delaying maternity, and this contributes to the exceptionally low fertility rates in the southern countries (Maloutas *et al.* 2002).

(2) Low residential mobility supports a high dependence among extended family members and reinforces the family's control over the individuals within it. This is clear in the case of delayed emancipation of the young, but similar problems of control accompany the difficulty of accessing housing for couples who wish to separate and divorce. There is no specific data in official surveys, but some couples who are separated *de facto* continue to share the same home. Other couples are confined within bad relationships for a long time by the difficulty of finding alternative housing for one of the partners. This is especially a problem for low-income households and, above all, for women who do not have a job. These problems are exacerbated by a welfare system that provides few direct social services and is reluctant to intervene in intra-familial relationships (Lewis 1997).

(3) Low residential mobility has an impact on the labour market, either by maintaining inequalities among regions or by imposing high travel costs on people changing the location of their jobs and unable or unwilling to change the location of their homes, given the high levels of attachment to neighbourhoods and importance of parental proximity.
(4) High house prices and poorly developed mortgage systems increase pressures on household incomes. In some cities with very high costs of living in addition to high house prices, households need two incomes in order to pay the mortgage and live adequately (Taltavull 2000). Increasing home ownership is one of the main reasons for the increase in the number of young women working outside the home. This, in turn, reinforces the decrease in fertility rates because of the lack of childcare services and inadequate social benefits.
(5) High levels of home ownership and low residential mobility generate specific processes of urban socio-spatial segregation, which differ from those found in countries with higher levels of mobility and more rented housing. Housing prices can be understood as a form of social control over the values of the urban space. This happens in all cities, but in the southern cities countering such segregation is not on the political agenda for two reasons. The first is that the very scarce resources available for building any social rented housing mean that more housing can be built in the cheaper locations, thus contributing to rather than countering socio-spatial segregation. The second reason is that until recently these cities were ethnically homogeneous and socio-spatial integration was not considered a problem (Leal 1999a; Maloutas & Karadimitriou 2001).

In summary, the problems of gaining access to housing in a housing system dominated by owner occupation are creating new forms of social cleavages in the southern countries. For example, in Madrid, more than 50% of households live in their own homes which are paid for in full. At the same time, new households under the age of 40 must devote more than 43% of their income to buying their house. Difficulties in obtaining access to housing prolongs the problem of integrating young people into full adulthood since the difficulty of getting a permanent job is just the beginning of a series of obstacles that last until they have completed the last payment on their mortgage. These differences between groups of home owners are becoming an increasingly significant dimension of inequality, negatively affecting the consumption power of indebted households and reducing the possibility of maintaining their standards of living, investing in their children's social mobility through education, and so on. The stresses on consumption by young households also undermine demand for any taxation-based expansion of welfare services and contribute to the specific nature of southern welfare regimes (see Chapter 4).

Production and promotion of housing

This section looks first at patterns of housing production in Europe to show how southern Europe is distinctive from the remainder of Europe. It then discusses the basis of this distinctiveness in housing promotion systems and in broader socio-economic processes associated with housing production.

The pattern of housing production in southern Europe is distinctive. Table 2.18 shows that in 2000–01, the rate of housing production in Portugal, Spain and Greece was only surpassed by Ireland among the European Union countries. In contrast, Italy ranked fourteenth among the 15 member states.

The historical pattern of production in the southern countries, shown in Table 2.19 and Figure 2.3, demonstrates both long-run and cyclical trends. Over the period between 1980 and 2000, there was a slight downward long-run trend among the other 11 European Union countries, compared with a slight rising trend in the four southern countries. Among the southern countries, Italy has consistently had one of the lowest rates of housing production in Europe and production has declined at the same rate as in the other 11 countries. Portugal had the lowest rate of housing production

Table 2.18 Rates of housing production, European Union countries, 2000–01.

Country	Dwellings completed per 1000 inhabitants
Portugal	10.5
Spain	8.9
Greece*	8.2
Italy*	2.5
Ireland	13.7
Austria*	6.8
Finland	5.9
France	5.1
Netherlands	4.6
Germany**	4.0
Luxembourg*	3.8
Belgium	3.7
Denmark	3.0
United Kingdom*	3.0
Sweden	1.7

Source: Eurostat (2002).

* data for 2000
** including former DDR

Table 2.19 Trends in housing production, southern Europe and remainder of European Union, 1980–2000.

Country	New dwellings completed per 1000 inhabitants				
	1980	1985	1990	1995	2000
Greece	14.1	8.9	11.8	6.1	8.2
Spain	7.0	5.0	7.2	5.6	9.1
Italy	5.1	3.6	3.1	2.9	2.5
Portugal	4.2	3.8	6.6	6.8	10.8
Southern Europe average	7.6	5.3	7.2	5.3	7.7
EU11 average	6.7	5.3	6.0	5.1	5.1

Source: Eurostat (2002).

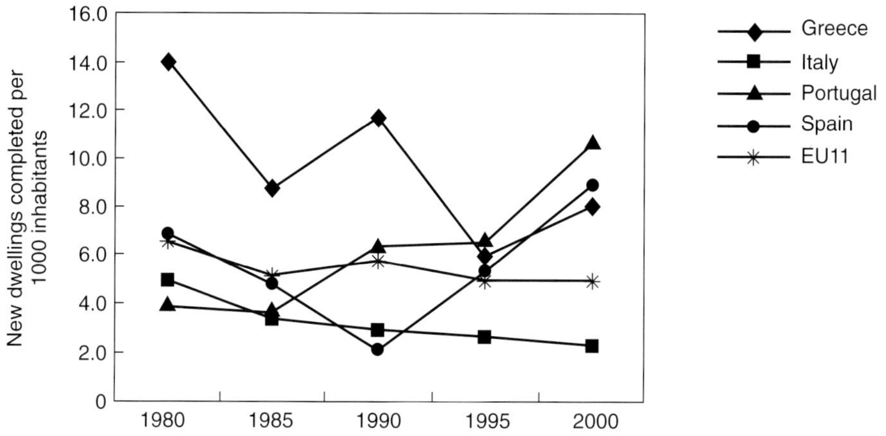

Fig. 2.3 Trends in housing production, southern Europe and remainder of European Union, 1980–2000. Source: Eurostat (2002).

among all the member states in 1980, but rose to second place by 2000. Spain has also shown a faster trend in growth than the remainder of the member states. Production in Greece has fallen more quickly than the remainder of the European states over the period, but still remains above the average. Greece, Spain and Portugal have shown the same cyclical trends as the rest of Europe. In Greece, these cyclical variations have been amplified in comparison to Europe, but they have been dampened in Portugal and Spain as a consequence of the strong long run trend to growth. Italy seems to have 'marched to a different drummer', with little cyclical variation.

At the same time, these rates of housing production are linked with relatively low levels of investment in dwellings in relationship to total capital formation. Table 2.20 shows this clearly. The average annual rate of growth in GDP between 1994 and 2002 was 3.3% in Greece, 3.2% in Spain and 3.0%

Table 2.20 Gross investment in dwellings as a percentage of gross capital formation, European Union countries, circa 2000.

Country	Gross investment in dwellings as % of gross capital formation
Greece (01)	21.0
Spain (00)	22.5
Italy (01)	23.0
Portugal (99)	21.0
Ireland (95)	33.0
Germany (01)	32.0
Austria (00)	27.0
France (00)	26.0
Finland (00)	25.0
Netherlands (00)	25.0
Belgium (00)	23.7
Denmark (01)	19.0
United Kingdom (00)	18.0
Luxembourg (00)	15.0
Sweden (01)	12.0

Source: Eurostat (2002).

The year to which data refer is in parentheses against the name of the country.

in Portugal, compared with 1.9% in Italy (Eurostat 2003). Thus, the most likely explanation for the similarity in capital investment among the four countries is that gross capital formation is very high generally in Greece, Spain and Portugal, reflecting a relatively high rate of economic growth while, in Italy, it reflects a lower rate of economic growth.

These data raise questions about the institutional structure of housing production in the four southern countries. Important aspects of this are discussed throughout the remainder of this book, and this section is intended to provide an introduction to some of the issues.

There are, roughly, two distinctive systems of housing production found in southern Europe. The first system is associated with large-scale housing development, generally multi-family housing, carried out by large construction firms and supported by a strong urban planning system which favours large landowners. Such large-scale development also requires a relatively highly developed residential mortgage system to guarantee credit for development and sale. The second system locates the initiative for development in households themselves and results in small-scale production, often of single houses or relatively small multi-family buildings. It is associated with small construction firms, a weak urban planning system, relatively easy access to small plots of land and a weak credit system for both building and purchase.

Both types of production system coexist in the southern European countries, but the balance between them is different. Barlow and Duncan's (1994) analysis, based on data for the late 1980s and presented more fully in Chapter 4, groups Italy, Greece and Portugal together as generally characterised by a system of small-scale production while Spain is characterised by large-scale production. However, more recent evidence suggests that Portugal is now also characterised by a system of large-scale production, facilitated by the development of a residential mortgage system and, possibly, the penetration of the Portuguese construction industry by large Brazilian firms.

In order to understand the balance between these two forms of residential development, it is useful to consider the ways in which housing development can be promoted in southern Europe. Housing promotion systems are ways of organising supply and demand for housing. They reflect the ways in which a wide range of institutions are co-ordinated in housing production: land ownership systems, planning regulation, subsidies, contracting firms, and financial and other resources supplied by extended families. Five distinctive forms of housing promotion, which are sometimes interlinked, exist in the southern European countries. It is the balance between these forms of promotion which distinguishes both southern Europe from northern Europe, and each of the southern countries themselves. They are:

- Self-promotion
- Co-operative promotion
- Direct public promotion
- Private promotion of publicly financed housing
- Private free promotion.

Self-promotion

Self-promotion has been widely used in all southern countries in the past and still makes a significant contribution to building in Greece and Portugal. Self-promotion is most extensive where the size of available land parcels is relatively small. Sometimes public land is used but, more often, it is private land without any kind of urban plan or the infrastructure required for housing, for example, in green or protected areas. Self-promotion is also sometimes related to illegal building, that is, building without obtaining the relevant building permits and/or planning permission.

It is difficult to generalise about the way of building which is used in self-promotion. Usually people use their savings as working capital. Mortgage loans are not commonly used. Sometimes the building process stopped part way through because of lack of resources and only resumed when more resources became available. The consequence was an urban landscape where unfinished houses were frequently seen.

The general process starts with a family buying a piece of land, usually on the periphery of a city. They look for a building company which presents them with a plan for the kind of house they want to build. The design is adapted to the specific needs of the family and to their available resources. There is a verbal agreement between the builder and the future owner. Sometimes, when the household does not have enough resources, their investment is limited to the materials only and the house is self-built with the help of friends and family. Many of the people who built their homes themselves were construction workers since many of the migrants from rural areas found their first urban job in construction, which also played an important role in integrating them into the urban production system.

Up until the mid-1970s, a substantial part of self-promotion was illegal (*abusivi* in Italy; *afthereta* in Greece; *clandestinos* in Portugal). Standards in these areas have been progressively upgraded in all three countries. Areas of poor-quality self-promotion in Athens have been progressively upgraded by processes of internal regeneration, through repairs, partial or complete rebuilding by the owners themselves, public provision of urban infrastructure, and so on. On the periphery of the largest Spanish cities, self-promotion was highly developed during the 1950s. After that time, controls over housing development were strengthened and self-promotion became marginal. In Portugal, self-promotion was important in the early phases of rural to urban migration, and there has been a rapid development of shanty town type self-promotion (*barracas*) in the 1980s associated with the influx of returners and refugees from the former colonies. There is now a large programme, centred on Lisbon and Porto, to relocate people living in *barracas* to newly built social rented and subsidised owner-occupied dwellings.

'Houses built overnight' were the most typical form of development of illegal self-promotion on the urban peripheries during the 1950s and early

1960s. In all four southern countries, there were similar laws that prevented the demolition of illegal houses if they already had a roof and people were living in them. Consequently, people migrating from rural areas bought a piece of land or illegally occupied a piece of public land and built a precarious house overnight, when the local police were off-duty or pretended not to know. This was possible because the self-builders were working in construction and had the help of colleagues as well as members of their families. In the morning when the police officer passed by the area, he had to acknowledge the house as built with people inside and not order its demolition.

These houses were subsequently improved, but some parts of the buildings remained in poor condition and could not be refurbished. In Spain, most of these areas were demolished and rebuilt some years later, and their residents were relocated in public housing. Around Athens, most of the areas built illegally were progressively rebuilt by the home owners who improved their construction, but could not alter the basic flaws associated with small parcel sizes, absence of public space and insufficient infrastructure, which remain as chronic problems in such areas. In Italy and Portugal, innovative programmes have been developed to improve the quality of these areas, involving demolition or upgrading, depending on the basic quality of the area and the resources available to residents and public authorities for improving the infrastructure.

There are also cases of self-promotion by households in the highest income groups. Here the process is usually legal. People looking for individual homes buy a parcel of land which is within the land use plans for the area and agree on a unique design with an architect. After the design is agreed, the project is given to a construction company to be built. All the large metropolitan areas in southern Europe have enclaves of this kind of housing. Where self-promotion is more frequent, as in Greece, this practice also extends to middle-class groups.

Co-operative promotion

Co-operative housing is a common way of promoting housing for low- and lower-middle income households in the southern countries and can be considered as a collective form of self-promotion. In Greece co-operatives primarily concentrated on acquiring land on which to build and provided the urban infrastructure necessary to develop it while building the houses was carried out through self-promotion or a mixed system of promotion. Co-operatives are, however, no longer active in Greece. In Spain, Portugal and

Italy, co-operatives carry out the full process of promotion, from acquiring land through to building the houses, which are then sold to the individual members of the co-operatives. In Spain, trade union co-operatives have grown rapidly in recent years and have promoted a significant amount of housing in the big cities.

Co-operatives are a way of getting a home using less household resources. Some proportion of the investment is paid by the prospective owner before getting their home, and the remainder at the completion of the co-operative's work. The principal purpose is to save the costs associated with private promotion and to profit from increases in the price of the land in the period between acquisition and occupying the completed property. This way of gaining access to a home is popular not only because households save money, but also for the opportunity to participate in the design of their new homes.

Because the southern countries generally have weak public institutions, co-operatives can play an important intermediate role between public and private institutions. They may vary in size, from locally organised endeavours to those organised by major trade unions or larger umbrella co-operative associations. In this way, they capture some of the advantages associated with public housing in other European countries, mainly by selling public land to them at less than market price on the condition that the future owners' income will be below a certain level. Co-operatives can also benefit from subsidies allocated by the central government to the promoters of housing for low-income households.

Direct public promotion

As the tenure figures given earlier in this chapter show (Tables 2.1, 2.2 and 2.3), direct state intervention in promoting new housing is much weaker in southern Europe than in the rest of Europe. There are important institutional differences among the four countries, but the generally weak role of direct state promotion of housing reflects the importance of the principle of subsidiarity in structuring welfare state institutions in these countries. It also reflects the general weaknesses of civil administration in the four countries. Both these issues are discussed more fully in Chapters 4 and 6. Italy, Spain and Portugal continue to build small amounts of public housing, and even less is provided in Greece. On the whole, this housing is designed to support other public programmes by providing for those displaced by large public infrastructure projects, victims of natural disasters or, in Greece in particular, those repatriated from former socialist countries. In the larger cities where demand for housing among poorer groups is most intense, there are some localised programmes of direct public provision for renting. Because the supply of such housing comes nowhere near meeting demand from low-income households, especially from young people and immigrants, there are complex issues around clientelistic practices in allocating it.

It is difficult to estimate the total volume of public house building over time and the current tenure figures understate the significance of direct public promotion. Much directly promoted public housing has been sold to its occupiers, either because it was always intended as promotion for sale to lower-income groups or because strategic decisions were taken in the past to divest state institutions of housing which they owned and managed (poorly) by selling it. Most of the public stock in Spain was sold to its occupiers in the last years of the Franco regime as a means of avoiding civil unrest at the time, and well over half the public-built stock in Italy has been sold in a more piecemeal fashion to its occupiers.

The dynamics of direct public promotion have tended to be more closely associated with macro-economic policy than with housing policy. The fiscal austerity of the 1990s, associated with the Maastricht criteria, have inhibited direct public building. Direct public promotion has also been used as a counter-cyclical policy, in which case building for sale has benefits due to the faster turnover of state capital investment and the ability to produce a larger quantity of housing for the same level of investment.

Private promotion of publicly financed housing

This form of promotion provides the main alternative to direct public promotion in Spain and Italy. It can be considered as a form of social provision, which is primarily organised through the private sector. Private promoters build housing for sale, using relatively large subsidies, paid directly to either the promoter or the purchasers. The subsidy system also sets conditions on the maximum size of the houses and the maximum income for purchasers. The price at which the house may be sold is also determined by the government. The main advantage of this form of provision is that it avoids direct intervention by the state in promoting and distributing the product. It is a more effective means of promotion within weakly developed state administrative systems. The disadvantage of this form of promotion is that, even with high levels of subsidy, the housing is not accessible to those in the lowest income groups.

Private promotion

It is difficult to establish the precise dynamics of private promotion which are highly dependent on the structure of the construction industry and the extent to which companies within it are capable of taking on the role of promotion. In general, only the larger companies have this capacity. The sector generally has a strongly localised character, so that even in the same country, there are different types of companies and variations can be found in different regions within a single country. Nevertheless, there has been a tendency in recent years for housing promotion to become concentrated in large companies. In Spain, reliance on large-scale private promotion dates from political arrangements under Franco, representing one of the key alliances supporting the regime, and the system has been strengthened by the development of urban planning and financial arrangements which are biased in favour of large-scale promotion. In Portugal, there has been increasing reliance on large-scale promoters associated with rapid urbanisation and housing development since 1980. In Italy, private promotion was on a relatively small scale until recently. In Greece, large construction companies are still only interested in public works, although this may change after the 2004 Olympic Games, which has supported the formation of larger construction companies.

Another important feature of private promotion by larger companies is the use of small subcontracting companies for the major portion of the building works. The labour-intensive nature of building is one of the features which makes subsidising construction an effective tool of counter-cyclical macroeconomic policy. For a relatively small subsidy, there is a relatively large and rapid effect on employment and consumption. Many of these small companies are based on familial structures, composed of the members of an extended family who specialise in specific crafts: masonry, flooring, roofing, iron works and so on. These small companies also use a high proportion of immigrants for unskilled building work, and increasingly in more skilled tasks, so that the construction sector generally provides a means of integrating migrants and immigrants into urban areas. Somewhat metaphorically, migrants and immigrants build the very cities where they come to live.

Housing promotion systems

What distinguishes the housing promotion systems in southern Europe is that they rest strongly on self-promotion, with its roots in familial and neighbourhood social structures, and on large-scale promotion systems in the larger cities (except in Greece). In comparison with northern Europe, the role of the state in securing housing promotion for lower-income groups is more indirect. There is little direct state promotion of housing for rent; the state prefers to sponsor promotion by other agents, either co-operatives or private promoters. The overall result is that there is relatively little new provision which is accessible to the lowest income groups throughout the four countries. Consequently, the pressure from relatively high rates of migration and immigration focusing on the larger cities is either absorbed by increased overcrowding in the private rented sector or by families where this is possible.

The balance between self-promotion, state-sponsored promotion and large-scale private promotion is different among the southern countries. This is most apparent in the dynamics of urban form in the largest cities. In Greece, where self-promotion and small-scale private promotion dominate, cities acquire extensive and sprawling peripheries dominated by single-family housing. In Spain and Portugal, where large-scale private promotion plays a bigger role, urban expansion is characterised by large-scale multi-family developments with strongly demarcated boundaries, often inserted into a surrounding rural hinterland or next to existing villages. In Spain, this urban expansion has a more planned character, but in Portugal even existing cities come to have an irregular character as large-scale new development jostles against older, single-family self-promoted areas.

Conclusion

Southern housing systems are distinguished from northern systems by four characteristics. They have both high levels of home ownership and very small social rented sectors. All four countries have large stocks of secondary homes. Issues of access to housing have an important impact on family and household structures. And, in three of the countries, self-promotion plays a significant role in the production of housing.

The configuration of these characteristics could be interpreted as simply a variant on a general European housing model. In contrast, we argue that they reflect fundamental differences in the way society is organised in all four countries. The social significance of these four aspects of southern housing systems can only be understood in this wider context. Chapter 3 introduces this argument by discussing the pivotal role of housing in articulating urbanisation and industrialisation in the four countries. Chapter 4 lays out the theoretical basis for our argument that the housing systems in the four countries constitute a southern system because they are set within a southern welfare system, based on a specific institutional structure which shapes housing policies, practices and outcomes. Chapter 5 shows how families constitute an important part of this welfare system and the strategies they deploy in accessing housing for their members. Finally, Chapter 6 draws out the implications of the southern welfare system for housing by showing how it shapes the public action space within which public policies are formulated and implemented.

3

Urbanisation and Housing Systems in Southern Europe

Introduction

The rapid urbanisation of the southern European countries after World War II was accomplished in the context of weak industrial development, minimal direct state involvement in housing and a welfare state that offered little to migrants from the countryside. What made urbanisation possible in this context? The answer is the role of the family and the nature of the housing provision system.

This short chapter outlines key features of the post-war urbanisation process and shows how it depended on family practices and strategies for accessing housing. It highlights the nature of these processes in two ways: by raising questions about their sustainability in the future and by comparing the different urban patterns in Athens and Madrid, which illustrate how similar structural processes can have different local outcomes. This chapter provides a synthesis of the main themes which run throughout this book and situates the detailed arguments about southern welfare systems, family practices and strategies, and housing provision systems which are examined in the next three chapters.

The articulation between urbanisation and industrialisation: the pivotal role of housing

There are important differences in the social reproduction processes in northern and southern Europe. In the north, where urbanisation was clearly associated with industrialisation, social reproduction was organised around the needs of industrial development for a skilled workforce (education, training), its location (housing and transport) and its condition (healthcare, housing quality, nutrition). It reflected the need to plan and organise the city and society around industry and urban development. The core element for social integration was waged work, the prerequisite for anyone wishing to move to the industrial-urban core. Housing and other social amenities followed and were usually secured by the state and/or employers: the family's role was reduced to simple, everyday tasks in the process of modernist individuation that disarticulated traditional attachments based on kinship, locality and so on in the transition between Gemeinschaft and Gesellschaft, following Tönnies and Simmel (Park 1925 [1957] & 1929 [1957]; Wirth 1938 [1964]; Tsoukalas 1987; Frisby 2002).

In the more recently, weakly industrialised south, urbanisation has not been led by industrial development. Rather, it was war and the progressive disarticulation of the rural economy that pushed large numbers of people towards the protective anonymity of urban living and the diverse opportunities that the city could offer. Although parts of southern Europe, in northern Italy and northern Spain, shared the northern European experience of industrially based urbanisation, Greece and Portugal as a whole, along with southern Italy and other parts of Spain, demonstrate the different historical path followed in the south.

Southern European urbanisation after World War II has therefore been driven more by the depletion of rural areas than by the relatively meagre attraction of an unorganised urban labour market. Instead of a labour market structured by industrial jobs, work opportunities in construction, personal services and public administration were the basis for urban growth in many southern European cities. Because the urban labour market offered insufficient and often precarious jobs, there was less need to invest in the reproduction of the labour force since there was no shortage of workers and the requirements in terms of the quality of the labour force were not high.

Meanwhile, the dualistic welfare state developed in the context of this fluid labour market (Padovani 1984 & 1996). It guaranteed support for public-sector and full-time workers but little protection for peripheral workers in irregular jobs in construction and personal services, offering no support for the new urban population (see Chapter 4).

Securing a job was not the key to integration into urban society as employment was usually not sufficient to guarantee a family's living requirements for any significant period of time. Since amenities were not guaranteed by jobs, through wages and benefits, it was preferable to secure a house and then search for casual and, later, permanent jobs. The house would have to be a dwelling that created no regular cost, such as rent, since jobs could not offer a regular income. Low-standard, owner-occupied dwellings, self-built or otherwise acquired, became a suitable solution. As a consequence, home ownership in southern Europe is very high among low-income groups (Cremaschi 1998). In Athens, in 1991, it was much stronger outside the area surrounding the city centre and especially in the western, working-class part of the city (Maloutas 2000, p. 66).

The high levels of unemployment in southern Europe after World War II also led to emigration to western and northern Europe up until the mid-1970s and reduced the incentive for southern governments to provide adequate rented social housing or any other form of public housing. Home ownership was the only feasible way for southern European families to access housing and, thus, the right to housing was conflated with the right to home ownership. Illegal housing construction was not considered to be antisocial. The policies of *condono* in Italy (Padovani 1988) and similar policies in Greece legalised the houses by simply imposing a fine (Leontidou 1990, pp. 137–71; Emmanuel 1975; Economou 1988; Maloutas 2003b). These policies promoted individualist and familialist approaches, against which the state was lenient since it did not provide any other basis, such as substantial social services, that could legitimate a strict enforcement of legality.

The pivotal role of housing for moving to and surviving in urban areas became a family concern since it was difficult to acquire individually. Consequently, immigration to the city was also a family strategy. The significance of housing as a means of integration into urban society meant that the house became a primary objective in family strategies for surviving in the city. Casual, insecure work could be found anywhere in the cities so there was no need to move home to work. The house could, therefore, remain a stable spatial reference point and kinship networks could be formed without substantial pressure from the labour market.

Demographic patterns, family and housing

The urbanisation model described in the previous section is related to demographic patterns and processes that have an important direct and indirect impact on housing.

The rapid urbanisation in the second half of the twentieth century, as the result of migration from the rural areas within southern European countries, affected different cities at different times. Although industrial activity was also developed within several parts of this region during the same period, urbanisation was instigated mainly by war, civil war and crisis in the rural economy. With no substantial industrial basis the southern European cities did not act as incubators of modernist social relations in the way that their northern counterparts did in earlier periods. The recent immigrants to the cities represented a vast group in which more traditional rural family structures and values were still strong. These structures and values were developed into assets for a particular type of welfare arrangement. The scale of rural migration overwhelmed local urban labour markets and, as the fordist industries elsewhere in western Europe were seeking cheap labour, some of the surplus labour in southern Europe moved to these markets where they secured steady jobs and welfare benefits over a long period of time. Although these immigrants seldom gained occupational and social status in the host societies, they benefited from the considerable difference between the cost of labour and living in the host countries and in their own countries, where most of them returned when the rate of industrial growth slowed in the rest of Europe.

Rural to urban migration, coupled with emigration to northern Europe, has formed part of individual family strategies. The benefits from these moves have contributed to increasing family assets, either as savings brought back by returning immigrants or as regular remittances to members of the family that stayed behind, and have helped to consolidate the family's role in social reproduction.

Household structures are closely related to the social institution of the family, which is their organising principle. In southern Europe the power of this organising principle is reflected in the comparatively greater number of family-centred household structures. The population of this region has a larger proportion of nuclear and extended families than the rest of the European Union (see Tables 2.12, 2.13 and 2.14). The close proximity of the homes sought by households related by kinship is further evidence of the strength of the family institution in solidarity networks. (This is discussed more fully in Chapter 5.)

Therefore, the strength and vitality of the family in southern Europe is related to its role in the context of a particular kind of rapid urbanisation. The dominant family culture, linked to a recent rural past and to the relatively high percentage of rural population, was an important asset in promoting specific forms of political and social regulation. The state has had less direct intervention in the organisation of social reproduction than in those countries where urbanisation was led by the expansion of fordist industries. The apparently weaker and different role of the state has been less the result of structural necessity than of political systems which allow clientelism and populism to flourish. Bargaining for political support allowed concessions to families in a process that reinforced the role of the family as a social and political agent.

In terms of housing, the family took the initiative in devising solutions within a sector that was shaped neither by state intervention in the form of social housing nor by private promoters and builders (except in Spain, where production is dominated by large construction firms). Self-promotion, suitable for family initiative and often illegal, remained important in most parts of the region throughout most of the second half of the twentieth century. However, the relationship between family and housing goes further than accessing home ownership. Families have also deployed equally important strategies during periods of reduced access to home ownership. Defensive strategies aiming at pooling housing resources meant that younger members delayed leaving home and widowed elderly parents lived within their children's households.

The origins of these practices which sustained family solidarity can be found in a complex relationship between socio-economic constraint and cultural predisposition. Family solidarity is a set of social practices which respond to current socio-economic constraints in ways that are based on predispositions formed in other contexts, most importantly the rural areas from which families came. Moreover, the relationship between constraint and cultural predisposition can be, and usually is, monitored politically. Therefore, the key role of the family in social reproduction in southern Europe has been the outcome of a combined social, political and cultural dynamic.

Family structures and practices are not immune to new developments. Households are tending to become less family-centred, although the increase of single-person and other forms of non-family households is slow. Women are beginning to participate much more in the labour market and this is a central problem in maintaining traditional family solidarity practices, which depend heavily on most women providing the domestic labour that underpins them. Traditional gender roles are becoming less sustainable not only because of economic pressure, which does not necessarily lead towards a modernisation of gender roles, but because of wider aspirations for self-fulfilment. These aspirations have been supported in other countries, especially in the Nordic countries, through the development of direct welfare services which have been slow to develop in southern Europe (Pantelidou-Malouta 1988; Esping-Andersen 1990 & 1999). Additional support for changing gender roles is now found in the recent wave of immigration into the southern countries, with foreign female labour filling traditional women's roles in the host societies (Maratou-Alipranti & Fakiolas 2000). However, these trends introduce new social divisions between the indigenous population and the immigrants as well as within the indigenous population, since both the aspirations for self-fulfilment and the resources to hire domestic help are more characteristic of the professional classes than the lower social strata.

The low birth rates in the region, especially in Italy and Spain, also represent a reduced base for the future reproduction of family solidarity. These rates can be interpreted as strategies used by middle- and lower middle-class families to maintain their standard of living. They can also be interpreted as an effect of the increasing numbers of economically active women and longer time periods spent in education, which have pushed the average age of first childbirth to the late twenties and reduced the opportunity for large families.

Another important impact of low birth rates is an ageing population, which will become a burden for social security systems and undermine traditional family solidarity practices as an imbalance develops between the growing need for and scarcity of domestic labour. Ageing also contributes to an increase in the number of smaller households in the context of slow or non-existent population growth. An ageing population creates a need for more and different types of homes.

However, the most important demographic impact on housing in the region originates from the wave of immigration in the past 15 years. The southern European countries stopped providing migrants to other labour markets in the late 1970s and began receiving immigrants from other parts of the world such as South America, Africa and eastern Europe. The percentage of immigrants in these countries' population is comparatively low, but their visibility is high because of the rapid growth in their number over a short period of time and their presence in a context that was ethnically and culturally homogeneous.

The impact of the flow of immigration on housing is important. This immigration has not been instigated by the needs of endogenous development but by growing flows from less developed regions in the world, despite increased immigration controls throughout the European Union. In contrast with the flows to western Europe in the 1950s and 1960s, current immigration flows have not been caused by employers searching for cheap labour but have come as a response to political and economic change elsewhere (Pugliese 2000). It has also produced unplanned housing situations. Immigrants to the southern European countries now face a housing market dominated by production for home ownership, which does not meet the needs of their largely transitory presence nor suit their limited resources. As a social rented sector which would suit their needs is poorly developed, they have to turn to the private rented sector where they occupy the least desirable areas and homes, often windowless basements and shanties. The growing immigrant presence in southern Europe and their unprotected status is increasing pressures for segregation in land and housing markets. As a consequence, inequality in housing conditions is growing as the housing stock becomes more socially segmented.

Similarity and difference in south European housing processes and urban patterns

In Chapter 2, we pointed to important similarities in housing patterns and arrangements among the southern European countries. In this we have stressed contextual homogeneity. However, there are also important differences that should be examined.

The striking difference between the layout of two cities such as Athens and Madrid is immediately visible and an example of some of the differences among southern countries. Athens is built around a central area, which is denser and sprawls in all directions, stopping only at natural barriers such as the coast or the mountains. It forms a continuum from dense to sparse and from high-rise to low-rise construction, and consequently, the city limits are blurred. Madrid is built more compactly around an old city nucleus in a dense and high-rise concentric zone with a series of suburban extensions, where the boundaries between land with and without construction are also clear. In Athens, the impact of planning has not been important and this is obvious in the street layout, the absence of functional zoning, the disordered orientation of buildings, the absence of public space and so on (Economou 1997). In contrast, Madrid reveals a structure that could not possibly be the result of spontaneous and uncoordinated construction but is rather the result of an important and long-term planning effort (Leal 1999a). Can two cities with such different urban patterns belong to the same housing system?

Behind the differences in the layouts of Madrid and Athens lie very different ways of organising the construction of cities. Madrid was built through corporate promotion after the 1950s. Large promoters developed important areas around the city and converted them into high-rise residential areas, providing affordable housing in a city that was growing fast due to internal migration. Athens was constructed through self-promotion in an unplanned and uncoordinated way that, nevertheless, was also effective in providing housing for a rapidly growing population that tripled during the first three decades after World War II.

Different patterns of housing and urban promotion are related to different social structures and to the role of landed property in building and housing. Large landed property owners around Madrid represented socially homogeneous and functionally concentrated social groups that could better valorise their assets through rigorous planning and large-scale house building. The land development regulations in Madrid favoured these large proprietors in the public decision-making processes about building and substantially reduced the autonomy of small landowners.

In Athens, the small landowners' interests prevailed, following the path used to solve the massive problem of housing refugees from Asia Minor in the inter-war period (Leontidou 1990; Economou 2000). Large tracts of public land were subdivided and distributed to the refugees for them to build their own homes. This solution became the model for the early period after World War II. The dominant position of the small landowner is reflected even in the laws and regulations that were meant to affect only specific areas where 'active urbanisation' would be implemented (EKPAA 2001). At best, the large landowner has been able to speculate on the conversion of land from rural to urban uses and its subdivision, but has been excluded from any kind of direct participation in important land development and housing operations. Small landowners and self-promotion have therefore dominated in Athens, while large landowners and operations were more characteristic in Madrid.

This important difference in land ownership and housing production between the two cities is partly due to the different historical paths that led to different social forms of land ownership but also has its roots in the political regimes experienced in the post-World War II period. Francoist Spain was an openly dictatorial regime that could impose solutions favouring the social groups, such as the large landowners, which had helped install it. The regime had prevailed in the Spanish Civil War and had little need to legitimise its power by concessions. In Greece, the Civil War followed World War II and the German occupation, and its outcome depended heavily on foreign military intervention. The authoritarian regime that was installed in the 1950s had weak legitimacy and became an ambivalent democracy after pressure from the United States (Nicolacopoulos 2001; Alivisatos 1983). Housing was one of the areas where concessions could be made in a complex balancing act between economic tolerance and political control.

Despite the physical differences between Madrid and Athens we will argue that they result from a similar housing system. The common element, even in cases as dissimilar as Athens and Madrid, is the production of affordable housing, without direct state provision, for a rapidly increasing urban population in the second half of the twentieth century. The absence of direct state provision in housing has left wider opportunities for the market and civil society. The state, although failing to intervene directly, has nevertheless heavily influenced the activities of the market and civil society.

In the parliamentary-clientelist Greek regime of the first two decades after World War II, the dominant conditions for social reproduction allowed diverse housing strategies to be developed by civil society, mainly by the family. Market forces were present, but were subordinate to state-sponsored family initiatives. This situation gave a free hand to the Greek family to develop housing strategies focused on owner occupation and mainly involving some form of self-promotion and often self-construction. The dictatorial Spanish regime depended more on the market to invest for profit, leaving less space for family strategies. Thus, in Spain, family strategies were developed in a market-dominated context and revolved around accessing home ownership through the market and managing the family housing stock according to the present and future needs of its members.

The dissimilarity between Madrid and Athens is reflected in their strikingly different patterns, the former being a planned city and the latter an aggregate of spontaneous sprawl. Spontaneous urbanisation is therefore not a distinctive feature of southern European housing. Planning and spontaneity are both present in the region, and sometimes their extreme forms are present in the same country (Milan or Turin versus the cities of southern Italy, for example). The planned city produced either through the spatial organisation principles associated with industrial development, as in northern Italy, or through the market and the political power of big landowners and developers, as in Madrid, coexists in southern Europe with the unplanned, spontaneous city based on the loosely regulated familialist-clientelist urban development found in Athens.

Therefore, the southern European housing system does not rely on similar urban patterns, or on similar processes of housing production. The search for its common features should be focused on the relative absence of *direct* state intervention in solving the acute housing problem generated by rapid urbanisation and how this shaped the housing solutions that were implemented. These processes occurred in the context of welfare states that focused mainly on pensions but failed to intervene in other ways to support families and which, thus, allowed a bigger role for the family in social reproduction. It is this configuration of key elements of social regulation in the region which is the main common feature in southern European housing systems.

4

Welfare Systems in Southern Europe

Introduction

Housing has famously been characterised as the 'wobbly pillar of the welfare state'. This phrase usually refers to the way that housing systems span the boundary of the welfare state and the market, but it also raises the question of what we mean by the welfare state and, more importantly, how we can delineate the role of the welfare state within more widely conceived ideas of welfare systems. These are key questions in a comparative study, especially if one is concerned with a set of countries in which the welfare state has a minimal role in the direct provision of housing.

This chapter argues that welfare systems have a distinctive form in southern Europe, which both reflects and shapes their housing systems. Three institutional structures shape the way welfare and housing are delivered in these countries: the capacity of the civil administration, an extensive irregular and informal labour market, and familialism. The argument weaves together two dimensions of comparison. The first sets the southern countries in a European context while identifying differences among them, and the second compares housing systems with other welfare state programmes.

Welfare systems and institutional complexes

It is important to start by distinguishing between welfare states and welfare systems. Abrahamson (1992) suggests the metaphor of a welfare triangle, comprising household, state and market, as a framing device for conceptualising welfare systems. He sees the organisations which comprise civil society as suspended within this triangle, and argues that changes in any one of the three sets of institutions represented by the points of the triangle will affect both civil society and the institutions at the other two points. Pereirinha (1996) points out that it is useful to distinguish between the extended southern family, conceptualised as including both kin and friends, and non-profit third sector organisations in discussing civil society. Alexander (1998) argues that the concept of civil society must be drawn even more broadly to include those bodies, such as trade unions, professional and civic organisations, which serve to aggregate political interests horizontally across society. These distinctions are important in capturing the specificity of southern Europe.

Kolberg and Uusitalo (1992) amplify Abrahamson's model. They define the institutions which make up a welfare system as family, labour market and welfare state, and argue that they are inextricably linked into a single, larger, institutional complex. Because these institutions are mutually dependent, then the changing configuration of relationships among them should be the focus of study. They observe that fifty years ago, each of the institutions could be seen as separate, but that a process of functional de-differentiation has taken place over the intervening period, leaving the three institutions completely intertwined and creating new forms of political cleavage, for example, between public and private sector employees in Scandinavia or between labour market insiders and outsiders in continental Europe. Kolberg and Uusitalo's argument reflects a Parsonian view of societal modernisation as functional differentiation, which implicitly raises the question of whether the southern countries have emerged into a tertiarised global economy in a state of pre-differentiation.

The ideas of Abrahamson and of Kolberg and Uusitalo are important in framing a study of southern housing systems. Housing is a field of practical activity which links the state (as direct supplier, regulator or generator of relevant housing, economic and social policy, or as the focus of political organisation), private markets (related to the provision of housing and to labour markets) and family (as occupiers of housing and as a resource in housing provision). If the institutional structures in these three areas are different, then we would expect the nature of the housing systems to be different too.

The remainder of this chapter uses these ideas to review a set of debates about welfare systems in southern Europe. We start by explaining Esping-Andersen's work on welfare regimes (Esping-Andersen 1990, 1996 & 1999) and looking at the ways it has been applied to housing. We then set Esping-Andersen's work in a wider context, largely drawing on the work of Castles (1994, 1995, 1998, and Castles & Mitchell 1993) and Castles and Ferrera (1996). This provides a basis for examining the debate on whether there is a separate southern welfare regime, which leads into a detailed discussion of the institutional context in southern Europe which shapes how welfare is delivered.

Welfare regimes, welfare states and welfare activities

If the notion of welfare systems is a way of framing the problem of welfare delivery in the broadest possible terms, then the concept of welfare regimes defines welfare delivery very narrowly and rigorously.

In *The Three Worlds of Welfare Capitalism*, Esping-Andersen starts by defining welfare regimes in the following way:

> 'Contemporary advanced nations cluster not only in terms of how their traditional social-welfare policies are constructed, but also in terms of how these influence employment and general social structure. To talk of "a regime" is to denote the fact that in the relationships between state and economy a complex of legal and organizational features are systematically interwoven.' (1990, p. 2)

The Three Worlds of Welfare Capitalism was the first large-scale, cross-national quantitative study of welfare policy. It was forged as a tool for analysing the dynamics of labour markets. The conceptual and methodological advances in this work sparked off immense debate throughout the 1990s. Two important strands centred on whether there was a separate southern welfare regime and on extending the analysis to examine housing provision systems. We look at both these issues later in this chapter. Our overall argument is that:

- Esping-Andersen uses the concept of welfare regimes to classify countries into one of three regime types on the basis of their income-maintenance systems. In contrast, we argue that the concept of welfare regimes is more fruitfully understood as a complex ideal-typical construct locating specific countries in terms of how they lie between different ideal regime types. Using the concept in this way helps us to understand the problems of extending it to other welfare state activities, such as housing, and to other countries.
- Analysing the way the concept of welfare regimes has been applied to housing points to the need to contextualise it. Different welfare state activities are linked to their societal context in different ways.
- There is no specific need to argue for a separate southern welfare regime in strictly defined terms, but the debate over a separate southern welfare

regime identifies key elements in the wider societal context which generate a specifically southern welfare *system*.

On the basis of this argument, three elements of the broader social context for the delivery of housing welfare can be identified: the capacity of the state's civil administration, the large irregular and informal labour market, and familialism. Each is discussed in turn later in this chapter.

Esping-Andersen and welfare regimes

In *The Three Worlds of Welfare Capitalism*, Esping-Andersen identifies three types of welfare regimes: liberal, conservative and social democratic. Each type is defined in terms of three components: the extent to which welfare state policies decommodify labour; the relationship between welfare state policies and forms of social stratification; and the split between state and market in the design and delivery of specific programmes. The typology of regimes is built up by identifying clusters of nations around each of these components. The analysis is based on data for 18 OECD countries. The empirical justification of the concept of welfare state regimes rests on the overlap in clusterings of nations. Each component in the typology is first defined in theoretical terms and, on this basis, a set of quantitative measures are selected. Most of the quantitative measures are drawn from income-maintenance programmes (pensions, unemployment, disability and sickness benefits). These quantitative measures are combined into complex indices which form the bases for identifying clusters of nations.

The main analytical issue in extending Esping-Andersen's work to other policy fields and countries is whether to start with the concept of welfare regimes as a pre-existing classification of countries or to dissect the concept in order to develop a method for analysing other policy fields. Is the concept a typology of countries or an ideal-typical construct? Although most of the debate is based on his classification of countries, for our purposes it is more useful to reconstruct the concept as an ideal-typical theoretical tool. In order to do this, we set out its theoretical base and the quantitative results which Esping-Andersen presents, then re-analyse his data to develop an ideal-typical tool. This procedure supports looking at specific countries and identifying the tensions within them which will influence their future development.

Decommodification

Esping-Andersen argues that welfare states are rooted in the manner and extent to which they decommodify labour, that is, they stand as a barrier or safety net between workers and their treatment in the labour market as propertyless wage earners. His index of decommodification is based on the relative generosity of old-age pensions, sickness benefits and unemployment benefits, which he regards as measuring the welfare state's potential for decommodification, that is, the extent to which an average worker is 'market independent' (1990, pp. 49–50). He concludes that there is a clear clustering of countries on the decommodification index into three groups: Anglo-Saxon (all six of the English-speaking countries), continental European (including Japan) and Nordic (including Austria, Belgium and Netherlands).

Social stratification

Esping-Andersen argues that there is a mutually reinforcing relationship between systems of social stratification and the welfare state programmes within any one country. Existing forms of stratification constrain the nature of programmes that can be adopted and, once adopted, these programmes tend to support existing forms of stratification. The argument is made more subtle in three ways. First, the adoption of particular social welfare programmes is mediated through existing political institutions and, in particular, the ways in which political parties aggregate social interests. Second, political parties develop their programmes in competition with each other, so that what is politically feasible at any point in time varies. Third, the development of modern welfare states extends at least as far back as the late nineteenth century. Welfare state programmes reflect the configuration of social stratification and party political competition at the time of their introduction. In short, while the principle that welfare state components and social stratification systems are mutually reinforcing is quite simple, present-day arrangements reflect path dependencies within each country.

Esping-Andersen analyses three strands of 'welfare thinking': conservative, liberal and socialist. Each incorporates a particular view of social stratification.

Conservative

Conservative approaches to social stratification are founded on maintaining traditional status distinctions, whether based in hierarchy, occupation or familialism. Vestiges of *noblesse oblige* are associated with a readiness to extend generous help to those requiring assistance. Conservative approaches are also associated with maintaining the authority of the state, *etatism*, and, thus, privileging the position of state employees. Conservative approaches have also been supported by the Catholic church, which has sought to steer a course shaped by its antipathy to liberal capitalism and socialism, on the one hand, and by its commitment to the family and subsidiarity, on the other hand. Esping-Andersen's quantitative indicators privilege the corporatist and *etatist* dimensions, measured by the number of occupationally specific pension schemes and by the percentage of GDP dedicated to pensions for state employees.

Liberal

Liberal approaches to social stratification arise from the belief that a healthy and unfettered market dissolves the hierarchies of tradition and the heavy hand of the state. Status differentials produced by the market are seen as essential to maintaining the spirit of competitive individualism on which markets rest. Poverty is a natural outcome of the operation of the market. Reform liberalism recognised, however, that maximising the efficiency of increasingly complex production processes depends on collective investment in human capital. Acceptable social policies resolve externalities and produce public goods which enhance private production. However, since welfare policies should also nurture self-help and thrift there is a strong reliance on needs testing in social assistance and a preference for private insurance schemes over state schemes. The outcomes reflect wage differentials, with only minimal levels of support for those unable to provide for themselves through the labour market. The quantitative indicators that Esping-Andersen uses measure the extent of means testing, private pensions and health schemes.

Socialist

Socialist approaches emerged with organised labour movements. Before universal suffrage, socialist thinking emphasised mutualist and co-operative approaches, drawn from conservative traditions, and self-help approaches associated with a liberal morality of self-reliance among the labour aristocracy. Universal suffrage meant mobilising a solid parliamentary party and required cross-class strategies, most commonly an agrarian-industrial coalition, leading to populist-universalist social policies. Two factors inhibited the shift to populist universalism in some countries. Where the labour movement enjoyed a strong collective bargaining position, there was no incentive to move towards populist universalism, and where trade unions controlled significant funds as a consequence of previously established corporatist schemes, they were reluctant to lose this source of power. Populist universalism adapted to economic growth and increasing white-collar employment by levelling up benefit levels, especially in the period following World War II. Esping-Andersen uses two quantitative measures of socialism: universal coverage in benefit schemes and low differentials in benefit payments. It follows that large benefit differentials should characterise both conservative and liberal regimes.

Statistical tests among the variables identified with each approach to stratification show that the relationships are as predicted by the theoretical analysis, except that there is no relationship between universalism and egalitarianism because some otherwise liberal countries have highly egalitarian welfare schemes (although the relationship between the two variables is close in the Nordic countries). Using just the high scores within each set of indicators, he classifies five of the continental European countries as conservative (Austria, Belgium, France, Germany and Italy). The liberal grouping contains only one European country, Switzerland, together with Canada, United States, Australia and Japan. The four Nordic countries, plus Netherlands, make up the socialist grouping. Three countries cannot be classified: Ireland, United Kingdom and New Zealand.

Programme design

This component of Esping-Andersen's concept of welfare regimes examines the relationship between state and market in the design of welfare state programmes. It is based on analysing the public-private split in pension schemes. He justifies his focus on pension schemes because they represent the largest single component of expenditure in all welfare states and, thus, should be the most significant element of expenditure contributing to the decommodification of labour. The analysis distinguishes four types of schemes: social security pensions available to all as a social right (linked to socialism), government schemes for civil servants (linked to *etatist* conservatism), private occupational schemes (linked to both conservative and liberal approaches) and individually purchased annuities (linked to liberalism). The quantitative indicators are based on the percentage of total pension expenditure within each of these schemes. In practice, he privileges social security and public employee pensions in his analysis and does not use the full data set systematically. On this basis, he classifies pension systems into three types:

- *Residualist*, in which market provision prevails over social security and civil service schemes
- *Corporatist state-dominated*, in which previous occupational status is the key element in the pension programme

- *Universalistic state-dominated*, in which social security schemes are the most important form of pension.

In classifying countries, Switzerland is the only European state considered as residualist. The others are: Australia, Canada and United States. The corporatist countries include: Austria, Belgium, France, Germany, Italy, Japan and Finland. Five countries are considered as universalistic: New Zealand, Norway, Sweden, Denmark and Netherlands. Ireland and United Kingdom elude classification, and Denmark, Netherlands and Finland are also difficult to classify.

Politics and welfare regimes

Esping-Andersen then explores the significance of party politics. His main hypothesis is that working-class mobilisation, expressed through mass parties of the left, contributes to creating more socialist welfare states while dominance by Catholic and/or Christian Democratic parties creates more corporatist welfare states. In other words, the structure of the welfare state is related to the structure of political relationships, as expressed through democratic party politics.

The basic statistical model tests the significance of party politics, relative to economic and demographic factors, in shaping welfare state activities. Three points summarise this analysis:

(1) Aggregate spending on social security and on pensions is best explained by economic and demographic structural variables. Party politics has little influence on total spending levels.
(2) Political power relations explain the structure of the welfare state as a whole and of specific programmes within it. Left party power accounts for decommodification and the general development of social democracy (operationally defined as the influence of left/labour parties in preventing the development of liberal measures). Catholic parties and a history of authoritarian statehood clearly account for corporatist and *etatist* biases in the structure of welfare states.
(3) There is a correspondence between political forces (as measured by party shares in cabinets or legislatures) and welfare state regimes. Conservative stratification principles in welfare state programmes are clearly explained by the presence of strong Catholic parties and a history of absolutism. Socialist stratification depends on the strength of left/labour parties, as does the avoidance of liberal stratification principles.

Esping-Andersen's overall argument can be summarised in three tables. Table 4.1 sets out the structure of ideas behind the theoretical argument. Table 4.2 sets out how the countries in the data set are classified on the basis of *each* of the three components which make up the concept of welfare regimes. Table 4.3 combines these two tables into a summary of the theoretical and empirical arguments. It includes *only* those countries which can be clearly classified as belonging to a particular regime type on the criteria associated with all three components. In other words, it identifies the archetypal countries associated with the concept of welfare regimes. Three

Table 4.1 The theoretical argument in *The Three Worlds of Welfare Capitalism* (Esping-Andersen).

Type of regime	Liberal	Conservative	Social Democratic
Level of decommodification	Low	Medium	High
Stratification principle	Liberal	Conservative	Socialist
Programme design principle	Residualist	Corporatist	Universalist
Associated political forces	Absence of social democracy	Christian Democrat: Absolutist periods	Left/Labour

Table 4.2 Classification of countries in *The Three Worlds of Welfare Capitalism* (Esping-Andersen).

Decommodification	Stratification	Programme design
Low	*Liberal*	*Residualist*
Australia	Australia	Australia
United States	Canada	Canada
New Zealand	Japan	Switzerland
Canada	Switzerland	United States
Ireland	United States	
United Kingdom		
Medium	*Conservative*	*Corporatist*
Italy	Austria	Austria
Japan	Belgium	Belgium
France	France	France
Germany	Germany	Germany
Finland	Italy	Italy
Switzerland		Japan
		Finland
High	*Socialist*	*Universalist*
Austria	Denmark	New Zealand
Belgium	Finland	Norway
Netherlands	Netherlands	Sweden
Denmark	Norway	Denmark
Norway	Sweden	Netherlands
Sweden		

Table 4.3 Regime types and archetypal countries in *The Three Worlds of Welfare Capitalism* (Esping-Andersen).

Regime type	Liberal	Conservative	Social Democratic
Level of decommodification	Low	Medium	High
Stratification principle	Liberal	Conservative	Socialist
Programme design principle	Residualist	Corporatist	Universalistic
Core countries	Australia Canada United States	France Germany Italy	Norway Sweden

points stand out in Table 4.3. First, it only includes eight of the eighteen countries in the data set and only five European countries. Second, all the European countries are classified as either conservative or social democratic. In other words, the global reach of the work understates the differences among the European countries. Third, Italy, the only southern European country in the data set, appears as having an archetypal conservative welfare regime, alongside Germany and France.

Welfare regimes: Groups of countries or ideal-typical construct?

The results discussed in the previous section suggest that Esping-Andersen's work must be looked at differently to examine differences within Europe and extend the results to Spain, Greece and Portugal. One way to do this is to set out the concept of welfare regimes as an ideal-typical tool, by re-examining how Esping-Andersen handles his data for each of the three components of the concept of welfare regimes.

First, the three-group categorisation for decommodification is not supported by the data. The natural breaks in the scale he develops suggest that five categories would be more appropriate. There is a clear break within the Anglo-Saxon group, with Canada, United Kingdom and Ireland lying closer to the continental countries than to Australia, United States and New Zealand. More importantly, Italy lies closer to the European Anglo-Saxon group than to the continental group. Figure 4.1 illustrates these two different readings of the data. The extended decommodification scale gives a more differentiated picture of the European Union countries and indicates that Italy may have been misclassified in Esping-Andersen's analysis.

Second, a more extended use of the stratification data set shows that only two countries fall unambiguously within the theoretically defined stratifi-

Esping-Andersen classification	Alternative reading of Esping-Andersen's data
	Very low
Low	Australia
Australia	United States
United States	New Zealand
New Zealand	**Low**
Canada	Canada
Ireland	Ireland
United Kingdom	United Kingdom
Medium	Italy
Italy	**Medium**
Japan	Japan
France	France
Germany	Germany
Finland	Finland
Switzerland	Switzerland
High	**High**
Austria	Austria
Belgium	Belgium
Netherlands	Netherlands
Denmark	**Very high**
Norway	Denmark
Sweden	Norway
	Sweden

Fig. 4.1 Analysis of the decommodification scales in *The Three Worlds of Welfare Capitalism* (Esping-Andersen).

cation types (Sweden (socialist) and United States (liberal)). All the other countries are more fruitfully classified in terms of the tensions they exhibit between two of the ideal type regimes. Figure 4.2 sets out the positioning of each of the countries in this way. This analysis indicates significant differences among the European countries. Germany still does not appear because it is evenly suspended among all three types of stratification. The position of Italy, suspended between conservative and liberal stratification principles, suggests that the suppression of communist opposition after World War II had a significant impact on shaping its welfare state. Both Rhodes (1996) and Ferrera (1996) make a similar point about the other three southern countries. Rhodes observes that they missed the *trentes années* and Ferrera investigates the specific problems facing the socialist parties after the return to democracy. Thus, the re-analysed stratification data also suggest that how the content of political debate is structured may be as important as the structure of party dominance in shaping political choices. This conclusion is more consistent with Esping-Andersen's theoretical analysis than his own.

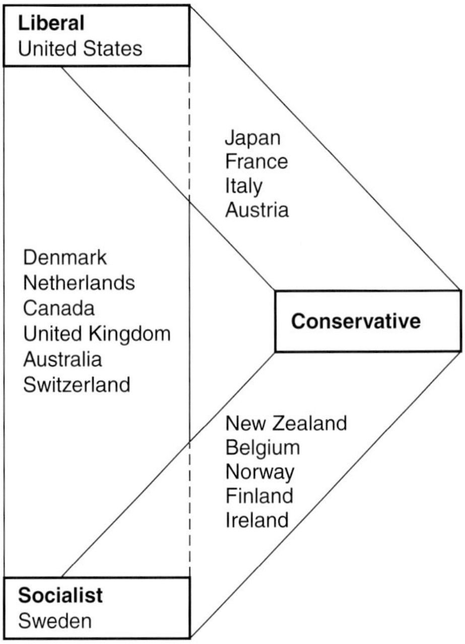

Fig. 4.2 Stratification principles: analysis of the classification of welfare states in *The Three Worlds of Welfare Capitalism* (Esping-Andersen).

Third, a fuller use of the data set on pensions gives a different classification of countries within the central types (residualist, corporatist, universalist). Thus, Figure 4.3 classifies countries in terms of their reliance on private sector schemes, down the left-hand side of the diagram, and in terms of their reliance on universalist social security schemes, across the top of the diagram. A high reliance on social security substitutes for the use of private pension schemes and roughly distinguishes between residualist-privatised pension systems and universalist systems, with Canada providing an archetypal residualist system and New Zealand providing the archetypal universalist system. The next step is to distinguish those countries that are more corporatist than the others. Those countries with an above-average use of occupational pension schemes are indicated in bold. Belgium comes closest to providing an archetypal corporatist system. The final step in the analysis is to distinguish those countries with pension systems which are *etatist* in nature. These countries are indicated in italics. The figure shows that *etatism* is semi-independent from corporatism. Even within the strongly universalist pension systems of Norway, Sweden and New Zealand, public employees have additional privileges, whereas in Ireland and Belgium public employees appear to be almost the only occupational group which is privileged.

Reliance on private sector provision (occupational and individualised)	Reliance on universalist social security		
	Low	Medium	High
Very high	Canada **Australia**		
High	**United States** ***Japan***	Switzerland *Denmark*	
Medium	***Ireland***	**Netherlands** **United Kingdom** *Germany*	
Low	**Belgium**	***France***	*Norway* *Sweden*
Very low		***Finland*** ***Austria*** ***Italy***	*New Zealand*

Fig. 4.3 Pension programmes: analysis of the classification of welfare states.

Figure 4.3 shows that using Esping-Andersen's full data set gives a more differentiated classification of European countries, indicated by the circles. There is a clear core grouping of corporatist *etatist* systems with little use of private pension schemes: Italy, Finland and Austria. These three countries also supplement the main schemes with some social security support. Norway and Sweden are clearly universalistic, but also *etatist*. None of the European countries could be characterised as fully residualist, and a significant grouping of countries (Denmark, Netherlands, United Kingdom and Germany) show very mixed pension systems.

Figure 4.4 draws together this re-analysis of Esping-Andersen's data. This approach privileges Esping-Andersen's theoretical analysis, but shows how specific countries embody tensions between regime types, which reflect their historical paths of development and which should influence their future paths. This approach contrasts with Esping-Andersen's use of welfare regime analysis in his later work, which, thus, assumes that each *regime* has its own internal dynamic, which determines the path of future development in the countries classified within it (Esping-Andersen 1996 & 1999). An additional advantage of the ideal-typical interpretation of Esping-Andersen's work is that it yields a more finely differentiated view of the European countries, whereas the classificatory approach simply divides them into two groups: conservative and social democratic.

Deconstructing Esping-Andersen's concept of welfare regimes into an ideal-typical framework helps with looking at housing in the four southern

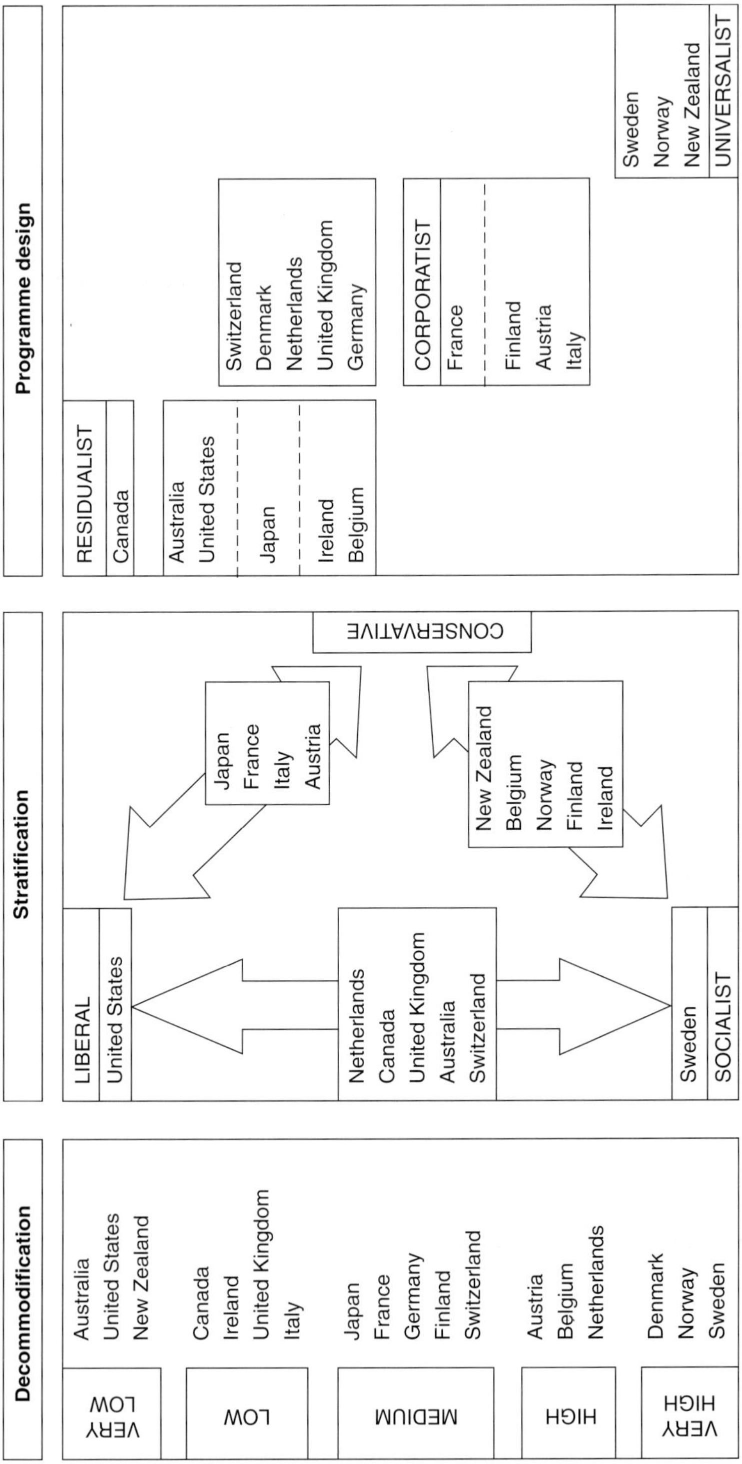

Fig. 4.4 Re-analysing existing welfare states using welfare state regimes as an ideal typical construct.

countries. The next section of this chapter examines how the concept of welfare regimes has been applied in comparative housing studies, as a prelude to examining welfare delivery in the south.

Applying the concept of welfare regimes to housing

Although many authors acknowledge the significance of the concept of welfare state regimes, only three extend it to a detailed analysis of housing provision: Harloe (1995), Barlow and Duncan (1994) and Arbaci (2002). Broadly, Harloe's work tackles the issue of decommodification, Barlow and Duncan focus on programme design, and Arbaci considers issues of stratification.

Decommodification

In *The People's Home?* (1995), Harloe presents the twentieth century history of social housing in six countries (Sweden, Denmark, former west Germany, France, United Kingdom and United States). He identifies social rented housing with decommodified housing and argues that it supports the decommodification of labour in the same way that cash benefits do in Esping-Andersen's analysis. Thus, the scale of provision of social housing provides an indirect measure of the decommodification of labour.

Harloe observes that mass provision of social housing characterised the periods immediately after World Wars I and II, but these were followed by much longer periods of residualised provision. His analysis also shows that where specific institutions were set up to own social housing, and where these institutions were buffered against direct political decision making, the contraction of provision was less marked than elsewhere. Mass social rented provision only occurs under two conditions: first, when the scope for private provision is limited, and second, when failure to ensure provision threatens the stability of the capitalist system itself. The swings between mass and residualised provision are reminiscent of the liberal/residualist and socialist/universalistic dimensions in Esping-Andersen's analysis of regime types. Given the selection of countries which Harloe studies, it would be reasonable to expect more structurally significant differences among them. Apart from raising issues about the ways in which tenure contributes to the decommodification of labour, his work adds little more to a welfare regime analysis of housing. Nevertheless, tenure issues are of great relevance in the southern countries with their small social rented sectors and widespread home ownership across the social spectrum.

Programme design

Barlow and Duncan (1994) use Esping-Andersen's work more systematically. They investigate the extent to which housing can be decommodified within the structure of housing provision, that is, the social processes which surround the production and consumption of housing (Ball & Harloe 1992) and provide detailed case studies of three European countries (Sweden, France and UK). They use the concept of welfare regimes as a theoretical framework to justify their selection of countries (cf. Doling 1997). They include only the European Union countries and add a fourth regime type, rudimentary, in order to include Greece, Portugal and Spain (cf. Liebfried 1992). They then specify the general nature of the housing systems they would associate with each type of welfare regime (shown in Table 4.4).

Their next step specifies a programme design component for a welfare regime-based analysis of housing. They elaborate the idea of a housing provision chain with four links: promotion, production, control of land supply and consumption. Each link is divided into specific elements, and these elements are related back to welfare regime types. Table 4.5 (a, b) sets out this line of reasoning. The elements in the housing provision chain form

Table 4.4 Regime types and housing provision systems.

Regime type	General principles
Liberal	• Overt intervention limited to stigmatised provision for a residual population unable to adequately participate in markets • Covert support for the better off (mainly owner occupiers) • State policy favours the market (large housebuilding firms and credit institutions) • State intervention aimed at consumption, not production
Corporatist	• More widespread overt state support is less ideologically symbolic • Does not disturb social differentiation • Used to solve temporary social problems • Self-provision is favoured because it avoids enlarging the public sector • State intervention aimed at consumption, not production
Social democratic	• Rented and co-operative housing are seen as an alternative sector open to all • Development profit is seen as undeserved • Strong intervention in the production of housing
Rudimentary	• Little tradition of direct state involvement in providing housing • Self-provision predicated on extended family systems substitutes for state role

Source: adapted from Barlow and Duncan (1994, pp. 30–31).

Table 4.5(a) Housing provision chains.

Links in the housing provision chain	Elements within each link of the chain
Promotion	• Speculative • Limited profit social housing • Self-promotion • Restricted profit private sector
Production	• Profit regime: short-term speculative gain or long-term productivity improvements • Size of firms: large or small
Land supply	• Development control • Zoning • Public and semi-public land ownership
Consumption	• Means tested subject subsidies • Price and/or rent reductions

Table 4.5(b) Welfare regime types.

Regime type	Associated with these elements of housing provision chains
Liberal	• Speculative promotion • Land supply regulated by development control methods • Consumption costs determined by market values and individual subsidies
Corporatist	• Self-promotion and restricted profit private promotion • Land supply regulated by zoning and binding land use plans
Social democratic	• Restricted profit social housing and private sector promotion • Land supply owned by public or semi-public bodies • Consumption costs determined by historic costs and universalistic housing allowances
Rudimentary	• Speculative promotion and self-promotion

Source: adapted from Barlow and Duncan (1994, pp. 32–5).

the basis for devising general criteria to assess state-market mix within housing provision systems. Not all elements in the chain can be directly related to specific regime types; some could occur in all regime types, and for some regimes, a specific combination of elements may be important. Because Barlow and Duncan's interest lies in how the organisation of housing production can promote decommodification, they do not pursue the consumption element in the housing provision chain.

Each element in the housing provision chain provides a scale along which existing housing systems can be measured. Barlow and Duncan present two of the six possible bivariate relationships along these scales in graphic form: size of firm versus profit regime, and size of firm versus land supply. These analyses also test whether their analysis of housing replicates the grouping of countries in Esping-Andersen's analysis. Sweden is a consistent outlier and, thus, it can be seen as an archetypal case. The clustering of the other European countries into groups is rather dispersed, but two strong groupings are invariant across both analyses. These are a southern grouping of Italy, Portugal and Greece and a corporatist grouping of Austria, west Germany and Belgium. These core groupings do not match those in Esping-Andersen's analysis of pension programme design. They also show that Spain has a very different housing provision system than the other three southern countries.

Barlow and Duncan's work illustrates some of the problems of applying the concept of welfare regimes to housing. First, the way that tenure is woven throughout the housing provision chain suggests that the concept of tenure is too complex to use within welfare regime models (cf. Jaffe 1989). Second, decommodified housing is defined as identical with state intervention to limit profits in either the consumption or production of housing. But does limited profit housing do any more than simply allow labourers to work for lower wages? Should the housing related measure of labour decommodification be the extent to which labourers can withdraw from the labour market because the terms on which they occupy housing are relatively secure? Third, focusing on limited profit housing also raises the question of who occupies it and may be more closely linked with stratification than with either decommodification or programme design. Other forms of state housing intervention, for example universal subject subsidies, may have a stronger impact on decommodifying labour. Fourth, focusing on the organisation of building new houses says little about the links between the whole housing stock and social stratification.

Barlow and Duncan's work also raises more general questions about the concept of welfare regimes. They have used the concept as a generalised ideal-typical construct by basing their selection of housing related indicators on their understanding of each regime type. The different grouping of countries which they obtain suggests that the classification of countries in welfare regime analysis is programme dependent (although this issue is partly obscured by Barlow and Duncan's introduction of a fourth, southern welfare regime covering Greece, Portugal and Spain). They use a fourth regime because Esping-Andersen's three regime types preclude an adequate treatment of self-promotion and self-provision in housing. In the south, both self-promotion and self-provision are strongly related to family practices, but Esping-Andersen's (1990) specification of regime types is based solely on state-market relationships. Using only his regime types, self-promotion and provision could feature only as an aspect of subsidiarity within a conservative welfare regime. The narrow question is whether they point to a fourth regime or to extending the concept of welfare regimes beyond state-market relationships to include a robust concept of the way the family provides significant elements of household welfare. The broader question is whether to use a different analytical strategy altogether, in which the state-market relationship is about decommodification and the family-market relationship reflects a kind of semi-commodification of labour, as the family also, in some ways, protects workers from full commodification within labour markets.

Stratification

In a remarkable piece of work building on Barlow and Duncan, Arbaci (2002) opens up some of the issues around defining a stratification component appropriate to housing within a welfare regime approach. Her aim is to analyse whether the diverse spatial settlement patterns for the poorest ethnic groups in a variety of European cities are shaped by the way in which the housing stock has been produced. She identifies scale of production as the most relevant dimension of Barlow and Duncan's models because it is most closely related to producing the spatial structure of the physical housing stock. She argues that large-scale development by large-scale builders produces large tracts of housing which can be occupied by minority ethnic groups. Small-scale, fragmented development produces a more spatially integrated pattern of settlement.

Scale of production, however, is only half the story. The second half relates to the conditions of access to housing. She observes that ethnic segregation is higher in those countries with dualist rental sectors. She extends Kemeny's concept of unitary and dualist rented systems (Kemeny 1995) by identifying self-provided, informal housing as the counterpart of a dualist rental system in the owner-occupied sector, which allows her to take the dominance of owner occupation in southern Europe into account.

Arbaci identifies the three key variables which govern the pattern of spatial insertion of poorer ethnic groups into cities as:

- Scale of provision, which is also closely linked to control of land supply and the balance between productivity and development gains in the building industry.
- The extent to which there is tenure neutrality or dualism within the institutions governing access to housing within and across tenures.
- Promotion forms, especially the significance of self promotion.

Three additional variables are included in her analysis in order to look at the socio-spatial distribution of specific groups within the whole stock of housing. These are:

- The range of quality standards across the stock
- Reinvestment programmes in the existing stock
- The physical house types in some cities which contribute to a vertical rather than horizontal pattern of social segregation (cf. Maloutas & Karadimitriou 2001).

Arbaci focuses on ethnic groups at the bottom of the social hierarchy, but her work raises broader issues of how different housing systems reflect different principles of stratification. She suggests that the main line of analysis should assess how dualisms within each tenure sector affect the quality and location of the housing which can be accessed by different social strata. Barlow and Duncan's work also suggests that these dualisms are, to some extent, embedded in the way that housing is produced. In contrast, Harloe emphasises the relationship between income and price, and the extent to which security of occupation depends on stability of income. Arbaci's focus on ethnic minorities also suggests that Esping-Andersen's view of stratification may need to be extended beyond class to encompass variables such as ethnicity and immigration.

Welfare regimes and housing

These three housing studies using the concept of welfare regimes raise two questions. How can the concept be adapted in order to apply it to housing? And what do they tell us about housing and welfare systems in southern Europe? The key to answering these questions depends on whether regime types are regarded as a means of classifying countries or as an ideal-typical construct. If regime types are regarded as a classificatory device, then Barlow and Duncan's, and Arbaci's work confirm that the idea clearly leads to fuzzy classifications of countries although the classification of countries varies with the specific welfare state programme under analysis. However, if the idea of welfare regimes is regarded as an ideal-typical tool of analysis, then it requires detailed answers to three questions. How do housing systems contribute to the decommodification of labour? How do housing systems reflect and/or seek to alter social stratification within society? And, how are different redistributive principles reflected in housing policy and programmes? Using the concept of welfare regimes as an ideal-typical tool also helps to identify how institutional configurations within a single country reflect tensions between different regime types (Brandsen 2001).

These housing studies also suggest three ways in which the concept of welfare regimes can be contextualised:

(1) Because it is founded on an analysis of decommodification of labour, the concept focuses on the relationship between state and market. But direct state provision of housing is hardly relevant in southern Europe and, more generally, it is not clear whether state intervention to limit profits supports the commodification or decommodification of labour. In northern Europe, the provision of social rented housing has been associated with the fordist commodification of labour, but it is not clear whether it would perform the same function in the context of economic change in southern Europe, where a largely agricultural population has moved directly into a rapidly expanding tertiary sector. What does the decommodification of labour mean in this context and what role could direct state provision play?

(2) The links between state and market in income maintenance programmes are easily measured by cash transfers. In housing, relevant state actions are much more diverse, including direct provision, regulation of private provision, provision of essential complementary goods, such as urban infrastructure, and so on, as well as symbolic interventions, non-intervention and non-implementation of policies. (The public action space for housing in southern Europe is discussed fully in Chapter 6). The variety of the links between state and market in housing raises questions about the capacity of states to manage specific kinds of programmes.

(3) Focusing on state-market interaction is procrustean in the context of southern Europe, because it ignores the function of the extended southern family in ensuring access to housing for its members and its role in protecting labour against commodification in a tertiarised economy.

The narrow rigour of the concept of welfare regimes makes it a sharp tool for dissecting the role of income maintenance programmes in shaping labour markets (Esping-Andersen 1996 & 1999). However, it becomes something of a blunt instrument when applied to housing. The main problems are, first, that the concept of welfare regimes focuses on market-state relationships and ignores the role of the family in welfare delivery and, second, analysing the complexity of the state's role in housing requires a more robust concept of welfare *systems*. Both these problems can be approached by looking at the wider societal context within which welfare regimes operate. We do this in two ways: the next section looks at a different way of framing a large-scale, cross-national study of welfare policy, and the subsequent section examines the debate over a separate southern welfare regime.

Castles and families of nations

Castles first set out his concept of families of nations in 1993. These were 'defined in terms of shared geographical, linguistic, cultural and/or historical attributes and leading to distinctive patterns of public policy outcomes' (1993, p. xiii; cf. also Therborn 1993). Although the initial set of three families only included Italy among the southern European countries, he speculated that there was a separate southern family, and the final set, found in Castles (1998, p. 8) includes four families among the 21 OECD countries:

- An English-speaking family: Australia, Canada, Ireland, New Zealand, United Kingdom and United States
- A Scandinavian or Nordic family: Denmark, Finland, Norway and Sweden
- A continental western European grouping: Austria, Belgium, France, Germany, Italy and Netherlands
- A southern European family: Greece, Portugal and Spain.

Two orphans, Switzerland and Japan, do not fit into any of these families and are treated as *sui generis*.

Two articles on welfare policy in southern Europe that Castles published in the mid-1990s provide a useful introduction to the cross-national study in *Comparative Public Policy* (1998). In a speculative piece of work, Castles asked whether religion matters in determining policy outputs (1994). He refers to the central Catholic doctrine of subsidiarity, which underlies corporatist approaches to social policy. This doctrine sees the family (rather than the individual) as the fundamental unit of society and as an organic unity resting on a gender-specific division of labour. Moreover, 'A doctrine of natural inequality reinforces the notion of status but is counterposed by the idea of the just wage, which leads to the belief that benefits for adult male employees ... ought to be characterised by a capacity to replace the family income at the level of the present status' (Castles 1994, p. 23). Such beliefs would lead simultaneously to high levels of welfare expenditure and highly gender-differentiated welfare outcomes. To test the hypothesis, Castles isolates a group of Catholic countries (Germany, France, Italy, Austria, Belgium, Greece, Ireland, Luxembourg, Netherlands, Portugal and Spain) and asks whether the relatively high level of social security expenditure in these countries is a function of real income or membership of the Catholic group of countries. A very simple model suggests that the Catholic effect was more significant in 1990 than in 1960. Fragmentary data on divorce, women's labour force participation and unemployment rates, women's and children's rights, and the scale of public sector employment are consistent with this interpretation. The problem, however, is to identify the specific political and policy processes which might lead to the outcomes he notes in these areas. Nevertheless, he concludes that religion appears to be a pervasive and deep cultural factor influencing everything.

In 1996, Castles explored the effects of democratic transition on social security spending in southern Europe. In 1960, Spain and Portugal spent less than the other OECD countries on social security transfers, while Greece fell within 2% of the OECD average. Italy was among the group of high spending western European countries. By 1990, Portugal spent just less than the OECD average, Greece and Spain were just above the average and had caught up with Italy. There was now a distinctive Mediterranean grouping, lying behind Scandinavia and the other high-spending western European countries but well ahead of the English-speaking countries. The statistical models show that within each of the four countries, growth in the elderly population, unemployment and economic growth were the most significant determinants of social security spending while partisan politics appeared to have no significant effect at all. The cross-national models present a very different picture. Between 1960 and 1974, 'The single most important factor accounting for variation in social security effort in the OECD lay in the very substantial differences in the degree to which different regimes permitted the political articulation of popular demands' (Castles 1995, p. 309). By 1990, general democratisation appears to make no difference among the OECD countries while partisan politics have a small effect compared with age structure and GDP per capita. In Portugal and Spain, the removal of the dictatorships released popular pressures and created a structural shift in underlying political relationships, allowing different forces to come into play to mediate popular demands. This shift apparently did not occur in Greece, and Castles argues that the period of military rule was too brief to have depressed spending much below the relatively high level prior to the colonels seizing power.

These two pieces of work illustrate Castles' primary interest in identifying the specific political institutions and processes which shape social policy instruments, outputs and outcomes in advanced capitalist countries. *Comparative Public Policy* presents data for a wide range of variables for three points in time, 1960, 1974 and the early 1990s, for all 21 countries in the four families. Castles traces the spread of democratisation after World War II, showing how political institutions, such as trade unions, electoral turnout, partisan competition and constitutional factors articulate public demands for welfare. Urbanisation, an ageing population and the influence of Catholicism are treated as general contextual variables in this approach. The division of countries into families facilitates understanding how each has proceeded at a different pace. After passing a threshold in economic development, then the way in which democracy has been institutionalised within the family group begins to influence the shape of the welfare state.

Castles' four-family argument works well for the big issues: the overall scale of government spending, levels of social security transfers, expenditure on health and education. The main divide in the 1960s was between the high-spending continental (Catholic) countries and the remainder (including southern Europe), which he labels as a two-family model. (For Castles, Catholicism is effectively a matter of domination by the Christian Democratic parties.) By 1990, a three-family model is more useful, with higher spending in the Scandinavian countries than in the continental European countries and very low spending in the English-speaking countries, nearly replicating the classification of welfare regimes in Esping-Andersen's work. However, for issues associated with gender and the family (including home ownership), the two-family model is still highly relevant. He argues that economic modernisation shapes the growth of the state in Catholic Europe and that cultural modernisation shapes policies which touch on gender and family matters (Castles 1998, p. 319). Thus, depending on the issue, all four families may be fully distinguished or they may be grouped together into fewer families. This conclusion resonates with Barlow and Duncan's analysis of housing provision systems, which did not reproduce Esping-Andersen's classification of countries.

The main line of Castles' argument broadly supports the approach taken in this book. Three of the southern European countries (Portugal, Spain and Greece) are distinguished by their late economic development and democratisation, but can also be seen as members of the Catholic group of continental European countries. Italy, one of the Catholic countries, would be categorised with the other three southern countries in a two-family model, but not in the four-family model. This finding is consistent with our re-analysis of Esping-Andersen's data, which highlighted the contradictory position of Italy.

Castles' historical analysis raises the question of whether the general pattern of political and economic change in the four southern countries implies that they are converging on a pattern of housing provision which is distinctive from the rest of Europe, or whether all four countries are converging on a continental European model of housing provision. Unfortunately, the analysis of housing policy in *Comparative Public Policy* does not permit a clear answer to this question. Part of the problem lies in the restricted terms of the analysis. The statistical models are designed to explain changes in the level of home ownership, which is assumed to be an inverse measure of state support for housing. This assumption only makes sense if state support is assumed to be identical with the direct provision of housing since the rate of home ownership could also be seen as a *direct* measure of state support through mortgage subsidy. The reason for specifying the model in this way is that the rate of home ownership is the only housing-related variable for which it was possible to construct an adequate data series for all 21 countries for all three points in time. The only independent variable running consistently through the four statistical models (one each for 1960, 1974 and the early 1990s, and one measuring change over time) is the level of employment in manufacturing. Different economic variables, generally reflecting the economic climate for housing investment, have affected home ownership at different points in time. While the models are not inconsistent with the dominant narratives of housing policy in the post-war period (cf. Harloe 1995; Power 1993), which is the line of interpretation Castles adopts, alternative lines of interpretation could be imagined, focusing specifically on the growth of owner occupation. In particular, the significance of the Catholic culture variable in the model for change between 1960 and 1990 suggests differences among the families of nations. Both the conceptual weakness and instability of the models over time suggest that an area of welfare state policy which depends on both private sector production and family activity reflects different underlying aspects of economic development and democratisation than those which are operationalised in Castles' analysis.

In terms of social security expenditure, Castles' work presents a picture of the welfare states in the four southern European countries as not dissimilar from the continental or Catholic European countries. Italy differs from the other three only because of their late economic development and political modernisation. The longer historical perspective in the cross-national study, together with his work on democratic transition and on housing, however, suggests that there are different underlying dynamics shaping housing systems, policies and practices in southern than in northern Europe.

Setting the south in a European context

Both Castles' and Esping-Andersen's narratives have the same main plot: subject to the level of economic development in a country, politics matters in shaping the nature of their social security systems. However, the cast of characters and the subsidiary plots are very different. Following Esping-Andersen strictly, there can be no doubt that the income-maintenance systems in all four southern countries are corporatist and *etatist* in nature (Guibentif 1996; Petmesidou 1991). The systems in Spain, Portugal and Greece have been called a 'discount edition of the continental model', sharing the same basic structure but with lower levels of benefit and coverage (Katrougalos 1996, p. 44). Our reconstruction of Esping-Andersen's data analysis suggested that future change in the Italian income maintenance system would be torn in different directions, as indeed it has been during the 1990s, as has the Greek system (Symeonidou 1996). Castles' historical analyses of democratic transition in three of the countries begins to suggest why the political systems find these crises so difficult to handle.

But, for a study of housing and welfare in southern Europe, more important conclusions can be drawn. The dynamics of housing systems are different from those characterising social security systems (Castles 1998). Barlow and Duncan's (1994) and Arbaci's (2002) work suggest that the welfare regime concept is too narrowly conceived to be extended easily to housing and that a more widely conceived analysis of welfare systems would be more useful. Such an analysis would need to incorporate both family practices and a consideration of how southern political systems articulate family and market to shape a public action space in housing.

There is sufficient evidence in this review of two large-scale cross-national comparative studies and the more detailed studies associated with them to support the conclusion that the welfare systems in the four southern countries are sufficiently different from those in the north to warrant further investigation. There is also sufficient evidence to suggest that what makes housing different in these four countries is the way in which it is set within its wider societal context. The dynamics driving housing policy in southern Europe appear to be different from those in northern Europe as a consequence of the configuration of the welfare systems in the south.

The problem with large-scale quantitative studies is that they are institutionally thin, unable to describe particular societies in any depth. Comparison is bought at the expense of understanding how institutions are articulated within specific societies. The remainder of this chapter addresses this problem. Many of the specific features of southern welfare systems were identified in the debate over a southern welfare regime. Following a review of this debate, the remainder of the chapter examines three features in more depth: the capacity of civil administration, the large irregular and informal labour market, and familialism. It is the interlocking relationship among these three socio-economic institutions which shapes the southern welfare system.

Is there a separate southern welfare system?

There are two broad approaches to arguing for a separate southern welfare system. The first takes the view that the concept of welfare regimes is both too narrowly based on income maintenance programmes and decontextualised. Arguments within this approach, therefore, look at a range of welfare delivery issues and stress the wider societal context. The second approach focuses on Esping-Andersen's work, and argues either that there is a fourth welfare regime, characterising the southern countries, or that the southern countries constitute a significant variant within his conservative regime.

A rudimentary Latin Rim regime

Liebfried (1992) argues that there are two variants of Esping-Andersen's conservative welfare regime: Bismarckian (Germany and Austria) and the Latin Rim (Spain, Portugal, Greece, Italy and, possibly, France). Four features distinguish the Latin Rim from the other European countries:

- They have an older tradition of welfare connected to the Catholic church, which is absent in northern Europe
- Disability pensions have been widely used, notably in southern Italy, as a form of basic income maintenance programme
- Their labour markets have a strong agricultural bias, combined with a subsistence economy
- They do not have a full employment tradition, especially for women.

On this basis, he characterised the southern welfare states as rudimentary, a 'semi-institutionalised promise' to create a modern welfare state and pointed to substantial institutional problems which would need to be overcome to extend them.

A separate southern welfare model

The most thorough argument for a separate southern model of welfare has been put forward by Ferrera (1996). He rejects Liebfried's rudimentary and Castles' Catholic characterisation, noting that a deeply rooted socialist/communist subculture in all four countries has sometimes been more important than the church and its social doctrine.

Ferrera bases his argument on four specific features of southern societies which affect the way corporatist income maintenance systems operate in the southern context. First, he stresses the interaction between income maintenance programmes and the labour market. Except for some minimal help from local authorities in parts of Spain and Italy, the system creates a polarised clientele. Workers in the core formal sector are hyper-protected. Workers in the informal and irregular sectors, young people and the long-term unemployed are under-protected. The labour market combines with the welfare system to place some workers in a highly privileged position while others, including new entrants into the labour force, are in a very weak position. The southern family holds this system together by acting as a clearing house between the labour market and the welfare system. Ferrera argues that it is vital for each family to have 'at least one member ... firmly anchored in ... *garantismo*' (1996, p. 21). Moreover, in the backward areas, the most sought after jobs are in the public sector, so that the 'deliberate expansion of state employment with a view to alleviating the chronic insufficiency (and territorial disequilibria) of labour demand ... [is] an additional peculiarity of the southern European model of welfare' (Ferrera 1996, p. 21). Families with no anchor in the guaranteed sector lose out altogether.

Second, southern welfare states combine fragmented income maintenance systems with universalistic approaches to health care. All four countries have attempted, with varying degrees of success, to develop universalistic health systems. Incomplete implementation, often layered on top of previously existing insurance schemes, has led to incomplete coverage and a variety of collusive practices between the public and private health sectors. The system combines micro-corporatist solidarities in income maintenance and aspirational universalism in health.

Third, there is a 'double deficit of stateness' in southern Europe. There is less direct provision by the state, and state welfare institutions are vulnerable to partisan pressure and manipulation. 'Welfare rights are not embedded in an open, universalistic, political culture and a solid, Weberian state impartial in the administration of its own rules' (Ferrera 1996, p. 29). Developing more targeted social policies, such as minimum income programmes, is not feasible when the administrative apparatus is not capable of verifying the effective needs of claimants/beneficiaries through standardised and impartial procedures and is inefficient in controlling tax evasion and verifying incomes.

Fourth, the combination of weak, unprotected sectors in the labour market and a 'soft' state is fertile ground for a 'clientelistic market, in which state transfers to supplement inadequate work incomes are exchanged for party support, often through the mediation of trade unions, at the individual level'

(Ferrera 1996, p. 25). In Italy, this works through the partisan penetration of welfare administration, both at the upper administrative echelons and at the point of delivery, and through bypassing the welfare administration via the creation of special review committees recruited from political parties with discretion to provide single benefits. Although there is no systematic comparative research, Ferrera presents evidence of similar processes at work in Spain, Greece and Portugal. Nevertheless, clientelistic practices have served important functions in the four countries. They have eased the restoration of democracy in three of them and managed to provide some income subsidies to backward areas in all four. More importantly, however, clientelistic practices have substituted for widening the range of welfare state programmes. The specific path to modernisation in southern Europe explains the persistence of clientelism. Its genesis lies in a strong Catholic church and resilient corporatist traditions, accounting for the restricted scope of welfare state programmes, and a family-centred social fabric linked to a segmented labour market, which has contributed to the uneven development of income maintenance programmes. The institutionalisation of clientelism is explained by three factors:

(1) State institutions are weak in terms of bureaucratic professionalism and autonomy. Failure to modernise the civil service before the expansion of income maintenance programmes supported the persistence of clientelistic relations and may have contributed to their further consolidation and sophistication.
(2) There is 'The prominence of parties as main actors for the aggregation of social interests' (Ferrera 1996, p. 30). The source of party dominance lies in the 'atrophy of southern Europe's civil societies and ... the specific modes of post-authoritarian democratic instaurations' (Ferrera 1996, p. 30; cf. Gunther *et al.* 1995).
(3) 'Ideological polarisation and, in particular, the presence of a radical-maximalist *and* divided left' has sustained clientelism (Ferrera 1996, p. 30, emphasis in original).

Housing in a southern welfare model

Castles and Ferrera (1996) extend this argument by looking at the policy mix between pensions systems, health provision and housing in southern Europe. They build on Kemeny's argument that home ownership is a substitute for old age pensions (Kemeny 1981). He argues that high home ownership redistributes resources from the young to the old and sets up a political constituency among the young which is opposed to extending the welfare state through taxation (because it would interfere with saving for home ownership), and in favour of private pensions, health care, and schools (because this allows a more flexible pattern of personal expenditure). The OECD data for the mid-1980s generally support Kemeny's proposition, but the four southern European countries show a different pattern. In Portugal, there was relatively low home ownership and relatively low expenditure on pensions. In Greece and Italy, there was high home ownership and high spending on pensions while Spain also shows high home ownership and is just on the margin of high expenditure on pensions.

The highly polarised system of social protection in the south sets them apart from the other continental European states. At the same time, workers in the guaranteed sector are not necessarily earning high salaries, but they have access to pension schemes with the highest income-replacement rates in the European Union. In contrast, workers in the non-guaranteed sector have the lowest income replacement rates for the benefits available to them when they are elderly.

The black economy also affects the trade-off between housing and pensions. It explains something about the propensity to invest in housing because black earnings cannot go into contributory pension schemes. Thus, acquisition of housing is also a form of savings available for investing black money. In addition, a proportion of housing is produced in the black economy. In this context, home ownership has two advantages: one to do with the operation of the black economy and the other with redistribution of income over the life-cycle.

In Italy, Greece and Spain, housing resources and welfare transfers are skewed in favour of the elderly at the expense of the young. The main effect is to lessen the priority given to other welfare state programmes. The major exception has been the expansion of health provision, almost the single issue that has united the fragmented political left. However, health provision is also skewed towards the elderly, and existing levels of provision are far from universal. At the same time, the left parties reinforce the fragmentation of the income maintenance system as part of their competitive attempts to retain core constituencies in the guaranteed sector. Coupled with fiscal austerity, there is, thus, systemic resistance to extending the range of welfare state programmes. The combination of high home ownership and social protection systems skewed towards pensions in the guaranteed sector creates a dualistic protection system which mirrors the organisation of the labour market, in a self-perpetuating system.

The main consequence of this dualistic system is that it creates intergenerational life strains, particularly around fertility and household formation. What eases these strains is the southern family, which is characterised by the high intensity and wide extension of kinship networks and very strong solidarity within these networks (see Chapter 5). In these circumstances, house purchase becomes an extended family operation, mobilising the assets of both households of origin for young couples. The strength of the family is also reinforced by its role in providing either direct employment in family businesses or the personal contacts which lead to employment. The gendered division of labour within the traditional family fills in the gaps in the formal welfare system. However, cultural and economic modernisation are creating strains on this arrangement and the main response is new strategies around the life-cycle. Household formation is relatively low, and fertility levels are below replacement rates. There are also severe problems for households who do not have at least one of their members anchored in the guaranteed sector. These households, especially in economically backward areas, are candidates for indigence and exclusion even if they own their own (illegally built) home.

Castles and Ferrera (1996) identify a pattern of articulation between housing and social security policy in southern Europe which is significantly different from that in the remainder of the OECD. The policy mix in southern Europe relies almost exclusively on social security transfers, has weak education and health sectors, and very scarce personal social services while housing policy has focused on the promotion of home ownership. The consequence of this mix is that the extended, gender-divided southern family fills in for the missing services. It plays a role which is as strong as the state's in the delivery of welfare to households.

The configuration of the welfare system in southern Europe has two important implications for analysing housing systems. The first is that understanding family strategies is as important as understanding formal housing policies in grasping the nature of the housing systems. The second is that, where family strategies are significant, then the nature of access to and the evolution of the labour market are of some importance in shaping family strategies and, thus, in shaping housing systems.

Southern welfare societies

Hespanha *et al.* (1997) present a very different argument for a distinctive southern welfare system which centres on the articulation between state and civil society. In Portugal, Spain, Greece (and Ireland), late modernisation has led to a specific kind of relationship between state and society. In Portugal, Salazar's *Estado Novo* relied on the maintenance of family and community solidarity in a rural population with low expectations in terms of consumption and quality of life, and delayed establishing the administrative and juridical infrastructure associated with modern welfare states. As a consequence, the welfare society, 'a whole permanent informal non-state system producing social practices' (Hespanha *et al.* 1997, p. 169), still operates alongside the state and the market. It:

> 'Can be defined as a configuration of networks of relationships of inter-knowledge, mutual recognition, and mutual help, based on kinship and community ties, through which small groups exchange goods and services on a non-market basis, and with a logic of reciprocity that approximates that of the gift relationship.' (Hespanha *et al.* 1997, p. 173)

The principle of universality does not exist in these networks. Exchange is based on a particularistic logic which rests on face-to-face interaction, and there is a need to continually invest in primary social relationships to maintain group cohesion.

Economic modernisation does not necessarily rupture primary solidarity ties. Instead, the increasing division of labour diversifies the resources available to mutual help networks. Nevertheless, modernisation also begins to create stress in the networks of primary solidarity, largely because of the pivotal role of women. Hespanha *et al.* discuss caring for the elderly and children in some detail, but also look at how these networks operate in housing provision in rural areas. In housing, the most significant contributions come from close relatives: parents, siblings and close collateral kin. They meet very diverse needs: providing living spaces, access to family plots of land, financial loans and labour. More distant relatives, neighbours and friends who are part of the family's wider social network also help but more occasionally, providing, for example, connections in municipal government, access to transport vehicles, masonry or electrical skills, arranging discounts with suppliers, lending money and so on. As with caring relationships, housing provision places a heavy burden for a long period of time on family relationships.

Hespanha *et al.* speculate that the most likely line of development in the welfare society is through a more formalised third sector, but this raises questions of negotiating the forms of state regulation and support for 'such flexible and relatively unstructured forms of co-operation and solidarity' (Hespanha *et al.* 1997, p. 181) without destroying their basic role.

All of the arguments for a separate southern welfare model highlight the importance of specific institutional arrangements in southern Europe. In contrast, the arguments against a separate southern welfare model rest strongly on the concept of welfare regimes and tend to assume that economic development will erase any significant differences between south and north.

Southern separatism and economic modernisation

Guillen and Alvarez (2001) argue that while the southern states may constitute a family of nations, they do not constitute a separate welfare regime because neither clientelism nor familialism is a sufficient reason for altering the basic definition of welfare regimes. They do not consider clientelism to be as widespread as Ferrera believes (given the lack of systematic evidence both views are sustainable), and they quote Esping-Andersen's comment that:

> 'A perverted use of welfare programmes and public bureaucracies may define the character of a polity, but it is difficult to see how it defines a welfare regime unless the entire system was from the very beginning specifically designed for the purpose of clientelism rather than social protection.' (Esping-Andersen 1990, p. 90)

They argue that familialism will wither away once public provision has closed all the gaps in provision and claim that Esping-Andersen's analysis of familialism supports their argument that there is no significant difference between the southern countries and the continental welfare states in terms of familialism (Esping-Andersen 1999). They ignore the very restricted definition of family in Esping-Andersen's analysis in order to draw on his authority in making this point.

Guillen and Alvarez's main argument, however, is that there is an emerging difference between Spain and Italy, on the one hand, and Portugal and Greece, on the other hand. Decentralisation in Spain and Italy expands welfare provision by releasing bottom-up demands and facilitates meeting demands for expansion from the European Union. Expanding provision also erodes the differences between insiders and outsiders in the labour market and supports managerial reforms aimed at limiting or ending clientelism. However, there is evidence that decentralisation has these modernising effects only in the north and central regions in Italy, but not in the south where clientelism persists (Fargion 1996).

Katrougalos argues that Greece fits the continental-corporatist welfare regime perfectly and predicts that any remaining differences will disappear as the southern countries imitate the welfare states of northern Europe and expand the scope of their programmes (Katrougalos 1996). In contrast to Katrougalos' theoretical fastidiousness, Symeonidou (1996) manages to fit Greece into all possible southern welfare models, including Esping-Andersen's corporatist regime.

Southern difference and welfare regimes

Esping-Andersen has commented: 'Typologies are problematic because parsimony is bought at the expense of nuance' (1999, p. 73). The price may also include relevance. If the aim of the analysis is to apply a strictly defined concept, then there is no argument for a southern welfare regime. The welfare state in southern Europe may be less developed than in the north, but a leaders-laggards model of modernisation will eventually erode any differences. If the aim of the analysis is to learn more about welfare *systems* in southern Europe, then three basic arguments may be made for a southern welfare model:

(1) Two variants within the corporatist welfare regime can be distinguished, a Bismarckian variant and a southern variant. This position is taken by Esping-Andersen, who comments that the distinctive nature of the welfare states in southern Europe affects their adaptation to post-industrial employment (1999).
(2) A fourth regime may be required to analyse housing programmes, as Barlow and Duncan's, and Arbaci's work demonstrate.
(3) Analysing broad social issues requires different approaches to distinguishing among European countries.

Much of the debate over the existence of a separate southern welfare regime interprets the concept as a way of classifying countries and points to significant differences between the wider socio-economic context in the southern countries and the continental European countries. Our analysis of Esping-Andersen's work shows that it is neither necessary nor helpful to distinguish a separate southern regime. What is important is to understand how the concept of welfare regimes can be used to develop a method of analysis which seeks to explain the position of specific countries along the dimensions of decommodification, stratification and programme design compromising the ideal-typical formulation of the concept. Of all the countries which Esping-Andersen considers, only Sweden can be considered archetypal in the ideal-typical formulation. In other words, deconstructing the concept of welfare regimes in the way we have in the first part of this chapter immediately directs attention to identifying those aspects of the wider socio-economic context in any one country which generate its position within the ideal-typical framework. From this perspective, the helpfulness of the somewhat diffuse and wide-ranging debate over southern welfare regimes is that it allows us to identify key elements in the wider socio-economic context of the southern countries which affect how the welfare state operates within them and how its operation is articulated with other institutional features in these countries to create a distinctive southern welfare *system*.

On this basis, we can identify three general features of southern societies which shape the way their welfare states operate within their wider welfare systems: the capabilities of the civil administration, the large informal sector in the labour market and familialism. These features shape what kinds of housing policies can be formulated, how they are implemented and what their impact will be. The next section of this chapter discusses each of these features in turn.

Civil administration, dualistic labour markets and familialism

The purpose of this section is to clarify some of the concepts associated with each of these features of southern society and set the context for the next two chapters which focus on how the nature of the southern family and the nature of the public action space in southern Europe shape housing systems in these countries.

The state and civil administration: clientelism

The cross-national quantitative methods used by both Castles and Esping-Andersen necessarily assume that all states have the same capacities to develop, implant and manage modern welfare state policy. Both of them explore the significance of political choices, but neither explores the social processes underlying how democracy has been institutionalised in different countries. This raises particular problems in southern Europe because of the very recent processes of democratic consolidation in Spain, Portugal and Greece, together with the democratic crisis in Italy in the early 1990s if this is seen as part of a delayed democratic consolidation (Malefakis 1995). In contrast to the other states in Europe, democratic consolidation in the south has occurred concurrently with a major structural shift from a rural agricultural society to an urbanised service sector society. In addition, corporatist income maintenance systems were institutionalised well before the process of democratic consolidation started in all four countries (cf. Linz & Stepan 1996; Gunther *et al.* 1995 and Diamandouros *et al.* 1995 for a discussion of the processes of democratic transition and consolidation). Thus, it is reasonable to expect that the specific paths followed by the four southern countries will have left an imprint on the operation of the civil administration which underpins formal democratic government.

The most common way of discussing the weaknesses in civil administration in the southern countries is by discussing clientelism. Although the specific practices can vary immensely, clientelism is essentially an exchange of services provided by the state in return for support for political parties. Such services may also include the failure to enforce regulations (cf. Ferrera 1966, Petmesidou 1991, Petmesidou & Tsoulovis 1994, Tsoulovis 1996, and Katrougalos 1996 for specific descriptions of clientelistic practices). Clientelism, thus, distributes services according to a particularistic and/or personalised logic, rather than the depersonalised and universalistic logic associated with professionalised Weberian bureaucracies in modernist welfare states.

The borderline between practices which are regarded as normal and proper, that is, clientelism, and those which are regarded as corrupt varies from society to society and may change over time within a single society (Mény & Rhodes 1997). Clientelism is most likely to emerge when the processes of social change lag behind political modernisation, and that even where clientelism is no longer a significant phenomenon, informal methods of patronage persist throughout most developed representative democracies. It is only in an ideal typical sense that the nature and functions of democratic representation run counter to those of clientelism since both can easily co-exist in the same historically institutionalised setting (Roniger 1998). While it is relatively easy to install formal democratic institutions, it takes longer to install the 'interior ground rules' associated with transparent political administration and may require reinforcing changes in other parts of the political system (Pérez-Diaz 1998).

The roots of clientelism lie in traditions of civil administration which predate the transition to democracy in the southern countries. Patron-client relations substituted for rational administrative interactions prior to the installation of democracy in the mid-1970s in three of the countries and were transposed into the new institutional structures (Mény & Rhodes 1997). The absence of a tradition of public service and a supporting administrative culture meant that access to rights functioned on the basis of personal connections and patronage (Martin 1996). Clientelism seems to linger longest in those regions with high levels of need relative to available resources (Fargion 1996), and where legislation creates administrative instruments allowing for great discretion or is so complex that it is opaque to an outsider (Katrougalos 1996). The highly fragmented corporatist pension schemes in Greece have facilitated a particularly organised form of clientelism linked to the necessity for the state to subsidise one scheme or another (Petmesidou 1991). The natural habitat of clientelism is one where 'organisational deficiencies, overstaffing and lack of work incentives for public employees (opportunities for second jobs in the informal economy, party political and other non-meritocratic criteria for appointment and promotion) contribute to poor provision of services and lack of any systematic policy' (Petmesidou 1991, pp. 39–40). In contrast, administrative transparency and the use of universalistic, versus particularistic, criteria in the allocation of funds give much less scope for the operation of traditional forms of clientelism (Fargion 1996).

Clientelism is based on the political articulation of the relationship between client and bureaucracy. It is, thus, also related to the strength of vertical channels of interest aggregation through political parties (Fargion 1996). Democratic transition in Greece led to deep conflicts over which social strata could enjoy access to the state machinery and provoked a crisis of legitimation. During the transition to democracy, PASOK rebuilt its clientelistic networks in order to strengthen its control over the state apparatus. One technique which it used was to alter the recruitment regulations for public sector jobs in the mid-1980s on the basis of criteria other than professional qualifications such as number of dependent children, handicapped dependent relatives, geographic origin and household income (Petmesidou 1991). The interaction between democratic elections and clientelism can vary. In southern Italy and in some regions in Spain, clientelism has been used to ensure the continued dominance of specific parties through the pre-electoral bargain (although the scope for this has been limited by the recent reforms in the Italian election system). In contrast, in Greece, where a spoils system operates, clientelistic practices intensify electoral competition (Katrougalos 1996). The statist spoils system redistributes state resources to those social groups who are the winners in the electoral struggle by giving them access to political power and the state machinery (Petmesidou 1991).

The vertical aggregation of interests through parties, linked with clientelistic political practices, also tends to inhibit the development of organisations in civil society which can aggregate interests horizontally (cf. Alexander 1998). Linked with authoritarianism, it provided an effective method of social control (Guibentif 1996). Two factors must be taken into account in assessing the extent to which the absence of strong horizontal organisations in civil society is a direct effect of clientelism. First, the absence of such organisations may also be a consequence of class structures.

For example, in Greece, the middle classes are dominated by petty traders and self-employed persons, and so do not represent a strong base for horizontal organisation (Petmesidou 1991). It is likely, as well, that some rural agricultural social structures inhibit the formation of civil society organisations and these may then be imported into urban areas with migration. This is suggested by the ability of the *multifundist* farmers in north Portugal to organise much more easily during the revolution than the *latifundist* farmers in the south although subsequently the *latifundios* have disproportionately benefited from European Union agricultural subsidies. More generally, high inequality structures inhibit horizontal organisation (Reis 1998). Second, within a system characterised by Catholic (or Orthodox) subsidiarity, a wide variety of civil society organisations already exist, some sponsored by the church itself, which may also inhibit the formation of mass horizontal organisations (Hespanha *et al.* 1997). Certainly, an important effect of a pervasive Catholic conservative ideology is to valorise the acceptance of existing status differentials (Castles 1994).

Four aspects of clientelism need to be considered in assessing its impact on the welfare of households:

(1) In a clientelistic system, access to the direct delivery of welfare services becomes a unit of exchange between political and social groups, including trade unions, especially at the local level (Martin 1996). The particularistic logic of clientelist systems makes it difficult to predict their distributive effects, but it is clear that in some systems, such as the statist spoils system in Greece, the effects will be more marked and deeply institutionalised than elsewhere.
(2) Clientelism is set within social systems which emphasise primary solidarities among kin and neighbours, and these solidarities widen access to clientelistic patronage to meet particularistic needs for specific services. The system allows households to derive revenue through access to the state and means that traditional support networks offer an alternative to widening the range and scope of welfare state policies (Katrougalos 1996). At the same time, however, this reinforces patriarchal power relations within families because access is mediated through the male heads of families.
(3) Clientelism operates more easily in the context of an informal economy. Universalistic distributive policies are difficult to implement if incomes (and tax liabilities) cannot be accurately assessed and verified. The informal economy also spans the boundaries between the public and private sectors. There is direct evidence about the black economy among those working in the national health service in Greece where the payment of backhanders facilitates access to services, but puts an

additional burden on family budgets for health care (Symeonidou 1996; Katrougalos 1996). Similar, although perhaps more formalised, mechanisms occur in the incompletely implemented national health systems in the other three countries, all of which mix public and private provision.

(4) The welfare effects of state employment should not be underestimated. While this is quite different from the Scandinavian model of welfare state employment, nevertheless such employment is sought after, either for access to other benefits in a clientelistic system or because it anchors families in the guaranteed sector (Katrougalos 1996).

There is a two-way relationship between clientelism and the types of policies which can be formulated and implemented. Excessively complex policies, those which depend strongly on administrative discretion, and policies which require working across the boundary between the public and private sectors provide opportunities for clientelism. But clientelism can also shape policy. The statist spoils system in Greece promotes fragmented corporatist policy approaches and incremental change (Katrougalos 1996). It also inhibits the development of horizontal interest aggregation which limits the approaches which can be taken to town planning (Petmesidou & Tsoulovis 1994). Certainly the informal and illegal settlements found in many parts of southern Europe attest to the absence of policy or failure to implement policies regulating the use of land.

What are the prospects for change in clientelistic systems? The answer to this question depends on the model of societal change which is adopted. The most common view is that economic and cultural change will erode clientelism as modernist and universalist policies are put in place. Fargion's evidence suggests that the modernist rationalisation of civil administration is possible although it is difficult to implement evenly and requires strong and stable political leadership. This view rests on a view of clientelism as a pre-modern undifferentiated social, political and economic system. Thus, Fargion characterises clientelism 'as both a privatisation of politics and the colonisation of civil society, which has frozen the confusion of roles between state and society' (1996, p. 149). Others are less optimistic about the possibility of a modernist differentiation between state and society and take a different view about the process of change. For example, the incremental development of the welfare state in Greece in terms of improved levels of benefits and extended coverage has been strongly shaped in response to electoral needs (Katrougalos 1996). Finally, others argue that a modernist state administered universalism is not an appropriate aspiration in southern Europe. They see change as coming, not through direct state provision, but by the development of meso-level organisations located in civil society, supported by state funding and regulation, and building on existing primary solidarities (Hespanha *et al.* 1997).

In the absence of systematic research, it is difficult to draw firm conclusions about how widespread clientelism is (Guillen & Alvarez 2001). Either some practices go unremarked because they are regarded as normal and proper (Mény & Rhodes 1997), or the wide variety of practices which have been documented suggest that clientelism is a leopard which changes its spots as political systems change.

In conclusion, therefore, the general political conditions within which civil administration is set, that is, a highly party politicised formal democracy, the absence of strong horizontal interest aggregation and a weakly professionalised pre-modern bureaucracy, may be more important in shaping housing practices and policy than the specific forms of clientelism which vary over time and from place to place, even within the same country. Nevertheless, specific forms of clientelism may have a very strong impact on the way housing is provided in specific localities and regions. We will argue in Chapter 6 that clientelistic practices have also provided state bureaucracies with a particular set of skills in regulating private actors which, in different political circumstances, can be a basis for developing locally sensitive, transversal policies mobilising a range of public and private actors.

Dualistic labour markets

There is a strong connection between corporatist welfare systems and dualistic labour markets. The insider-outsider distinction is reinforced by the high levels of contributions required to finance social insurance schemes yielding high income replacement levels as well as regulatory biases against all but the standard adult male breadwinner worker. Within corporatist systems, there is a vicious circle which sustains the dualistic labour market. Both employers and employees have strong incentives to use informal employment relationships which do not require the payment of social contributions. Consequently, atypical and often black market activity provide the main strategy for those locked out of the core sectors (Esping-Andersen 1996).

The re-analysis of Esping-Andersen's data at the beginning of this chapter shows that, among the corporatist countries, Italy stands out from all the others by having *both* a low level of decommodification of labour *and* exhibiting a tension between conservative and liberal principles of stratification. In addition, the pension system is also strongly *etatist*. Income replacement rates are the highest in Europe for the pension schemes. In other words, the division between insiders and outsiders is especially sharply drawn in Italy. As Ferrera remarks, this is not *garantismo*, but *iper garantismo* (Ferrera 1996). This same pattern of corporatism and strongly divided labour markets is the case in all four southern European countries (Castles & Ferrera 1996; Katrougalos 1996; Petmesidou 1991).

Castles presents data which explain the genesis of the sharply dualistic markets in southern Europe. While the level of service sector employment in the southern countries is not as high as in the other corporatist countries, the *rate of growth* in such employment has been exceptionally high. The average rate of growth in tertiary sector employment in the four southern countries between 1960 and 1993 was 101.8%, compared to 63.9% in the other countries categorised as corporatist by Esping-Andersen. In the southern countries, growth in the service sector was achieved by a process of de-ruralisation while, in the other corporatist countries, it was achieved through a process of de-industrialisation which has generated more pressure for the social protection of service sector employees.

Characterising the labour markets in southern Europe as dualistic is over-simplified. An important segment of these labour markets, state sector employment, is not formal employment in the same way as in fordist manufacturing industry. In a 'not very Weberian state' coupled with a large informal sector, multiple employment by state employees is common (Ferrera 1998). The poor pay of civil servants, compared to the private sector, especially in Italy and Greece, contributes to their participation in the underground economy (Castles & Ferrera 1996). In Greece, the state is the 'employer of first resort', especially in rural areas (Katrougalos 1996) and employment by state and public corporations constitutes half the so-called formal sector (Petmesidou 1991).

The picture of the informal sector is also more complex than a simple dualistic labour market model suggests. In Spain, a four-cornered society is created by different job/income and welfare opportunities: protected core workers, temporary and irregular workers, an underground sector, and ex- and unemployed workers (Ferrera 1996). A segmented rather than dualistic labour market model helps to account for changes in employment patterns in agricultural areas as well (Pereirinha 1996). In Portugal, there is a shortage of labour in the most modern sectors and firms in urban areas co-existing with increasingly precarious and flexibilised employment in the other sectors (Pereirinha 1996). Portugal is, however, distinctive in that there is a shortage of labour, rather than a shortage of jobs, which partly accounts for the very high labour force participation rates for women (González *et al.* 2000, p. 12).

Four general phenomena contribute to structuring the informal employment sector:

(1) The first is multiple employment. This is not confined to poorly paid civil servants. In the rural areas in northern Portugal, 80% of farmers work part time in agriculture, 47.5% at less than half time (Pereirinha 1996). Self-employment favours multiple employment in both rural and urban areas in Greece, which has the lowest level of salaried workers and highest proportion of self-employed workers in the European Union (Symeonidou 1996). Multiple employment practices which span the formal and informal sectors protect workers during economic downturns, but also tend to fragment the middle and lower-middle classes, inhibiting horizontal solidarity and demands for the expansion of welfare state programmes (Tsoukalas 1987; Petmesidou 1991).

(2) The existence of a large black economy in all of the southern countries contributes to fragmentation and fluidity in the informal employment sector. The official estimate of the size of the black economy in Italy is 15% of all economic activity but similarly firm estimates are not available for the other countries although they have, rather implausibly, sometimes been estimated as high as 60% (Ferrera 1996). Esping-Andersen (1996) reports estimates in Italy and Spain of around 10–20% of GDP and assumes that most of this activity is either multiple employment or by those who have recently retired.

(3) The structure of the social insurance programmes themselves promote particular forms of informal employment. Half of early retired workers in Italy continue to work in the informal sector (Esping-Andersen 1996). Partial flexibilisation of the social insurance regulations may also strengthen informal employment, deepening the insider-outsider divide. In Spain, temporary workers accounted for most of the net job growth in the 1980s because firms regulated their labour force at the margin by using easily dismissible temporary workers (Esping-Andersen 1996).

(4) Immigration affects how the informal labour market functions. Illegal foreigners have no social rights and are much more vulnerable to exploitation in the labour market (Katrougalos 1996). Greece and Portugal, in particular, have absorbed very large numbers of both legal and illegal immigrants, including returners from the former Soviet Union and the former Portuguese colonies.

Set against processes which intensify the insider-outsider split in the labour market, some changes tend to soften the division. The attempts to implement a universalistic national health system have lessened disparities in the availability of these services between workers in the formal and informal sectors (Guillen & Alvarez 2001). Despite the financial and other difficulties in fully implementing these reforms, once started they become difficult to retract and contribute to developing a stronger concept of social citizenship than has existed before (Liebfried 1992; Venieris 1996). Also, spurred on by the European Union, all four countries are attempting to introduce some form of minimum income policies although whether this can be achieved without evoking a strong backlash is unclear. Ferrera (1998) is pessimistic about the potential for change, but Fargion (1996), surveying the gains made within the highly heterogeneous and spatially fragmented 'local citizenship systems' in Italy, is more optimistic.

In conclusion, the dualism in southern European labour markets is different from the dual markets associated with northern European corporatist welfare states. In the south, dual labour markets run alongside welfare states with exceptionally generous pension schemes in the formal sector and relatively scarce or non-existent provision in most other areas of welfare state activity (with the exception of the incompletely implemented national health systems). Strong networks of primary solidarity embodied in family, kinship and neighbourhood both compensate for this pattern of welfare state provision and facilitate the functioning of the informal employment sector.

The highly dualistic labour market creates strong biases in housing policy towards home ownership, both as an anchor of security for those outside the formal labour market and as a significant form of investment within the black economy (Castles & Ferrera 1996). In addition, self-provision and illegal provision also create flexibility in the pattern of payments for housing in circumstances in which income streams are uneven over time and unpredictable. In contrast, the financing of social rented housing requires either that the majority of tenants are in guaranteed sector employment or that the state shows a high level of willingness to subsidise such housing.

Familialism

The central argument in this book is that the distinctive relationship between family and housing in southern Europe shapes the nature of housing policy and provision in all four countries. The comments below, therefore, are primarily concerned with clarifying some of the key conceptual and methodological difficulties associated with how the southern family is dealt with in the cross-national studies. It draws largely on single country studies in southern Europe. While the southern authors do not always agree among themselves, they speak from a set of common assumptions which are important. Martin comments that most research on comparative welfare systems is carried out by Anglo-Saxon researchers, who '*Imagine* that social welfare measures adopted in southern Europe correspond approximately to those already found in northern and western Europe' (1996, p. 23, our emphasis). It is the failure to *imagine* what is meant by family in southern Europe that is the heart of the problem.

The persistence and significance of primary solidarities in the provision of social protection is 'Based on personal connections, affective links, networks of exchange and sociability, bartering and a non-cash economy' (Martin 1996, p. 34: cf. Hespanha *et al.* 1997). The network of social relationships between the extended family, kin and neighbourhood is an indispensable resource because it is a way of accessing other resources. For example, despite the failure of the Italian welfare state to provide any formal support for lone mothers, they are less likely to be poor than in Germany or the United Kingdom, because the Italian *parentela* operates as a clearing house mediating the relationship between a segmented labour market and a fragmented income maintenance system (Ruspini 2000). In Portugal, 50% of the very long-term unemployed reported that their families were their source of support while only 12% reported unemployment benefit as their main source of income (Pereirinha 1996). Kinship and social networks are more important for young people looking for jobs in both Italy and Spain than in the rest of Europe (Guerrero & Naldini 1996). The operation of the family is the main reason why poverty does not lead directly to social exclusion in southern Europe (Ruspini 2000; Katrougalos 1996). At the same time, family networks show a strong gender division of labour. Internal caring work is, in principle, women's work while external relations with the labour market are men's work (Symeonidou 1996).

Three points emerge from these observations. The first is that the family in southern Europe cannot be understood as a self-contained unit. It is first and foremost a nexus of affectively significant networks extending through a wider kinship circle and into the neighbourhood and locality. Second, those who are outside these networks lose their access to significant social and economic resources. A corollary of these first two points is that different methods of research and types of data are required to study such networks than are required to study households. Even the most advanced work on the family in southern Europe admits that this is an intractable problem at the moment (Gonzáles *et al.* 2000). The third point is how family solidarities are seen in the context of social and economic change. Are they seen as 'archaisms, a hangover from a traditional rural society that is sometimes thought to be disappearing, or ... as the foundation of the social and civic bond at the present time when only these private forms of solidarity seem to be able to compensate for the state's withdrawal' (Martin 1996, p. 35)? Are they a traditional, pre-capitalist social structure which will be eroded by further economic development (Katrougalos 1996)? Or are they a key institution which adapts to, but also shapes, other elements in the societal structure within a welfare society (Hespanha *et al.* 1997)?

This brief discussion of how the southern family is socially constituted is fundamental to assessing the cross-national studies reported earlier in this chapter. Although *The Three Worlds of Welfare Capitalism* asserts that welfare regimes are 'qualitatively different arrangements between state, market and the family' (Esping-Andersen 1990, 26), the book pays scant attention to family. Esping-Andersen addresses the question at some length in *Social Foundations of Postindustrial Economies*, largely in response to feminist critics of his earlier work (1999). He defines de-familialisation as the degree to which households' caring responsibilities are relaxed by transferring care for children, the sick and the elderly from the family to the state or market and uses what data are available to extend his analysis of welfare regimes (Esping-Andersen 1999). Identifying the problems with this analysis helps to clarify some basic issues in constructing a view of southern welfare systems. Four problems require attention:

(1) The identification between household and family is unproblematised. What is transferred to state or market in the analysis is only a small part of the family's function, domestic work done by women within households.

(2) The analysis is very much shaped by the gender equality agenda of his critics. There is a strong unspoken normative assumption that differentiated gender roles within the household are less satisfactory than undifferentiated roles. More precisely, what is missing is an ethnologically informed analysis of role differentiation within different household types, especially if the analysis is to cover multi-generation households operating within the context of the extended southern meaning of family (cf. Hespanha *et al.* 1997).

(3) There is the wider question of what is meant by welfare. The concept of decommodification provides a clear, if somewhat narrow, normative guide in *The Three Worlds of Welfare Capitalism*. The welfare state provides services, mainly income transfers, which protect the worker against commodification in the labour market. But, who is protected? The worker, the household, or the family? With the concept of defamilialisation, it is even less clear who is gaining what, except that women may be more free to become commodified by entering the labour market.

(4) There is a hidden meta-narrative behind extending the welfare regimes concept to issues of de-familialisation, which can be summarised in a Habermasian frame. In the highly decommodified, de-familialised (Nordic) social democratic welfare regime, the lifeworld of the family, understood in the extended southern sense, has been deeply colonised by the systemic world of state and market. Seen from another perspective, this could be a Faustian pact with modernity. While this formulation no doubt overstates the problem, it draws attention to a significant set of methodological issues. Not only is there a problem about how family is to be defined for the purposes of cross-national analysis, but there is also a problem about how it is to be conceptualised in relationship to the narratives of modernity and postmodernity which are relevant to understanding the different paths to postindustrialism taken by the de-industrialising northern countries and the never very industrialised southern countries.

In contrast, Castles' cross-national treatment of issues related to the family is much more open and straightforward. He concludes that explanations based in economic and political development do not explain much about those areas of welfare state policy which have an effect on personal life (Castles 1998). Castles' work on the role of Catholicism, also taken over by Esping-Andersen, is criticised by Guerrero and Naldini (1996) on the basis of the differences they document between Spain and Italy showing that the family is not valued in the same way in all Catholic countries (1996, p. 60; Castles 1994; Esping-Andersen 1999). Katrougalos (1996) complains that Orthodoxy cannot really be directly compared with Catholicism. But beyond these points, Castles accepts that a robust concept of family means that it cannot easily be fitted into the framework of an analysis which focuses on how economic growth (measured by growth in per capita GDP) and partisan politics shape welfare state policy, because the family is a way of redistributing cash transfers and combining them with other resources in a particularistic rather than universalistic logic (Castles & Ferrera 1996).

Economic change does affect the role of the family, but a more institutionally grounded concept of economic development is necessary to identify the mechanisms at work. For example, rural to urban migration is one process associated with economic growth which has significant impacts on the family. The networked particularism of the southern family opened possibilities for diversifying and multiplying the welfare resources which rural to urban migrants could make available to their families (Hespanha *et al.* 1997). But these effects seem to have also depended on the method of settlement in urban areas. In Portugal, social rented housing disrupts or attenuates many of these networking resources, while self-promoted and self-built clandestine housing helps to sustain them (Costa-Pinto 1998). The interaction between gender and labour markets is also important in understanding family strategies. As women enter the labour force in larger numbers, familial networks become more dependent on cash transfers as a substitute for women's unpaid labour in the family (González *et al.* 2000).

We argued in Chapter 3 that housing provided an important spatial anchor for migrants and we argue, in Chapter 5, that rural to urban migration has been an important part of family strategies to increase their welfare and social position. However, what is clear is that in the context of weak civil administration and segmented labour markets, family strategies are shaped as much by the pattern of resources available to them as the scale of those resources. The significance of structural economic change is that it alters the pattern of resources available to families. But if the family is accepted as an active agent in welfare systems, then the outcomes will reflect their actions as much as the actions of the state and market.

Conclusion

In conclusion, both clientelism and the family, in the context of a labour market characterised by irregular and informal labour practices, provide a particularistic way of distributing limited cash-based transfers from the welfare state. They do this in a way which partially compensates for the limited scope and coverage of welfare state programmes. Clientelism reflects the weak capacity of the state to administer universalistic programmes, and the party-based political articulation of the relationship between state and family both limits the professionalisation of civil administration and enhances the significance of the extended southern family in the distribution of welfare. In the context of a dualistic labour market, clientelism also provides a means of access to welfare, mediated through families, for those working in the informal sector and, thus, outside the scope of the formal income maintenance systems. The *etatist* nature of the corporatist income maintenance systems also inhibits the professionalisation of civil administration, since access to state employment is itself one of the significant mechanisms for the distribution of welfare among families. At the same time, the extended and extensive southern family provides a mechanism for aggregating and redistributing resources among its members according to a particularistic, rather than a universalistic logic. Thus, the primary solidarity of family determines the logic of distribution to individuals and households within the family. In this context, the strategies that families deploy in gaining and using resources are an important key to understanding how specific institutional relationships create a specifically southern welfare system.

The question is, therefore, how will this interlocked institutional system change? It is not sufficient to argue that economic modernisation will lead to a more universalistic and de-personalised system. Economic modernisation in Europe at the beginning of the twenty-first century rests on the development of the tertiary sector, characterised by informal and atypical employment patterns. This pattern of future economic development is already presenting considerable problems of adaptation in the more fully developed welfare states in northern Europe. At the same time, Hespanha *et al.*'s (1997) alternative vision of the regularisation of the array of civil society organisations into horizontally organised meso-institutions requires more strategic capability than the highly party-politicised democracies of southern Europe may have at the moment. The most likely course of change is that presented by Fargion (1996), who argues that decentralisation has the potential to capture the strengths of family and locality in responding to change, provided there is sustained political leadership at local and regional levels. This path of change would also represent a distinctive southern way, in contrast to the way in which northern European welfare states were consolidated in the context of the centralisation of state power.

The southern European welfare system

The argument for a separate southern European welfare system rests primarily on three institutionally specific features of southern European society: the capacities of its civil administration, the role of a large irregular and informal labour market within a dualist structure, and the significance of familialism in aggregating and distributing resources. What makes southern Europe different from northern Europe is this configuration of social institutions in which the extended southern family is the key link between the welfare of households and individuals, the labour market and the state.

The arguments for a separate southern welfare model raise two general issues:

(1) The scope of comparisons: as Kolberg and Uusitalo argue (1992), it is necessary to conceptualise the welfare of households more broadly, looking at the overall configuration of institutions and programmes, in order to make a well founded comparison between those countries in northern Europe, particularly in Scandinavia, where the state is the

dominant source of welfare provision, and the countries of southern Europe in which the state plays a more restricted role. This is a particularly important point if the aim is to understand how a significant element of household welfare, the provision of shelter, is organised.

(2) The implicit narrative of modernisation which lies behind comparing countries: both the major cross-national studies are characterised by a leaders-laggards model of welfare state development, which arises out of the selection of quantitative indicators which they use. This model is also taken over in some of the country specific literature on welfare and southern Europe.

However, the social institutions which distinguish a southern model of welfare suggest that the narrative of modernisation in the southern countries is different from that in northern Europe. This can best be illustrated by reflecting on Esping-Andersen's approach. His aim is to explain the role of different kinds of welfare states in decommodifying labour. His entire approach rests on the assumption that labour has already been commodified through a process of fordist industrialisation and that, as a consequence of this process, families consist of households who are not able to provide more than the simplest reproductive services for themselves. In this context, the welfare state steps in to provide a range of services supporting the welfare of households who are, by and large, participating in highly regulated formal labour markets. Furthermore, state administration is characterised by a Weberian bureaucratic rationality, able to deliver such services in a depersonalised and universalistic way. The focus of current debate within this modernisation narrative is about the capacity of state welfare services to adapt to the more fluid and less regulated labour markets characterising a post-fordist, service-based economy.

In contrast, it would be difficult to characterise the southern economies as post-fordist since they were not widely industrialised anyway. Rather, there is a different narrative of modernisation in these countries. Their economies have moved from being rural and based in agriculture to being based in an urbanised service sector. The majority of the labour force, thus, could be characterised as pre-commodified. Formalisation within the labour market, and hence, commodification of labour, affected only a proportion of workers in the core sectors, and there were different processes of formalisation for industrial and state sector workers. Welfare services were primarily provided within the extended family, and the welfare state was restricted to income maintenance programmes addressing the formal sector in the labour market. The strong *etatism* within southern income maintenance programmes does not reflect the formalisation and Weberian rationalisation of state employment, but rather the only semi-formalised nature of state employment and the role of state workers in articulating the relationship between political parties and families. Within this concept of the state, state employment *itself* is seen as a form of welfare delivery, rather than being seen as the means to deliver welfare state programmes to the population as a whole. The irregular and atypical forms of employment which characterise the service sector, as well as the reliance on extended families, show important continuities with the recent past in the southern countries. This description of the southern welfare system suggests a very different path of future change than in the north.

Since familialism forms a very robust element in southern welfare systems, any treatment of housing systems must set it alongside the roles played by state and market. Chapter 5, therefore, outlines the role of the family as a social institution in housing. Chapter 6 looks at the nature of the public action space in housing, a concept we have developed to indicate that state policies and activities are as much shaped by familialism as they are by markets.

5

Family and Housing

Family, tradition and culture

The family institution has been an important agent in the shaping of the social and territorial organisation of communities, especially in pre-modern times when tribes were organised around kinship. Its role in human reproduction still facilitates naturalist and essentialist explanations of its social role, which are contradicted by the extensive changes in its form and function in the wider social context. The importance of family and kinship as organising principles of social relationships has been reduced as modernity, the division of labour, spatial mobility, wage labour and commodification, led to the emergence of a strong focus on individual identities. This has profoundly affected household structures by progressively diminishing their family component. The gradual disappearance of the extended family household, the emergence and proliferation of non-family households and the decreasing importance of wider family networks all reflect the diminishing role of the family in social reproduction.

Stripped of its economic function, the family has been reduced to a micro-environment in which members have relatively more independent lifestyles and choices in terms of education, employment and housing. This process of individuation, supported by the labour market and, later, the welfare state, has been reflected in household formation. Household cycles have become shorter, more segmented and varied. The size of households has shrunk and their number increased. Their housing needs could not be met unless the housing market took these changes into account or the state intervened to remedy the market's failure to do so.

The classic texts in urban sociology linked the declining role of the family in social reproduction with urbanisation, and particularly with the emergence of the modern metropolis:

> 'The family is now in process of change and disintegration in every part of the civilised world.... Changes in the family, however, are taking place more rapidly in cities than elsewhere. Everything that is characteristic of city life, a mobile population, a wide division of labour, and the multiplication of municipal institutions and social conveniences of all sorts have contributed to bring about these changes. Schools, hospitals and all the numerous agencies for personal service which have taken over, one by one, the functions once performed by the home and in the family have contributed indirectly to undermine that ancient institution and diminish its social importance.' (Park 1929 [1957, p. 84]).

Wirth evoked some important consequences for the family of this transfer of activities to specialised institutions:

> 'In cities mothers are more likely to be employed, lodgers are more frequently part of the household, marriage tends to be postponed, and the proportion of single and unattached people tends to be greater. Families are smaller and more frequently with less children than in the country. The family as a unit of social life is emancipated from the large kinship group characteristic of the country, and the individual members pursue their own diverging interests in their vocational, educational, religious, recreational, and political life.' (Wirth 1938 [1964, p. 80]).

In southern Europe, the continued importance of the family in social reproduction and the strong extended family element of household structures can be seen as an unfinished project of modernist development. It is tempting to attribute this to a belated and relatively weaker industrialisation compared with other parts of the continent. However, the underlying assumption of a linear process in which southern Europe lags behind on a common path is, at best, simplistic and does not take account of the specific and intricate ways in which family structures and practices form part of the process of industrial development and urbanisation described in Chapter 3.

The family is usually equated with tradition, since in traditional societies it usually has a wider role in the economy and in social reproduction. Most concepts of the process of modernisation have been based on a view of economic development as led by large-scale industrialisation and with an enhanced role for the central state in organising social reproduction. Modern market and state regulation has reduced the role of the family, by occupying a substantial part of its vital space and by defining society as an aggregation of individuals rather than groups, such as families, tribes and sects. However, modernisation has seldom developed in this ideal type form since new cultural identities, especially national, have been boosted with modernity and have reduced or channelled in a different way the 'liberating' impact of individuation. Traditional elements of social structure have often persisted, being changed in the process but, at the same time, altering the characteristics of the modernisation process.

The family's importance is often attributed to culture. There is no doubt that family is part of southern European culture, but if its importance is mainly attributed to culture the explanation becomes tautological: southern Europeans live and operate in families because they like to or are accustomed to. Culture should not be easily evoked as 'some sort of ultimate explanation of social and political behaviour' (Rose 1996, p. 251). There are many other, more tangible conditions that help to preserve and develop family roles in southern Europe. However, once a successful reproduction of family roles is established, a positive cultural predisposition is created that can contribute to their further development or inhibit change in them for some time if these wider social and economic conditions become less supportive.

Regional specificity in family, housing structures and practices

Housing practices are households' responses to need in specific contexts and depend on different material, institutional and organisational resources. These practices are central to understanding southern European specificity if we assume that, compared with the north, they have a stronger family element, a wider role and, thus, have an impact on housing conditions in a greater variety of ways. The object of this chapter is to stress the link between this wider role and family solidarity, and consider a housing model that takes account of family solidarity.

There are striking similarities between southern European countries in the form of housing consumption and in the underlying processes. These similarities are a relative phenomenon, since they show smaller differences among the four southern countries than between them and the other countries in the European Union. But there are also differences in housing conditions among these countries, especially in terms of basic amenities. The two smaller countries are in a much worse situation, while Italy and Spain surpass the European Union average (Eurostat 1997b).

As discussed in Chapter 2, southern European housing has a number of common features:

- High rates of home ownership that have increased substantially since World War II

- High rates of housing construction
- Low percentages of social rented housing and social housing expenditure
- The important role, although not everywhere, of individual promotion and production (legal and/or illegal)
- High percentages of second and vacant homes.

There are also striking similarities between southern European countries in terms of household structures and practices. Table 5.1 gives some indication of these similarities and the differences from the rest of the European Union.

In summary, the southern European household structure is distinguished by a substantially stronger family element compared to the rest of the European Union. There are more nuclear families and the average household size is bigger, whereas all forms of non-family household (single-person households, couples in consensual unions, and family dissolution (divorce rates, single-parent households, births outside of marriage) are significantly fewer.

We can obtain a clearer synthetic account of this similarity by performing a principal components analysis on the above mentioned variables[1]. The results of this analysis are shown in Figures 5.1 and 5.2. The first and most important principal component emerging from this analysis accounts for more than 52% of the variation in the data set, meaning that it summarises that amount of information contained in the initial variables. The content of this first factorial axis, or principal component, is a precise reflection of the major differences in family structures and practices in European Union countries. On the positive side of the axis there is a cluster of higher percentages of one-person households, divorce rates, births outside marriage, single-parent households and social protection expenditure. On its negative side there is a smaller cluster including larger average household size, higher percentage of nuclear families and high percentages of the elderly living in family households. The second axis, far less important with 13% of the total variation, refers to marriage patterns and more precisely to the younger age at first marriage correlated with higher percentages of single-parent households. Figure 5.1 illustrates this analysis.

If we position each of the European Union countries on the first factorial axis, there appears to be a clear geographical structure with 'more family' in

[1] Principal components analysis is a statistical technique where the object is to give a summarised account of the information contained in a data set by reducing its dimensions, that is, by reducing the number of variables. This is done by calculating a small number of new synthetic variables, called factors or principal components, that usually account for a substantial part of the information contained in the initial data set.

Table 5.1 Family-related variables in southern European countries and the rest of the European Union, early 1990s.

	Greece	Italy	Portugal	Spain	Rest of the EU
Average household size (1995)	2.7	2.7	3.0	3.2	2.4
One-person households (1995)	21.0	21.0	14.0	13.0	29.3
Percentage of persons in one-person households (1991)	5.5	7.3	4.4	4.1	12.2
Young women (20–29) in one-person households (1995)	7.0	4.0	3.0	1.0	12.3
Young men (20–29) in one-person households (1995)	8.0	6.0	2.0	1.0	15.8
Elderly women (over 74) in one-person households (1995)	44.0	69.0	30.0	26.0	59.7
Elderly men (over 74) in one-person households (1995)	16.0	22.0	17.0	9.0	25.7
Percentage of couples with children in households (1990–91)	62.2	62.6	61.5	68.1	52.3
Percentage of persons in non-family households (1991)	9.6	9.8	6.5	4.4	16.4
Percentage of elderly (>65) in three or more person households (1991)	38.7	30.1	35.7	40.7	16.9
Percentage of single parent family households (1996)	7.0	11.0	12.0	8.0	9.6
Mother alone as percentage of family households (1990–91)	6.1	8.7	8.3	8.6	14.5
Children under 16 living with one parent (1994)	4.0	6.0	7.0	5.0	10.6
Percentage of couples in consensual union (1994)	2.0	2.0	3.0	3.0	10.8
Births out of marriage (1995)	3.0	8.0	19.0	11.0	28.5
Crude divorce rate (1994)	0.7	0.5	1.2	0.7	2.2
Age of men at first marriage (1992)	29.3	28.6	26.3	28.1	28.4
Age of women at first marriage (1992)	25.0	25.7	24.3	25.6	26.2
Social protection expenditure (in 1985 ECUs) per capita (1995)	1643	4491	2313	2960	5577
Family protection expenditure as % of social expenditure (1980)	4.5	7.3	8.0	4.4	11.5
Family protection expenditure as % of social expenditure (1992)	1.7	3.9	5.6	1.8	9.5

Source: Eurostat (1996, 1997b, 1997c).

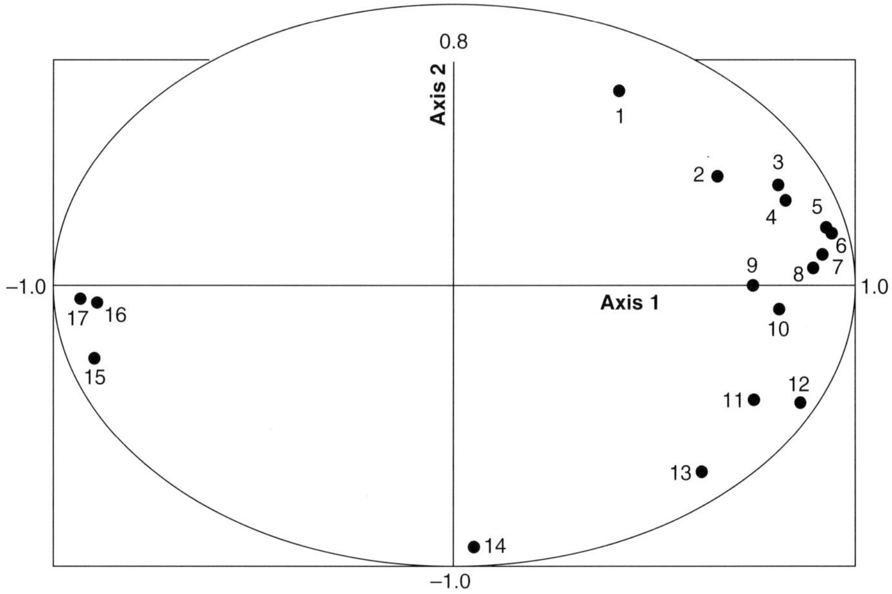

1 Average age for men at first marriage, 1992
2 Average age for women at first marriage, 1992
3 Single person households, young women 20–29 (% of households), 1995
4 Single person households, young men 20–29 (% of households), 1995
5 Persons living in single person households (%), 1991
6 Persons living in non-family households (%), 1991
7 Single person households (% of households), 1995
8 Social protection expenditure per GDP, 1995
9 Unmarried couples, age 30–44 (% of couples), 1994
10 Births outside marriage (%), 1995
11 Children under 16 living with one parent (%), 1994
12 Crude divorce rates, 1990–94
13 Single parent households (% of family households), 1996
14 Mother alone (% of family households), 1990–91
15 Average household size, 1995
16 Couples with children (% of families), 1990–91
17 Persons over 65 living in three or more person households (%), 1991

Fig. 5.1 Position of variables on the factorial plan defined by the axes of the first two principal components.

the south and less in the north as shown on Figures 5.2 and 5.3, where southern, central and northern Europe are clearly divided.

This small exercise, which does not include some important variables and lacks an explicit theoretical foundation, illustrates what we already know, that the presence of the family is a more important constitutive element in

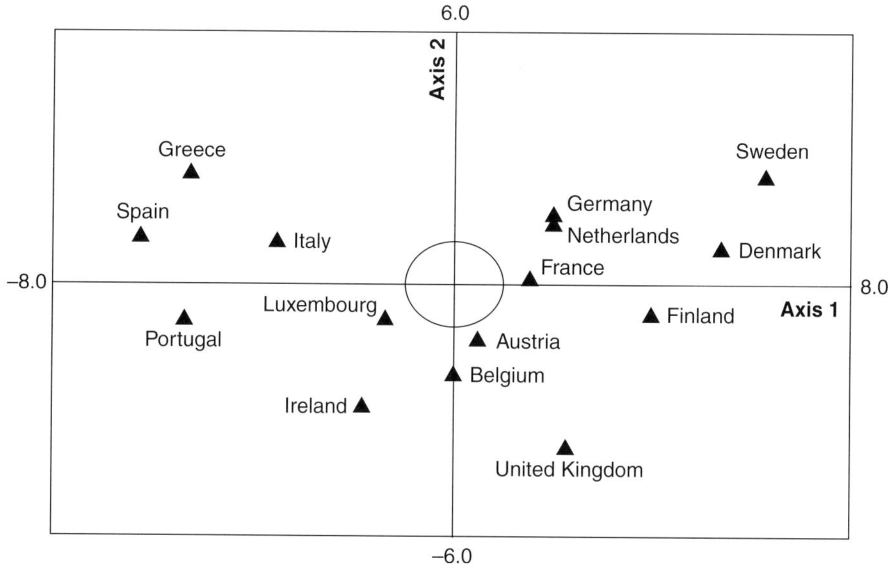

Fig. 5.2 Position of European Union countries on the factorial plan defined by the axes of the first two principal components.

the organisation of societies in southern European countries than in northern Europe. Common features, however, are not sufficient to devise a southern European housing model unless we study processes.

Strong family presence may characterise southern Europe, but the family has an impact on housing in all societies. We can crudely distinguish two main ways in which the family affects how housing is produced:

(1) Changes in family structures reshape the demand for housing products. Such changes have been far more important in northern European countries and are an important pressure for readjusting the housing supply. In this case, the family's impact on the demand for housing is an unintended consequence of wider demographic changes, which are only marginally related to the availability of housing.
(2) Families plan strategies for housing. Strategies for accessing home ownership, locating near self-help networks, preserving positions in the housing market and intra-family property transfers all affect housing. The impact on the aggregate level of demand for housing remains unintended but in this case the family, through its housing strategies, creates the conditions for its own reproduction. Southern European countries are much closer to this type of relationship between family and housing.

Therefore, the relationship between family and housing must be seen in

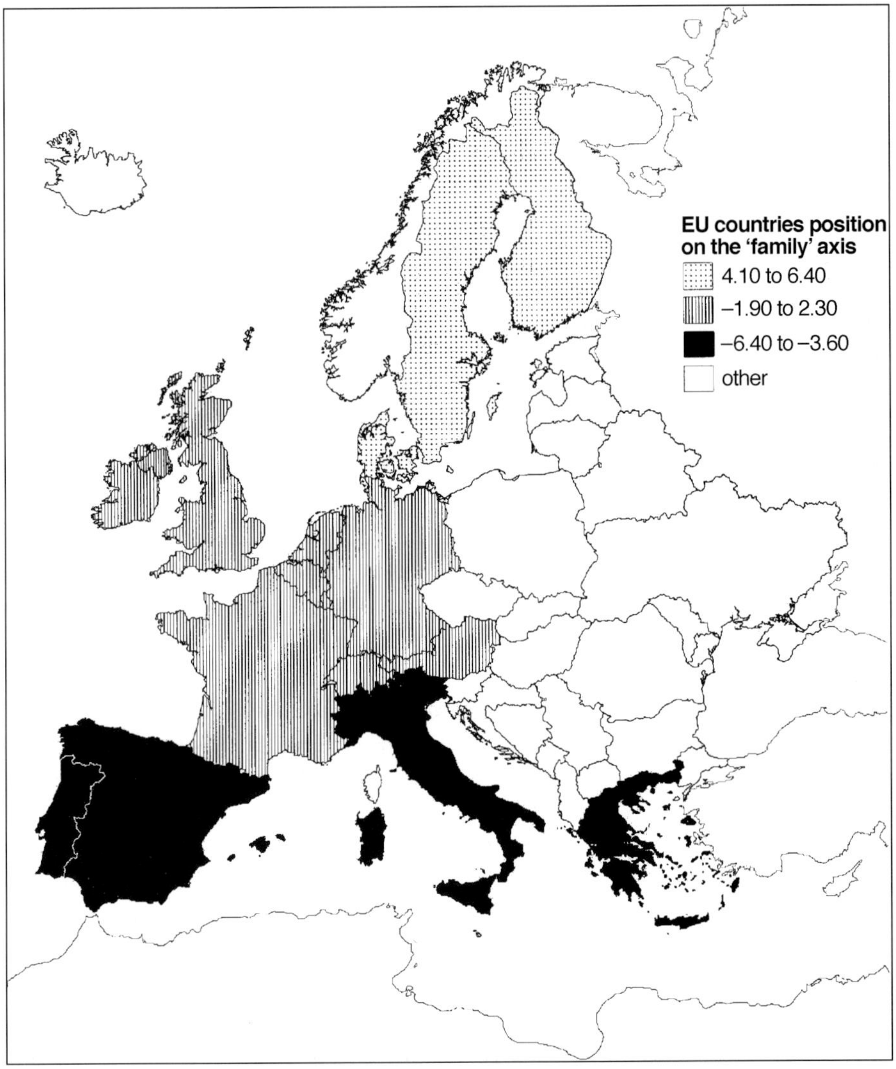

Fig. 5.3 Groups of European Union countries defined by their position on the 'family axis' of the principal components analysis.

terms of specific models of social organisation and development in order to investigate the respective roles of each and their interaction in terms of causality. The initial hypothesis for such an investigation in southern Europe is that the weaker and more recent development of welfare states in these countries has given more room to the family as an institution of social organisation and reproduction. Equally, weaker market forces have also given more room for the family. Family emerges, then, as an important organising principle, alongside the state and the market, and housing is one of the domains where its role is more developed.

Despite important differences between the southern European countries, some common aspects in their recent histories can be traced. Late and weak industrialisation, with the partial exception of north-west Italy and northern Spain, has produced late urbanisation and a different model of social integration in the new urban societies (see Chapter 3). Economic and political changes have produced massive flows to the big urban centres (see Tables 2.4 and 2.5) and flows of emigration during the three decades after World War II. Thus, the main problem for these countries during this period was housing rural migrants in the urban centres. (These changes occurred after 1975 in Portugal.) The rather rapid urbanisation is responsible for the high rates of construction (see Table 2.19) as well as for the growing number of vacant homes left behind in depopulated regions. The increase of vacant houses, more recently, is mainly due to the production of leisure homes for both natives and foreigners, and has taken place mainly outside the urban areas (see Tables 2.8, 2.9 and 2.10).

There was also increased social mobility during this period. Education levels increased sharply and the ratio of manual to non-manual work changed considerably (NSSG 1975 and 2001). This has had an important effect on expectations of housing standards, reflected in substantially improved housing conditions, and contributed substantially to the modernisation of southern European societies.

How can this apparent housing success story be explained? It is intriguing that significant numbers of people gained access to urban housing without substantial intervention by the welfare state. Moreover, the ways in which they accessed it and the reduced presence of homelessness and social exclusion add to the puzzle.

The place of the family in the southern development model and welfare system

Important economic and organisational resources, neither directly provided nor immediately controlled by the state or the market, were available to implement this massive social access to urban housing. The economic resources relate to the low degree of proletarianisation in these societies and the high levels of independent economic activity, usually through family businesses. Thus, some of the specific economic resources which could be mobilised by families include: the family patrimony in the place of origin; extensive access to public employment, which is a form of resource allocation to families through clientelist networks and which increased the number of public employees far beyond what the administration required;

emigrants' remittances from countries with higher wage levels during the 30 or so years after World War II and, since accession, European Union subsidies for weaker economic regions. The organisational resources available to families derive mainly from the role it plays in social reproduction and in housing in particular.

The low level of welfare state development should not be understood as an absence of state policies. In fact, the resources available to families were directly related to state policies, including: protectionism of small, unproductive family businesses; laissez-faire regulation of housing construction; increasing numbers in unnecessary or unproductive public employment jobs as a way of selectively transferring public funds to families and so on. The role of the family was enhanced with the help of the state.

The sharp increase in the need for urban housing occurred at a time of an intense focus on economic development. Since states considered industrial development to be the main vehicle of modernisation, their efforts concentrated mainly on that. Even the policies that directly favoured housing construction were dictated by the aspiration to promote economic development rather than promote housing *per se* (see Chapter 6).

Social regulation in southern Europe did not depend on the development of a welfare state because it could capitalise on other social and political structures that articulated the power relationship between the family and the state. As discussed in Chapter 4, clientelism and populism have been common characteristics of the political cultures in the southern European countries (Diamandouros 1991 & 1994; Lyrintzis 1987; Mouzelis 1987). Clientelist practices brought together local deputies and their political associates with the heads of extended families in a mutually empowering process where family votes were exchanged for a wide range of favours distributed in the form of jobs in the public sector, individualised lenience in regulating illegal housing development and priority for health care when health systems were congested. Clientelism, thus, contributed to maintaining and reinforcing family hierarchies and patriarchal power as a socially and politically stabilising force.

These kinds of social and political arrangements were associated with the authoritarian regimes in Spain, Greece and Portugal until the mid-1970s and with incomplete democratisation in Italy. The pattern of social programmes within their welfare states promoted a familialist and corporatist organisation of society and were developed in this context. The family's role in social reproduction was strongly supported by corporatist welfare state arrangements that focused on male breadwinners.

It is not sufficient to argue that the family has acted, and still acts, as a type of functional equivalent to a weakly developed welfare state. The family's role in southern Europe has been greatly enhanced by the distinctive pattern of industrialisation and urbanisation discussed in Chapter 3. This has particularly affected housing in the southern context as industrial manufacturing development has not driven organised urbanisation and there is no scarcity of labour requiring state support for its reproduction. Housing, rather than jobs in industry, has helped newcomers to integrate into the growing urban areas. The pivotal importance of housing and the absence of direct state intervention shaped the relationship between family and housing in southern European countries.

This relationship leads to housing being seen as a family concern, linked to the lower degree of proletarianisation of southern European societies, especially in Greece and Italy. In northern Europe, waged work is commonly seen as a duty towards society which, in turn, creates the necessity of rights to housing, health care, education, etc. In contrast, in social contexts where work is mainly a family concern, that is, where self-employment and small family business form a large part of the active population, the moral obligation of society to provide such services is less obvious.

Demographic parameters and trends

An important element affecting the relationship between housing and family in southern Europe has been external migration. During the three decades after World War II, people migrated from all four southern European countries to meet the demands for labour in the expanding fordist manufacturing industries in western Europe. Southern European immigrants, coming from low-wage economies and planning to return eventually, preserved strong family ties in their home countries, supported by regular remittances home. The difference in wages and living costs between the countries of origin and the host countries made it possible for them to accumulate significant savings over a period of 10–15 years. On their return, these savings allowed them to invest by setting up their own business and/or buying a house in a way that would not otherwise have been possible. Thus, emigration at that time could be considered as a family strategy for social mobility, seeking resources that could not be extracted from the local labour markets in order to attain, in the medium term, integration into their national urban societies mainly through the acquisition of an owner-occupied house.

The second aspect of external migration in southern Europe occurs in the more recent period, during the 1990s, when the flow was reversed and immigrants from the Third World and eastern Europe arrived in the four countries. The presence of a growing number of immigrants in the lower social strata of southern European societies creates the need for new kinds of strategies for gaining access to housing. Traditional family strategies for acquiring and managing housing assets do not work for immigrants since they have neither family networks nor housing assets to build on. Most recent immigration has been illegal and these migrants have no citizenship and fewer social rights. In societies where housing is the key to social support and where the family provides the means of access to housing, social groups outside this pattern are in a doubly difficult situation: they do not conform to the family-based social norm and have few alternatives in gaining access to housing (cf. Mingione 1993 and Benassi *et al.* 1997 about this double disadvantage). This change also alters the link between family and social cohesion since the family is no longer an asset for those who need it most.

Another important demographic development involving family and housing is the change in household structures and fertility. Southern European household patterns are now becoming closer to those in the north. Since 1965, fertility rates for Europe as a whole have fallen from 2.72, but have now stabilised at 1.45. There has also been a transition from larger to smaller household sizes. In sociological terms, the European household moved from the 'orthodox Parsonian family' of parents and children to a more mixed pattern, where the nuclear family now represents less than half of the total number of households. The question is whether it is just a matter of time before southern countries match the fertility levels and household structures of the rest of Europe or whether they are following a separate path. This is important because forecasts of population trends and household types and sizes, on which housing plans and policies are founded, assume that the southern countries are on a path to convergence.

The answer is not straightforward. On the one hand, fertility rates in southern Europe, which were 2.94 in 1965, have fallen faster and further than the rates for Europe as a whole. They have now stabilised at around 1.17. Household size, although larger than the European Union average, is shrinking. In Spain and Italy, fertility rates have reached a record low and the trend is related to a number of socio-economic variables. It can be interpreted as a sign of modernisation in societies with a more recent rural past. It can also be interpreted as the result of socially diffuse strategies to preserve a recently attained, but still insecure social status. It can be related to pressure from the labour market and the increased cost of education and improving lifestyles. It can also be related to the weak development of the welfare state, which generates feelings of insecurity about future generations.

Nevertheless, household structures in southern Europe are changing at a slower pace and still differ from those in the rest of the European Union. The primary difference is that they continue to be much more family-centred. People who live together as couples and raise children are more likely to be married and divorce rates are much lower. Culture and religion may help explain this but socio-economic factors are equally, if not more, important. Family solidarity can be boosted where the welfare state is weakly developed and the specific patterns of welfare state programmes may directly affect the shape of household structures. The delayed age at which young people leave their parental household, discussed in the next section, is probably the most important case in point.

Demographic trends are related to housing since they affect the required size of the housing stock and the need for particular types of dwellings in future. Forecasting these trends, however, must take account of the impact of social mechanisms in readjusting and harmonising housing and family cycles in a context of limited welfare state development.

Household cycles and housing

As discussed at the beginning of this chapter, the important role of the family in social reproduction is one reason for the difference in household structures and cycles between southern and northern countries. The more recent agrarian past of the urban population and the relatively reduced pressure towards individuation resulting from the lower level of development of manufacturing industry within the overall economy have created a favourable socio-cultural context for preserving and developing new family roles. The economic function of the family, especially in the countries and regions where self-employment and small family businesses remained important, constituted an equally, if not more important, support for the family. The importance of the family in social reproduction in southern Europe is also related to the relatively weak development of the welfare state, for which family solidarity has operated as a type of functional alternative.

The way in which older family roles were preserved as a basis for the development of new roles in southern Europe, especially in the urban environment, is reflected in household structures that include a greater number of nuclear and extended families than single-person households, cohabiting couples or lone parents with children. This obviously affects household types (see Table 5.1) and household cycles. Thus, individuals tend to move through fewer household stages, because they seldom live outside a family group before marriage or after separation or widowhood. The individualised forms of household found in northern countries do not occur so frequently because the broader pattern of southern families incorporates these stages. It is characteristic that in Greece almost 10% of all men and women aged between 18 and 49 are living in extended households, that is, in households with at least two other generations (Symeonidou 2002).

Historically there have been national and regional differences in the process of children leaving home. Their emancipation related to different modes of inheritance and especially of landed property, in societies that mainly depended on agrarian production. Modes based on the indivisibility of the property, usually transmitted to first-born males, imposed an obligation on the heir to house and cater for other members of the family (Grafmeyer 1993). These inheritance systems favoured multi-family household forms, in opposition to systems that favoured the segmentation of wider families into smaller household units (cf. Reher 1996 for a discussion of regional differences in Spain). However, in the eighteenth and nineteenth centuries, apprenticeship, temporary work and other forms of preparation for adult life and the formation of a new household often induced spatial mobility that also presented a strong regional variation. Such mobility was sometimes more frequent for women who worked as servants in urban areas, but this type of movement began to decrease at the beginning of the twentieth century (Reher 1996).

In Spain the average age of emancipation is higher in the north than on the Mediterranean coast. In 1991, 28.6% of Galicians aged between 16 and 39 were emancipated from their parents' household; in the Balearic Islands, the proportion was 46.2%; in Madrid it was 33.1% and in Barcelona 38.5% (Leal 1997). Historical differences in inheritance laws and practices are not a sufficient explanation for these differences since the non-division of landed property through inheritance was also a common practice on the Mediterranean coast, especially in Catalonia. More important explanations lie in the proportion of rented housing, the price of housing and youth unemployment, which vary among the regions.

The settlement pattern in different regions provides some further insight. Dispersed populations living in the countryside, in the cattle-farming north, favoured multi-family households and delayed emancipation. On the Mediterranean coast, a higher percentage of the population lived in cities and villages, and it was less common for young married people to live with their parents.

Despite the differences in household patterns among southern European regions, the four countries present a common overall tendency expressed by the stronger family-centredness of their household structures compared with the rest of the European Union and, especially, by the delayed emancipation of the young from the parental household. Current trends should, therefore, be related to their more recent common features, mainly to the articulation between their recent urbanisation, the weak development of their manufacturing industry and their weak welfare states, rather than to their agrarian past.

The delayed emancipation of the young is a common feature of the four southern countries compared with the rest of the European Union. Living in family households leads to a reduced percentage of single-person households and this is reflected in comparative data which show that the southern European countries, and especially the Iberian ones, have a significantly lower proportion of single-family households than the European Union average (Tables 5.2 and 5.3).

Table 5.2 Single-person households in the European Union, 1990 and 1995.

	Single-person households as a percentage of all households		Percentage of population living on their own in 1995			
			Age 20–29		Age 75+	
	1990	1995	Men	Women	Men	Women
Greece	18	21	8	7	16	44
Italy	20	21	6	4	22	69
Portugal	14	14	2	3	17	30
Spain	11	13	1	1	9	28
EU15	26	28	12	10	22	56

Source: Eurostat (1997b, p. 38).

Table 5.3 Single-person households by age in Spain, 1991.

Age	% of all single-person households	% within age group who are:	
		Men	Women
19 or less	0.9	52.7	47.3
20 to 34	11.7	58.2	41.8
35 to 49	11.6	59.4	40.6
50 to 64	20.8	40.1	59.9
65 to 74	27.4	20.6	79.4
75 or more	27.5	18.7	81.3

Source: calculated on the basis of the INE 1991 population census.

Another noticeable difference with the rest of the European Union countries is the smaller number of couples living in consensual union. This may be regarded as a traditional conservative practice related to culture and religion (especially Roman Catholic but also Orthodox), but it is also related to other, more practical difficulties that delay the emancipation of young southern Europeans. As a consequence, their move from the parental household usually coincides with their decision to form a new family household, sanctioned by marriage.

In Madrid, the average interval between leaving the parental household and getting married is 1.4 years, which is partly due to the increasing number of young people studying away from home. Couples living in consensual union were only 1.6% of almost 9 million couples in Spain in 1991 in spite of the increasing institutional change in marriage patterns in other countries. Below the age of 29, only 1.2% of men and 1.6% of women living in couples were not married in 1991. These percentages increased a little for the ages between 30 and 39, reaching 2.1% for men and 1.8% for women. The proportion of young adults living in such an arrangement is less than 0.5% for the age group of 20 to 29 (Garrido & Requena 1996).

Again, in Madrid, only 21% of the people who are or have been married had formed their own household before their first marriage, while 7% left their parental household after their marriage, meaning that they continued to live with their parents for some time after being married. In the remaining 72% of the cases, marriage and emancipation occurred at the same time. In Athens, most young people only leave the parental household when they get married. According to a recent survey, 51% of males and 68% of females had only stopped living in their parental household at that point (Maloutas *et al.* 2002). According to Symeonidou (2002) and the findings of the 1999 family and fertility survey in Greece, emancipation from the parental household is not particularly delayed since 50% of young women leave home around the age of 20 and young men do so around the age of 23. However, partnership formation occurs much later, four to five years later for both men and women, and since young people leave home when they get married and consensual unions are very rare, the only explanation for this rather early emancipation is the departure from home following the massive expansion of access to higher education. The entrance examinations to Greek universities produce a geographic distribution of students which is mainly dependent on their performance and only marginally dependent on their residential location. Leaving home to study can hardly be considered as emancipation in the Greek context where most expenses, and especially housing, have to be provided by the family. Moreover, students return home between terms and on long weekends.

Consensual unions before marriage are rare in southern European countries. In Spain and Portugal, only 3% of the total number of couples are not married while in Greece and Italy this percentage is even lower, at 2%, against a considerably higher percentage in the rest of the European Union, at 8% for the EU12 according to Eurostat estimates (see Table 5.4).

The trend in household formation in southern Europe indicates a slow decline in the family-centred structure (see Table 5.8). However, this is not a simple trend since in Spain, for example, the age of leaving the parental household is increasing (Table 5.5) instead of decreasing (Leal 1997). Longer job training periods may be one reason but can only be a partial explanation, especially as young people are delaying leaving home until they reach the age of 30. In recent years, the average age of emancipation has constantly increased, and in 1996 it was three years higher than in 1981 (Leal 2002).

Late emancipation from the parental household can be considered a feature of the southern European socio-cultural context related to the weakly

Table 5.4 Couples living in concensual union, percentage within age groups, southern Europe and EU12, 1994.

	Age group				
	Total Aged 16+	16–29	30–44	45–64	65+
Greece	2	9	1	1	1
Italy	2	6	2	1	1
Portugal	3	10	2	1	2
Spain	3	14	4	1	1
EU12	8	31	8	3	3

Source: Eurostat (1997b, p. 40).

Table 5.5 Percentage of young adults emancipated from their parental household, by age group, Spain, 1987 to 1995.

Age group	1987	1991	1993	1995
16–18	1.2	0.4	0.3	0.2
19–21	4.5	3.2	3.0	1.9
22–24	18.8	13.0	12.1	8.9
25–27	45.8	32.6	31.5	27.6
28–30	68.3	58.0	57.2	52.9
31–33	77.0	74.5	73.6	69.7
34–36	81.7	82.2	82.1	79.4
37–39	85.2	85.6	84.7	85.1

Source: INE *Encuesta de Población Activa* (1987, 1991, 1993 and 1995); all figures are from the second quarter of the year.

individuating impact of poorly developed welfare services, a comparatively recent agrarian past and the nature of the urbanisation process in the region, all of which allowed traditional social structures and practices to persist. However, these features do not explain why the average age of emancipation is increasing. The explanation of the increasing age of emancipation is mainly rooted in related trends in the labour and housing markets which make it difficult for young people to access housing. The growth of unemployment and insecure forms of employment have particularly hit the young, reducing their opportunities for self-sufficiency. Unemployment and long-term unemployment are hitting young people in southern Europe the hardest (Table 5.6).

Between 1981 and 1996, the unemployment rate for young people increased alongside increases in the cost of housing in relation to earnings (Vergés 1997). Table 5.7 clearly shows the negative relationship between temporary work contracts and the emancipation process. Precarious employment not

Table 5.6 Unemployment and long-term unemployment (12 months or more) for total active population and young people under 25 in southern Europe and the European Union, 1996.

	Unemployment rate (% of economically active population)		Long-term unemployment (% of total unemployment)	
	Total population	Aged under 25	Total population	Aged under 25
Greece	9	28	57	54
Italy	12	34	66	64
Portugal	7	17	53	41
Spain	22	30	53	43
EU15	11	22	48	39

Source: Eurostat (1997b, pages 94 and 98).

Table 5.7 Percentage of employed young people with temporary jobs in relation to their emancipation, Spain, 1995.

Age group	Emancipated	Not emancipated	Total
16–19	59.9	86.3	86.0
20–24	68.6	74.5	74.0
25–29	46.5	54.9	51.8
30–34	31.5	39.8	34.0
35–39	23.2	30.5	24.3
Total: 16–39	32.2	61.3	47.1

Source: analysis by author based on INE *Encuesta de Población Activa* (1995) (second trimester).

only affects those looking for jobs at the lower end of the service sector. The importance of the longer period of education and training required for highly skilled jobs also lengthens the period of time required to find secure employment. A period of uncertain employment is, therefore, created even for those entering highly skilled careers that eventually lead to stable employment (Lles & Tobio 1990). These changes in the process of entering the job market contribute to the generalised delay in the emancipation of the young. The reduced presence of precarious jobs in Greece, as expressed by the low percentage of temporary work contracts in official statistics, is not necessarily an indication of the opposite trend. It is rather an indication of a greater degree of inflexibility in the formal labour market which especially affects unemployment rates among the young and therefore does not favour emancipation.

The low proportion of the housing stock for rent reflects the lack of development of the social rented sector and the shrinking private sector over the past 20 to 30 years. Although the majority of young people in southern Europe are home owners, a large part of those leaving the parental household live, for some time at least, as tenants. In Spain, about 50% of young people do this. Therefore, there is a significant demand for a reduced and shrinking supply. Moreover, most of the housing stock for rent is in the private sector, which does not necessarily take into account the needs and incomes of young people.

Students form an increasing percentage of the age group in which emancipation from the parental household usually takes place. French or British students have a number of subsidised options such as student halls of residence or public housing (Godard & Bloss 1988; Rugg 1999), but Italian, Spanish and Greek students must seek housing in the expensive private rented sector. In Madrid, for example, it is difficult to rent a studio for a price below the minimum wage. While French students often choose universities that are far from their parents' home (Clark & Dilleman 1996), those in southern European countries usually seek universities as near as possible to their family's house because of the increased cost of independent living. Young people from middle-class families can more easily rent a house at the beginning of their working life than can those of working-class origin. This implies that the often belated entrance of young people from the middle class into the labour market is in some way compensated for by their comparatively increased opportunity to live independently as tenants.

There are also impediments for young people entering the housing market as buyers since they must consider the financial problems they will face if they decide to move again in the future. In Spain and Greece, the tax on buying a new house represents some 10 to 15% of its price. This has two consequences:

(1) It generally discourages residential mobility. The mobility of Spanish households living in large cities is about 5.5% (Modenes 1998). In Athens, there is a similar level of mobility (Maloutas 1990; Maloutas 2004). This level of residential mobility is lower than in most cities in the rest of Europe and substantially lower than in the cities of North America (Knox & Pinch 2000).
(2) Most young buyers consider their purchase as a very long-term investment, often a once in a lifetime purchase which, therefore, has to cover their future needs in terms of size, layout, location and so on. This requires a bigger investment than that needed at the moment of the purchase. High taxes and the marked similarity between the size of young people's houses and the average are, therefore, interrelated. The longer stay in the parental household for prospective home owners is often due to the need to accumulate the required down-payment. At the same time, the other side of this coin is that relatively few young people live in rented housing. Renting a home is considered an option only in those cases where a family project is not in sight and is most frequent among those who live by themselves for the first time and among those who are divorced. More than 25% of people in these groups are tenants in Spain, while overall only 15% of all households rent.

Prices, interest and unemployment rates are the most important macroeconomic factors affecting the process of emancipation in countries dominated by home ownership. Interest rate reductions in the first half of the 1990s did not have any visible effects on the increasing age of emancipation. However, when decreasing interest rates were accompanied by lower unemployment rates during the second half of the 1990s, the average age of emancipation stopped rising. In the second half of the 1980s, however, the drop in unemployment rates did not prevent the average age of emancipation from rising since there was a strong increase in house prices at the same time. The age of emancipation stabilised only when the decrease in unemployment was followed by the stabilisation of house prices and decreasing interest rates. Between countries with similar unemployment and interest rates, for example Italy and France, the age of emancipation may vary considerably. The way that the structure of the housing sector and housing policies affect the young, in particular, largely accounts for this variation.

Among the southern European countries, Spain has the lowest percentage of non-family households (see Tables 5.1 and 5.2). This is probably due to the rigid market forms of housing provision related to the dominance of large promoters and builders with access to housing credit from large private banks. These forms of housing production and credit have, at the same time, prevented the development of more flexible forms of housing provision, such as self-promotion, found more in the other countries of southern Europe. Therefore, they have encouraged the more frequent use of defensive housing strategies keep, such as delayed emancipation from the parental household, which focus on the redistribution of housing assets among family members rather than on securing new assets.

Delayed emancipation from the parental household has a number of important consequences:

First, it has a demographic impact by contributing to the reduction of fertility rates in southern Europe. Lower fertility eventually contributes to a

Table 5.8 The changing dynamic of family structures in southern Europe, 1970 to 1996.

		Greece	Italy	Portugal	Spain	EU15
Average household size (persons per household)	1985	3.0	2.9	na	na	2.6
	1990	2.9	2.8	3.1	3.4	2.6
	1995	2.7	2.7	3.0	3.2	2.6
One-person households (% of all households)	1988	16	19	na	na	25
	1990	18	20	14	11	26
	1995	21	21	14	13	28
Non-family households (% of all households)	1990–91	21	24	16	17	30*
Children under 16 living with one parent (% of all children under 16)	1994	4	6	7	5	9*
Couples in consensual union (% of all couples)	1994	2	2	3	3	8*
Crude divorce rate (per 1000 population)	1970–74	0.4	0.4	1.0	na	1.0
	1990–94	0.7	0.5	1.2	0.7	1.7
	1995	1.1	0.5	1.2	0.8	1.8
Live births outside marriage (% of all live births)	1970	1	2	2	1	6
	1980	2	4	9	4	10
	1990	2	7	15	10	20
	1995	3	8	19	11	23
Women's economic activity rate	1990	35	35	48	33	43
	1996	37	35	49	36	45

Source: Eurostat (1996, p. 44; 1997b, pp. 36–50, 76).

* Data refer to EU12.

decrease in average household size. Table 5.8 shows that the average household size in the EU15 remained at 2.6 between 1985 and 1995, while it was falling in all four of the southern countries. Delgado (1997) argues that up to 40% of the decrease in fertility rates in Spain is explained by the delay in having the first child. Postponing the time of the first childbirth implies a decrease in the potential fertility rates for the mother, even though the proportion of children born by mothers aged over 40 has increased slightly. In southern Europe, the decline in the fertility rate is strongly correlated with the increase in the average age of emancipation. This declining trend will probably cease and fertility stabilise at a higher rate than currently, once the impact of the gap between the procreation ages of generations no longer exists. Delayed emancipation as well as the reinsertion of the elderly into their children's households both affect the household structure in southern European countries by reducing the potential proportion of single person households and that of couples in consensual union.

Trends in the labour market, and unemployment in particular, have helped to delay emancipation. At the same time, the rigidity that delayed emancipation imposes on the spatial mobility of the workforce partly explains regional differences in unemployment rates. One of the biggest problems for labour force mobility is the difficulty in accessing housing in the areas of increased employment prospects, that is, in the large cities. This is especially true for Spain where regionally-based nationalism and localism are further impediments to internal migration.

The decreasing proportion of young people living independently also has an important influence on the housing market because it reduces housing demand as a whole, and for specific types of housing, and explains why housing production was lower than expected during the 1980s and the first half of the 1990s. In Madrid, it has been estimated that housing production was 20% less than expected throughout the 1980s and 1990s. This represents 140 000 dwellings, or 9% of the stock in the region (Leal 1999b).

Delayed emancipation is part of a reciprocal solidarity whose other component is the high percentage of elderly people living in their children's households. This pattern of inter-generational help also includes further assistance from parents in housing matters, that is, through taking over part of the cost of a new house for young households and actively supporting their children's new households over a long period of time. Such a pattern of family relationships makes residential proximity between family-related households necessary and forms another important parameter in the relationship between family and housing.

Delayed emancipation also influences the young person's definition of their personal identity. The process of their socialisation is enmeshed within contradictory pressures from the coercive family framework and broader social pressures towards more individuality. Sometimes this contradiction leads to alternative forms of self-expression through individualist consumption patterns and behaviours that influence housing practices and residential space (Bonvalet *et al.* 1999). In Spain, the lack of housing space within which young people can develop leisure-time activities means that such activities are transposed to public spaces, which puts pressure on public spaces and can induce conflict with other groups of users. The absence of private space at home and the difficulties in securing other spaces for the young add to the pressures they experience in a difficult labour market and partly explain the growth of violence, increased alcoholism and drug use as expressions of a growing feeling of dissatisfaction and exclusion.

The folding of more individualised steps in household cycles into those that are family-patterned is a distinctive feature of the southern European countries in the broader European Union context. This feature is related to labour and housing market conditions that do not favour or even actively obstruct the early emancipation of the young and the ability of the elderly to live separately. It is also related to welfare policies and to housing policies, in particular, that do not counteract these conditions.

An important characteristic of these practices is that they are socially diffused. The southern European societies experienced rapid social mobility in the three decades after World War II, through the *trente glorieuses* and rapid urbanisation. Sustaining a new middle-class social and economic profile, without the support of well-developed welfare mechanisms, has forced broad social strata to deploy defensive housing strategies based on their available assets, which include family networks. Economic restructuring since the 1970s has reinforced such strategies by increasing the pressure on these social strata, who believe that their social status and security is under threat.

Family solidarity contextualised or the circumstantial role of the family

The massive urbanisation in southern Europe after World War II was followed by powerful upward social mobility; the number of manual workers fell and tertiary employment grew. After a rather brief period of industrialisation starting in the late 1950s and early 1960s, and a longer period in Italy which began after World War II, expanding employment in manufacturing industry was overtaken by the dynamic increase of employment in the tertiary sector. The broad transition from agrarian to service sector employment made it easier to transfer and adapt traditional rural family values and ways of living to more middle-class forms of life in urban areas. In contrast, the forms of working-class family life and solidarity developed in countries that industrialised much earlier and more fully can be characterised as more of a survival strategy. Such proletarian families were more destitute of resources and so were reduced to performing simple tasks related to the reproduction of their members. The state in which they lived, most highly exemplified in company towns, ensured that they lived under conditions of surveillance that also limited their options (Tsoukalas 1987). The southern European family has not experienced the same extreme forms of poverty under capitalist development as occurred elsewhere, and, wherever this did happen, it never became a tradition, except in some regions of northern Italy. The resources that remained at the family's disposal allowed the development of strategies targeted at social mobility, not merely survival. Therefore, family-based solidarity can be distinguished from proletarian solidarity (cf. Pahl 1988 for a critique of the concept of working-class solidarity) because it pursues the family's goals rather than goals related to raising general living standards. Family-based solidarity provided a way for many poor households to overcome the difficulties of industrialisation and urbanisation after World War II, but at the same time contributed greatly to the formation of a political culture that constituted the basis of populism and clientelist systems (Diamandouros 1983; Tsoukalas 1987).

This problematic legitimisation of family solidarity produced a contradictory outcome: family solidarity, in the form of illegal house building, for instance, was comprehensible as a survival strategy for rural immigrants but it created problems for the organisation, planning and infrastructure provision in fast-growing cities. It also created moral and legal dilemmas for the state and society. Leontidou (1990), for example, discusses the way that the social diffusion of (legal) urban land ownership and the ambivalent policies about illegal house building functioned to legitimate the latter. The extended reproduction of the model of family solidarity to satisfy needs that were less pressing, for example, widespread vacation house building in Greece after illegal building was largely checked in urban areas, and its use by wider social strata, has further reduced its legitimacy but has also led to a sense of complicity between society and a de-legitimated state.

Family is generally supposed to promote social cohesion and southern European societies' social cohesion is often attributed to the powerful role of the family and of family solidarity in particular. Nevertheless, family and family solidarity are resources which also reflect class divisions and their reproduction contributes to the reproduction of established social hierarchies. Moreover, the introverted nature of family solidarity is not, in principle, consistent with the promotion of social cohesion since concern is limited within the group and outsiders are considered either indifferent or threatening if they are bound to draw from the same social resources. Thus, the promotion of social cohesion by family solidarity should be understood as limited to regulating lower social strata through respect for dominant family norms and values, imposing the care of family members in need and so on. This form of social cohesion is a limited version of social equality and social justice (Harloe 2001; Maloutas & Pantelidou-Malouta, forthcoming). In southern Europe, the link between family solidarity and social cohesion acquires more importance, since the weak development of the welfare state otherwise leaves people in need without any safety net. Nevertheless, the effectiveness of the link obviously depends on the family being a socially diffused asset and raises the question whether this situation is changing in southern Europe.

An important element of the family model in southern Europe is that it is organised around a set of norms and values related to gender relations (Pfau-Effinger 1998). Mothers are the focus of solidarity networks, taking responsibility for childcare, care of the elderly, the ill and, eventually, for grandchildren. In Greece almost 50% of working mothers with children under three years old rely on their mother or on their partner's mother for childcare (Symeonidou 2002). It is not by chance that there is a strong matrilocality in housing practices, as illustrated in the choice of residential location near the woman's parents and the return of the widowed elderly to their daughter's household, although there is a growing tendency of inter-generational proximity independent of gender (Maloutas *et al.* 2002). An obvious assumption of this model is low levels of employment for women (see Table 5.8), whose work is restricted to domestic labour for the family. Today, women's employment in southern Europe is growing and the distance from countries with traditionally higher activity rates for women is decreasing (European Commission 1998), but there are still vast numbers of economically inactive women, especially among the older cohorts and the lower social strata (Pantelidou-Malouta 2000). Middle-aged generations of women have suffered the double burden of employment and traditional domestic divisions of labour, while younger women are increasingly socialised away from traditional roles. In the future, therefore, the sustainability of the family solidarity model and its support for a traditional form of social cohesion is increasingly in doubt.

Another important question related to family solidarity in southern Europe is whether solidarity practices are declining in this region, as they have in the rest of the advanced capitalist world. Family structures are converging with those in the rest of the European Union. There are increasing numbers of one-person households and single-parent families and a decrease in the proportion of nuclear families and large households and so on. The proportion of one-person households in Italy has increased from 10.3% in 1961 to 21.3% in 1997, while large households with five persons or more have decreased from 25.6% to 7.7% of all households over the same period (Cremaschi 1998). There are similar tendencies in Greece, with large households decreasing from 20.4% in 1971 to 13.2% in 1991, and one-person households increasing from 11.9% to 16.2% over the same period (NSSG 1975 & 2001). This change has been more delayed in Spain, where one-person households only increased from 13% in 1991 to 18% in 2001.

Cortes, nonetheless, argues that the changing structure of the southern European family should be attributed more to demographic changes, especially to the ageing of the population, than to changing social relations since solidarity practices, such as the delayed emancipation of the young and the return of the elderly to their children's households, remain strong (Cortes 1995). This claim is partly correct, in that the increase in one-person households should not automatically be interpreted as a sign of increased independence from the family (Abellán 1996, cited in Cortes 1998). However, Abellán's argument is based on a strong distinction between social and demographic factors and focuses on the current situation without considering the dynamics of change. Lower birth rates, for instance, result from choices that are, at least partly, socially determined: delaying the age of childbirth, because of longer training and insecure employment, and having fewer children either in order to maintain living standards or because the childbearing period for women is reduced. In this sense, pursuing or even strengthening solidarity practices may be interpreted as an immediate response to increasing difficulties brought about by demographic changes and reduced resources in a context of favourable socio-cultural predispositions to the deployment of such practices. In the longer term, however, demographic changes will impose a new situation, leaving an increasingly large number of people outside family solidarity networks. Resources, such as women's domestic labour, will tend to become scarcer, and assumptions about the gender and the inter-generational division of domestic labour, on which the southern European family model stands, will inevitably be challenged.

Family strategies for housing: northern and southern Europe

Housing practices have a more or less pronounced element of strategy. This strategy can vary in scope from a mere survival strategy, as in many Third

World countries, to strategies of wealth accumulation, social mobility and a hedonistic appropriation of living space. Strategies consist of managing resources in order to attain goals. Resources for housing strategies can be of two main kinds. The first consists of material and economic resources such as income, borrowing potential, marketable property, social aid for housing, self-help and mutual aid networks, and the second relates to institutional and organisational resources defining the rules governing the management of material and economic resources.

The northern European pattern of resources for housing strategies relies more heavily than its southern counterpart on available material resources (higher incomes, more borrowing potential, more substantial social aid and perhaps more marketable property) but lacks variety (less self-help, less mutual aid networks and so on). In addition, northern European housing strategies are more rigidly regulated. Strategies have to be deployed in specific schemes moulded by the state and the housing market, whereas in southern countries wider margins for the development of such strategies seem to exist.

Another difference between northern and southern countries refers to goals. The goals of housing strategies depend on the form and the relations between the members of the social unit or household that produces them. The more atomised household structures in the north, weaker family ties and smaller households reduce the scope of housing strategies in terms of the number of people concerned and the range of the anticipated solutions. Greater atomisation, especially when associated with greater social fragmentation in terms of weak mass democratic organisations, denotes a civil society, in the Gramscian sense, with less organising principles of its own, that is, principles not imposed by the state. Southern European societies show less atomisation with more highly developed family structures and practices constituting a strong organising element in their civil societies. This organising element in southern Europe is both an asset, promoting some forms of social cohesion and solidarity, and a problem, because of its uneven distribution and internally repressive hierarchy and because its goals may be antagonistic to the development of broader social concerns.

With fewer material resources but wider institutional margins, housing strategies in the southern countries are more diverse and produce more unintended consequences. The looser regulation of housing practices by the state and the market leaves more room for family regulation and, at the same time, the existence of powerful family structures makes more room for family regulation. In this process family structures and relations are empowered, especially when combined with the other major source of empowerment, family-based economic activity.

Less regulation of housing practices by the state does not necessarily mean that this partial self-regulation occurs against the state. In most cases, the state has promoted such arrangements through supportive legislation and/or through its reluctance to oppose illegal housing practices. These arrangements have freed public funds for industrial development and have gained political support. The unintended consequences of this relationship between family housing practices and the nature of state regulation in the southern countries have been especially strong in contexts where self-regulated housing practices have been enmeshed in populist policies. Such policies have given excessive support to individual family housing solutions (as in Greece) without concern for the aggregate result, leading to a serious deterioration in urban living conditions in terms of environmental and aesthetic degradation and a lack of infrastructure (Maloutas & Economou 1992; EKPAA 2001, Economou & Maloutas 2002; Maloutas & Deffner 2002).

Aggressive and defensive housing strategies

Family strategies shape housing practices in a number of ways. Aggressive strategies refer to gaining access to new housing and accessing home ownership. They presuppose the existence of the required resources and they are usually part of an upward social mobility. These strategies acquired particular importance in the post-war southern European urban context, since home ownership became the touchstone of a housing solution. Defensive strategies, on the other hand, refer to preserving existing housing assets and making them adequate to cover changing needs. They relate to the scarcity of new resources but presuppose the existence of some housing asset, however inadequate.

Aggressive family strategies relate to accessing home ownership through self-construction, self-promotion and buying a house as a finished product. Self-construction relies on recent family experience of rural housing construction and on the additional skills acquired by urban newcomers in construction works, where they usually found their first employment in urban areas (see Chapter 6). Self-promotion requires business-like organisational skills, transferred from rural family management experience and its sequel in the urban context in independent economic activity and/or family business. There are important differences among the southern European countries in terms of the significance of self-promotion. In Italy, it has been estimated that self-promotion accounted for 40% of house building activity in the early 1980s, and 30% in the 1990s (Cremaschi 1998). In a housing survey carried out in Athens in 1986, almost 30% of owner-occupied houses had been produced by self-promotion (Maloutas 1990). In Spain, however, self-promotion is only marginally important in urban areas due to the dominance of large construction firms (Leal 1999b). Buying a house as a finished product depends on having the financial resources to be able to do it either independently or with the help of public and/or private institutional schemes.

In all of the above ways of accessing home ownership, the family plays an active role. Three forms of family support are especially important:

(1) *Financial aid*
In the southern countries, home ownership usually occurs with emancipation from the parental home at the time of marriage. Thus, difficulties in accessing home ownership refer mainly to the problems of young households in dealing with the requirements of the housing market. Structural impediments, such as a welfare model focusing on the elderly rather than the young (see Chapter 4) and circumstantial impediments, such as high youth unemployment, make access impossible for young households without substantial family help. Thus, financial help from families is very significant throughout southern Europe. In Lombardy, Tosi (1995) reports that 27% of home owners have received financial support from their families for their housing investment. Families in Italy contributed between 50% and 70% of total housing investments from the 1950s to the 1980s (Padovani 1998a). In Athens, a housing survey in 1986 showed that family financial help had been received by 27% of owner-occupiers either directly or in the form of family patrimony sold for that purpose. Housing credit from merchant banks or state institutions was used in less than 25% of the cases, the rest having financed their acquisition from personal and/or family savings (Maloutas 1990).

(2) *Self-construction*
Families also play an important role in self-construction. It is not an operation that can be carried out individually. In most self-construction operations, the services of members of the wider family were offered and were eventually reciprocated (Cremaschi 1998; Tosi 1995; Leontidou 1990; Maloutas 1990).

(3) *Acquiring a site on which to build*
Finding and often procuring a construction lot, in the context of easy and socially diffuse access to urban land, effective popular control over urban land in Leontidou's terms (1990), was especially important in the years after World War II, when rural migrants moving to the city followed migration networks based on family and places of common origin. In 1986 in Athens, it was found that in almost 35% of cases of self-promotion and self-construction, the construction lot was provided by

> the family (Maloutas 1990). This practice has created patterns of spatial proximity for family members, which also support the creation of residential solidarity networks (Vrychrea & Golemis 1998; Costa-Pinto 1998).

Aggressive family strategies for housing were more characteristic of the earlier post-war period of intense urbanisation and massive access to home ownership. More recently, home ownership has become less accessible and more socially differentiated. In Spain, house prices more than tripled between 1985 and 1997, while wages only doubled over the same period (Cortes 1998). In Greece, the progressive withdrawal of traditional ways of accessing home ownership, like self-construction, rather than price changes, introduced social differentiation in access (Maloutas 1990). Practices of self-promotion and, even more so, of self-construction have been diminishing as the housing sector modernised, costs increased and construction skills were lost with employment growth in the service industries. These practices declined first in Spain, where they were never especially important. They have also declined in Italy and Greece, where self-promotion has become a practice increasingly reserved for affluent households. They are still present, but also declining in Portugal.

Thus, the only remaining aggressive housing strategy is accessing home ownership through the housing market using formal systems of housing credit. This reduces family solidarity to money transfers while, at the same time, it reserves these practices for more affluent families. Thus, in a context of reduced affordability, access to home ownership becomes a middle-class concern. The more recent increase in the proportion of home owners shows an increasing social homogeneity as access becomes more limited to the middle classes. This tendency has been shown in Athens (Maloutas 1990; Emmanuel 2002). Guerra (1998) also provides evidence of class differences in using housing credit facilities in Portugal. Policies of tax relief for home owners and first-time home buyers are therefore assisting mainly middle class family solidarity as Emmanuel *et al.* (1996) have shown in the Greek case.

As aggressive housing strategies become less feasible for wider social strata, families tend to replace them with defensive ones in an effort to cater for their members' housing needs through the redistribution of existing assets rather than through new acquisitions. These defensive strategies include intra-family housing property transfers, house sharing and residential propinquity.

A significant and rising proportion of home owners have obtained their property through family transfer. In Italy, 23% of home owners had been given or had inherited their house (Tosi 1995). In Athens, 23% of households in 1986 had acquired their houses in this way, with a rather even social distribution, slightly declining for households with higher income (Maloutas 1990). It should be noted that often these transfers have a clear strategic character, since they are not the temporally unpredictable product of inheritance but of traditional practices such as dowry and its more contemporary and gender-free forms intending to provide for the housing need of newly formed young households. In 1986, more than 70% of such transfers in Athens were found to be of this strategic type (Maloutas 1990). Strategic property transfers are state assisted, with favourable taxation arrangements compared with the normal transfer and inheritance taxes. In Spain, the most common form of family solidarity in housing is through cash payments to meet the deposit on a mortgage. There are also some incomplete forms of property transfer, as in the case of the owner allowing the long-term use of a property by family members without any form of rent. In Athens, this accounted for 6–7% of all households in 1986 (Maloutas 1990). Property transfers presuppose the existence of property, and strategic transfers, in particular, presuppose more than one housing unit, although in some cases even a single house owned by the family may be transferred to younger members of the family for tax or other reasons. Such tax-based transfers tend to occur more among the middle class, so that tax relief mainly benefits the middle classes.

Access to home ownership through family help is certainly not a southern European privilege. Inheritance, in particular, is expected to be important as a means of accessing home ownership wherever the latter is substantially developed. In France, for instance, 28% of owners had family backing in their purchase and strategic transfers and 'anticipated inheritance' is also a common practice (Cuturello 1987; Cuturello & Godard 1980 cited in Tosi 1995). Although France may not be a good example, since it can be considered as partly southern European, such practices are important in southern Europe in making access to home ownership possible in a context where alternative ways of attaining it are limited.

House-sharing is a more popular form of asset distribution between family members. It is mainly practised by families with fewer resources and whose children are waiting to acquire a home. House-sharing is also a means of protection for vulnerable forms of household, such as single-parents returning to their parents' house after divorce, or lonely, elderly people in widowhood rejoining their children in their new households. Table 5.1 indicates that in Spain and Portugal, in particular, the proportion of widowed people living on their own is very small compared with the rest of the European Union. In Greece, the proportion is higher primarily because elderly people often tend to live in a separate dwelling in the same building as their children as a consequence of a particular housing production system (*antiparochi*, cf. Leontidou 1990; Prevelakis 2000). In Italy, the figures are closer to the European Union average and reflect the extent to which elderly people tend to return to their villages of origin after retirement. In all four countries, there is relatively little institutional provision of specialised housing for the elderly. It is difficult to distinguish these new types of house-sharing from the more traditional forms of extended family, where generations coexist in more permanent terms, and it is not always possible to estimate directly the extent of extended family practices from census data on house sharing, since a large part of extended family functions can be performed without house-sharing. However, the issues of delayed emancipation and the return of the elderly have acquired some political significance in Spain, reflecting the restrictions on families' ability to use the more flexible strategies of self-construction and self-promotion in a market dominated by large construction firms.

One way of securing some extended family functions without sharing a house is residential propinquity. This is structurally related to the urbanisation of the early post-war period, since it was almost a built-in element in self-promotion and self-construction. This situation permitted the development of family solidarity in areas such as child rearing, housekeeping, care for the elderly, the sick and the mentally ill. Solidarity in such areas remains in contexts where adequate social services have not been sufficiently developed. Residential propinquity for families remains an important factor in residential location choice even in the new, more commodified housing market conditions. In many cases it is the prime factor in households' residential location preferences, substantially overriding considerations such as proximity to work or to social and other services. In Athens in 1986 and Volos, a medium sized city in Greece, in 1993, 59% and 65% of households chose their location in order to be near their families (Maloutas 1995). In Italy, only 8.5% of households gave being closer to families and friends as the main reason for their choice of location, compared with 30% who gave getting married and 17.6% who gave access to home ownership as their main reason. These low scores are not, however, an indicator of lesser importance or greater distance between family members, but rather a factor of the scale of choice of residential area that is so pervasive that it ends up being taken for granted. In Italy, 43% of married children live within one kilometre from their parents and 78% of these married children visit their parents at least once a week, while most unmarried children live with their parents. In Spain in the early 1990s, 45% of households declare having very frequent contacts with other family members and only 12% do so rarely (Cortes 1998). Residential propinquity as the basis for the formation of kinship solidarity networks has been greatly facilitated by the reduced housing mobility in southern Europe, and to a large extent, the reduced housing mobility is a consequence of kinship solidarity networks in the southern European context of social reproduction. In Italy in 1993–94, only 3.9% of households moved to another house. The potential of kinship solidarity networks is exploited by dense contacts between the family members.

New conditions and changing context for family solidarity

It seems undeniable that family structures and family solidarity play a far more important role in the reproduction of southern European societies than in the rest of the European Union. Important questions, then, are whether family solidarity is increasing or decreasing, or whether the family is dissolving in southern Europe as it seems to be doing in the majority of post-modern societies.

Two major factors influence the future of the family's role in social reproduction: changing employment structures and women's employment.

Changing employment structures

Changing employment structures in a globalising economy make independent nuclear family formation more difficult due to the increasing scarcity of permanent and secure jobs. This is leading to the further dismantling of pre-existing family structures, witnessed by the steady increase in southern Europe of non-family and one-person households shown in Table 5.8. A further consequence is that the individualisation of poverty is intensified, bringing new kinds of problems for the welfare state. In southern European conditions, where there is a tradition of family solidarity, the pressure from the labour market tends to be absorbed by the family. In this process, family solidarity seems fortified through practices such as the delayed departure of youths from the parental house (Cortes 1995). At the same time, however, this means both the familiarisation (*stricto sensu*) of poverty and the pauperisation of the family in terms of diminishing available resources as the analysis of Mingione and Morlicchio (1993) has indicated in the case of the Italian south.

Both the individualisation and the familiarisation of poverty are products of the poorly developed welfare services in conditions where family solidarity is becoming less socially diffuse and the resources available to different family networks are increasingly unequal, since market services are usually taking over what the family can no longer cater for. Childcare provision in Greece is revelatory in this sense. For children under the age of five, childcare is provided in most cases within the family, mainly by the mother or the mother-in-law of the working mother. The second provider after the family is the private sector. Private nursery schools cater for 25% of three to five year olds (Symeonidou 2002). The socially dividing market provision of services is increasingly taking over what the family can no longer provide mainly because of the decreasing availability of women's domestic labour.

Increasing levels of employment of women

An important specific characteristic of changing employment structures, partly produced by the need to increase the number of employed members of households, is the growing employment of women. This trend is present in southern European societies, especially in the sharp differentiation in the rate of activity between different age cohorts of women. In Greece, for example, this rate in 1991 was 54.5% for those between 25 and 29 years old; 48.4% for those aged 35 to 39; 33.3% for 45 to 49 year olds; and 26.1% for those between 50 and 54 years old (calculated from data in NSSG 2001). The change is even more important if we distinguish between urban and rural areas. In the latter, women's activity rates were traditionally high since women in the small family agricultural exploitation (the paramount form of economic activity in Greek rural areas) have long been considered as economically active in the official statistics. Thus, it is not surprising that in 1997 the rate of activity for women in rural areas was 60.1% for those between 25 and 29 years old and 54.5% for those between 45 and 64 years old. A more important change takes place in urban areas where, for the same year, the activity rate for young women (25–29 years old) was 70.5% against only 28.6% for more mature women (45–64 years old) (calculated from data in NSSG 2000). Thus, although employment rates for women at the national level seem rather stable in the post-war period (Symeonidou 2002), the change is important both in urban areas and for younger cohorts, where it is corroborated by the official statistics, and in rural areas, where nominally employed women are progressively replaced by really employed ones and the increasing shortage of women's domestic labour is not reflected in official statistics. As a consequence of similar processes throughout southern Europe (with the exception of Portugal where the activity rate for women is well above the European Union average), there is a decreasing gap between southern Europe and countries with higher employment rates (European Commission 1998). The impact of this change on the southern family is to reduce one of its substantial assets, women's domestic labour, which deepens the pauperisation of the family. At the same time, it disturbs the family's gender-based hierarchical cohesion by destabilising, potentially at least, the internal division of labour through more autonomy for its dependent members.

Family solidarity in southern Europe is experiencing more strain and less resources and is increasingly being expressed in defensive patterns. If this can be considered a sign of vitality, it is not enough to prevent the family's decline in future. The internal cohesion and the role of the family in southern European countries have been consolidated on the basis of the management of considerable resources, while its decline elsewhere was linked to reductions in the resources available to it. Over a long period of time, the reproduction of social structures and practices creates cultural predispositions, which become partly independent of the material conditions under which they were created. However, if these material conditions then change over a substantially long period of time, it cannot be expected that these cultural predispositions will carry on unaffected indefinitely. In this sense, we should pay some attention to recent changes in family structures throughout southern Europe, indicating the increase of non-family household structures (Table 5.8). Under the present material circumstances affecting the family's role, we should regard the current situation as reinforcing defensive forms of family solidarity due to the reduced resources available to families. In the longer run, however, there is evidence that such defensive strategies are not sufficient to prevent family solidarity being undermined, with subsequent major changes in the role of the family and in its structures.

The family model and the housing system in southern Europe are mutually reinforcing. Access to housing demands large initial financial or other resources, for instance in the case of self-construction, that young households cannot provide on their own without family support. Thus, family support in facing housing need reinforced family solidarity and simultaneously reproduced the housing system. Decreasing interest rates and the development of long-term housing credit systems are changing the shape of access to housing, making family support less necessary. At the same time, an important asset for the development of family solidarity in housing, popular control in the form of cheap access to urban land, has been greatly reduced in Italy as well as in Greece, and thus the potential of the less affluent in particular for self-promotion has been substantially reduced (Maloutas 1990; Emmanuel *et al.* 1996). These changes undermine the continuation of existing family solidarity practices, the mutual reinforcement of the family model and the housing system. Only defensive family strategies for housing, maintaining and redistributing scarce assets among family members, especially for poorer families, have a feasible future. However, even this future is threatened by the changes in the family model and the increasing employment of women.

The familialisation of poverty and the pauperisation of the family, which have been produced by economic restructuring in the pre-existing conditions of the enhanced role of the family and family solidarity in social reproduction, raise a further issue. Does the role of the family, and of family solidarity in particular, have the same social content and impact in the present conditions of reduced resources and defensive attitudes?

The socially cohesive impact of family solidarity in southern European societies relied on a large proportion of the population being located within family networks and on the widespread social diffusion of family resources. Thus, the impact of wider changes alters as the conditions and forms of family solidarity change. There are three main factors affecting the social character of family solidarity and its impact:

(1) Decreasing resources affect families in a socially selective manner. In housing, it is the popular and working-class households that have been most severely affected by reduced accessibility to home ownership and which have had to limit themselves more to defensive practices such as house-sharing. More generally, poor families have been deeply affected by the considerable reduction of social resources (land, public jobs and so on) and control they received through localised and/or non-official processes. The reduction in these resources can be traced to either a shortage of public resources or the problems created by this earlier model in societies that are trying to modernise. Greek urban areas, and Athens in particular, are an illustration of such problems. Middle-class households, in contrast, possessed more resources to begin with and, favoured by tax relief policies, can continue their practices relatively unaffected. Thus, decreasing resources have a socially differentiated and differentiating impact on the content of family solidarity.
(2) Changing family structures are responsible for increasing numbers of people finding themselves outside of family solidarity networks. Even if these numbers represent considerably smaller proportions than in the rest of the European Union, their social impact, in situations and processes that presuppose family solidarity, is far more important. Thus, increasing numbers are left out of family help in a context of poor and inadequate social services.
(3) The growing immigrant population in the region can be considered as a further increase of the part of the population not protected by family solidarity and facing poor social services. Furthermore, immigrants are facing additional problems related to citizenship, ranging from simple discrimination to xenophobia and racism. These relatively new problems for southern European societies are further undermining the socially cohesive potential of family solidarity.

Conclusion: Family solidarity, housing and social cohesion

The reality behind family solidarity in southern Europe is sometimes distorted through romanticised versions that stress its historical role in promoting social cohesion and neglect its anti-democratic constitution and consequences (Barrett & McIntosh 1982). These romanticised views get far more attention in a period of welfare state crisis, when conservative discourse rediscovers the family, contrasting a version of the family deadlocked in welfare dependency on the state with a supposedly more spontaneous, democratic and successful version (cf. Leontidou 1996).

The family, forced into defensive strategies or stripped of access to wider social resources, can become the breeding ground for individualistic and selfish attitudes, socialising its members in caring and providing only within their small family world by securing the maximum of possible resources and being indifferent or hostile to those outside the family boundaries, where solidarity stops. This kind of selfish individualism, derived from family solidarity and not opposed to it, is also a cultural heritage of the region. It provides the necessary dispositions for the rapid building of xenophobic and racist attitudes in societies that did not, until recently, have any experience of immigration, leading them to forget their own extensive emigration experiences.

However, the family in southern Europe undeniably represents an asset that should not be neglected, especially in times of difficulty for social cohesion. Family solidarity can be considered as a resource if it can be established that it has contributed to increasing decisional autonomy and capacities in the fulfilment of aspirations and the satisfaction of needs. This means that the countries of southern Europe should not be exempt from the task of building a new democratic welfare state, because they have some kind of alternative solution, but that they eventually have additional resources for building if they succeed in putting the potential of family solidarity to wider social use.

6

Public Action in Housing

Concepts

The concept of public action is a way of looking at housing issues and housing policies as the outcome of systems of relationships among the different actors involved. Its nature may change over time or in different contexts. Public action also involves looking at both direct and indirect forms of action, and its boundaries are drawn to include forms of deregulation or decontrol, and even the systematic non-implementation of existing rules. Such a perspective is designed to operate horizontally rather than vertically, to look at the constellation of institutional actors rather than the hierarchical structures of public bodies and to be more open towards unintended consequences. Thus, the notion of public which it draws on is one which refers to the social nature of actions and their effects, independently of the public or private status of the active subject.

Using a public action approach builds on the perspectives developed earlier in this book. Chapter 4 argued that housing in southern Europe can only be understood in the context of a welfare system in which the family plays as strong a role as the state in ensuring the welfare of households. It also argued that there are specific characteristics of the state in southern Europe which shape how it acts and how it is linked with both family and market. Chapter 5 has examined the role of the family in some depth, showing how it performs its role in ensuring housing for its members. This chapter develops themes from the previous two chapters and continues our argument by examining how the state operates in the field of housing.

Is it possible to identify some distinctive common features of public action in housing in the southern countries? The four countries have experienced different processes of political, economic and social development that have affected how each views public action in housing. But, as we show in this chapter, they share some common features that can be seen as a distinctive pattern. Nevertheless, it would be difficult to maintain that they share the same set of policies in housing. Rather, common concepts and operational circumstances underpin the way housing policies are formulated and implemented in the four countries.

This book argues that it is worthwhile studying these patterns within a broader perspective than has characterised previous research. Most analysis of housing policies in southern countries has been based, both inside each country and in comparative European analysis, on a predefined set of assumptions about what constitutes sound and effective public action. The dominant perspective in most industrialised societies has tended, until recently, to conflate public action in housing with the development of a significant social rented sector and to evaluate the effectiveness of public policy primarily in terms of the size and quality of management in this sector.

The consequence of this reductive perspective is a tendency to see the four southern countries as lagging behind what is assumed to be a universal path along defined phases of housing policy development, each phase implying identifiable profiles of housing needs and problems that could, and should, be addressed through a consolidated set of practices. The concepts of rudimentary, undeveloped and incomplete have also been used to evaluate housing policies in the southern countries. This conceptual framework may explain the low level of interest, both inside and outside these countries, towards the public action systems in housing in southern Europe. Researchers focused on what were seen as more advanced, rather than backward, policies and practices.

We argue that if the analytical perspective is changed, some lessons may be drawn by looking at how public action in housing has developed in the southern European countries. Two changes in analytical perspective are necessary. First, we need to shift from the long dominant concept of state-centred housing action towards a wider perspective, in which we can see how mobilising a variety of actors within different social contexts affects access to housing and housing provision. Second, what is seen as the aim of public action must shift from providing a *commodity* to be consumed by households, the social rented sector, towards that of providing households with *resources* that can be used to improve their welfare and quality of life.

To look at systems of public action in housing in the southern countries and assess their success and failure along these lines seems promising for at least two reasons. The first, more limited in scope, lies in developing a frame of analysis to look at housing policies in southern countries that does not work as a procrustean bed, but is more appropriate for a critical understanding of their specific features. The second reason, broader in scope, looks at practices developed in the southern countries in the frame of the current European debates on housing issues and policies.

Three elements of the present housing debate in Europe seem pertinent. The first is a discussion of the impact of a post-fordist society on housing needs and on the nature of housing policies. The second relates to growing criticism of the rational, top-down, state-centred approach to public policies. The third is linked to the increasing weight that concepts of subsidiarity and governance have in defining public policies.

First, in a post-fordist society, labour flexibility and capital mobility are producing new and different patterns of housing advantage and disadvantage which affect more social groups and geographical areas in ways which are different from the past. Cross-border mobility at the upper and lower levels of social stratification has helped to create a greater diversity of patterns of habitation, ranging from exclusive, gated settlements to squatter settlements. These changes modify the nature of housing need as well as the role of the family. People are required to perform a more active role in organising their lives and housing assumes a more extended range of functions. Not only is it a private place for the reproduction of the household but it is also an economic resource, a place for work, and a tool for defining social status and a sense of community (Padovani 1991; Clapham 2002). The multi-faceted role performed by housing increases the gap between institutional and personal definitions of housing needs (Tosi 1994a) and raises questions about the effectiveness of traditional housing policy aims and instruments.

A second consideration arises from the changing role of central government in housing policies. Criticism of the rational, top-down approach and the interest in multi-actor, transversal, participative local action leads to questioning the state-centred concept of housing policy. The debate around the privatisation of the public housing stock promoted by the Thatcher Government in the United Kingdom has shown how different interpretations and other types of actions, not necessarily in line with the original policy, can be produced in the implementation process. Some outcomes were quite different from what was expected. This has shown the importance of the role of various actors in the so-called implementation process, even in a policy as centralised and top-down as the sale of council housing to its tenants. Actors are not simple executors but are also agents within a defined frame of behavioural and professional rules.

Third, the growing importance assumed by supra-national actors, such as the European Union, and local actors empowered by the principle of subsidiarity, introduces multi-level forms of governance. These forms of governance require central governments to shift from providing so-called public goods for their citizen-users' consumption to enabling a variety of actors to produce these goods for themselves and others. This implies that central government acts as only one of a set of actors. The concept of subsidiarity extends the role of actors to households and citizens.

Three main features of the housing systems in southern countries make it interesting to place them within the framework of public action: less direct state intervention, less targeted intervention and a polymorphic conception of housing. Together, these features comprise a shared pattern of public action in housing in southern Europe.

Less direct state intervention

The southern countries share a tendency to develop public action in housing in an indirect way. Using the concept of public action helps to see how different forms of support have been given to a variety of institutions and actors involved in housing provision and access. In this way, it is more useful than perspectives which focus on promoting or implementing systems of direct housing provision. Using the public action perspective draws attention to a much wider variety of actors from the market, public institutions and the third sector or the informal sector. The family is also included among these actors and recognised as a key agent in housing provision.

Less targeted

Housing policies are more pervasively spread and there is a laissez-faire, sometimes liberal, perspective rather than a direct-state view. In common with income-maintenance programmes discussed in Chapter 4, housing policies are also based more on cash than services. Compared with other western European countries, a disproportionately large part of public resources for housing is allocated to direct or indirect money transfer to support families' access to homes. Housing policies promote home ownership rather than other forms of housing supply, in contrast to most other European countries.

Polymorphic conception of housing

The concept of public action in housing is broader than a sectoral housing policy. Housing is seen as a multi-faceted resource. The home is not only a place for the reproduction of the household's life, but also a safety net for the family's welfare. Housing is also an economic activity that can play an important role in some phases of economic development, serving as a training ground helping in the change from an agricultural to an industrial and/or tertiary sector society and providing a source of income for the new urbanites. And, occasionally, under specific political circumstances, housing has been seen as a right. This transversal concept of housing is paralleled by a multi-functional conception of housing policies, which influences the aims and criteria used to evaluate the efficacy of these policies. They are evaluated against a range of politically disjointed issues and aims, rather than in terms of their economic consistency or response to specific housing issues.

The first two features raise controversial issues about inequalities in the destination of resources and the sustainability of current policies in the future. Another issue relates to the assumptions about how to look at similarities and differences in housing policies and institutional housing structures within the four southern European countries and between them and other European countries. The perspective adopted here is an attempt to understand the links between housing policy and its supporting institutional structure, on the one hand, and the social context, on the other. In contrast to convergence and divergence arguments, which tend to 'reduce to a residual important factors which explain evident differences between countries' (Clapham 2002), the concept of public action in housing can be seen as socially constructed in different and changing national and local contexts. Thus, it directs our attention to the links between housing actions and their contexts. In this way, we may be better able to understand and evaluate the variety of practices that have been developed in different countries.

Ideologies, political systems and conceptions of public action in housing

Public policies and public action in housing in the southern countries have been developed within different contexts. After World War II in all four countries, the dominant political ideology supported the centrality of the family in social life, and this was further reinforced by the strong role of the Catholic and Orthodox churches in national and local affairs. This was the case in Italy, when the Christian Democrats won the national elections in 1948 after a sharp confrontation with the left-wing coalition, as well as throughout the period of the fascist regimes in Spain and Portugal, and after the civil war in Greece. By supporting these conservative political regimes, the Cold War gave further emphasis to this ideology of the family. It was in this atmosphere that public action in housing was redefined after World War II.

In Greece, housing and housing policy discourse has not been closely related to political change. Since the 1920s, the definition of housing need and housing problems has been restricted to emergency situations, such as natural disasters (earthquake, flood) or national disasters (refugees from Asia Minor in the 1920s, civil war in the late 1940s). After the emergency conditions produced by the combined effects of World War II, the German occupation, and the subsequent civil war, housing progressively disappeared from the social policy agenda. Instead, housing provision was seen primarily as a method of promoting economic growth and played a more important role in debates on the model of growth to be followed in the country. In this context, since the early 1950s, housing has been a controversial issue between two conflicting groups. The first includes those who advocated a development model based on heavy industry and considered that housing investment would deprive the manufacturing sector of funds. The second group includes those who promoted lighter industrial development and viewed housing investment as a way of promoting growth for industrial products, such as building materials, housing equipment, and furniture, and in the commercial and tourism parts of the service sector (Economou 1987 & 1988).

In Italy in the first phase of the reconstruction after fascism and the war, housing was defined in a broad context: the first post-war plan to provide social housing was promoted by the Ministry of Labour with the explicit aim 'to promote blue-collar employment by subsidising housing production for the workers' (Di Biagi 2001). Under this scheme some 300 000 dwellings were produced between 1949 and 1963, employing 500 000 white- and blue-collar workers. The idea that *va tutto bene quando l'edilizia va bene* has been a recurrent theme in Italian post-war history, and it was at the heart of a fierce debate during the 1970s when questions were raised about the capacity of the building sector to redistribute resources to other sectors, industry in particular (Indovina 1981). However, in more recent years, the building sector has regularly been suggested as a tool for economic development.

In Portugal, the positive effects of employment in the building sector have always been a prominent issue. In Spain, public action in housing has depended on the assumption that house building promotes growth and is an important component of counter-cyclical economic policies promoting employment and consumption.

In the southern countries, housing policies, in any strictly defined sense, have not been at the core of political debate. Housing investment has been viewed through the lens of its effect on building activity rather than as a social problem. Access to housing was not a problem to be addressed by housing policies. It was considered more important to promote an economic climate that supported increasing employment and family wealth and that allowed households to satisfy their own housing needs. Urbanisation also played an important role in supporting this perspective. After World War II, a large part of the population was still engaged in agriculture (see Table 2.4), and the building sector played a central role in the shift from agriculture to industry and from rural to urban.

Overall, it would be fair to say that the important goal of public action in housing in southern Europe was not to develop an important social rented sector, but to give strong support through promoting the vertical social mobility of the population and supporting its geographical mobility. The possession of a dwelling was considered an important indicator of households' general welfare and the strong emphasis on home ownership can be seen as a device to render households more independent from fluctuations in the economy and employment. Home ownership was a way to give families a level of welfare that had no direct connection with personal, local or national cycles of economy, employment or wages, thus promoting social stability which was a very important strategic goal for the governments in southern Europe in the first three decades after World War II. The family, not the individual, was seen as the most important agent and ownership was considered as a safety net for the family to counterbalance a weak welfare state system, especially in the immediate post-war period. In other words, the longstanding and strong promotion of owner occupation can be seen as a strategic decision about how to construct a welfare system, given limited resources and the need to establish the legitimacy of governments following a period of considerable turmoil.

Distinctive features of public action in housing in southern Europe

In Chapter 2, we discussed a number of distinctive features of the housing systems in the southern European countries. In this chapter, we argue that these features rest on the institutional configurations within which housing policy is set and which determine their outcomes.

Three main themes characterise public action in housing in southern Europe:

- A low interest in the development of a large and effective social rented housing sector
- A large role for the private rented sector in housing provision
- The specific role of land development policies and land use control systems in providing homes, especially, but not only, for the less affluent.

Low interest in the development of a large and effective social rented housing sector

For a variety of reasons southern European governments did not set up policies to provide an important social rented sector, while great support has been given explicitly or implicitly to families to extend home ownership. Compared with the rest of Europe, the four southern countries have the smallest social rented sectors, the highest incidence of home ownership and the highest incidence of secondary homes (see Tables 2.1, 2.3 and 2.8). What needs to be explained, from a public action perspective, is why there was so little action to promote and develop a social rented sector. In Greece, the total number of social rented dwellings amounts to a few thousand units provided by the Ministry for Health, Welfare and Social Security for people in severe need, such as refugees and victims of earthquakes. In Spain, the number of social rented dwellings is also limited, about 85 000 units in 1991, or 0.7% of the total occupied stock. However, there is a larger social rented sector in Portugal and Italy, 4.6% and 5% respectively, of total occupied dwellings. In these two countries, institutional structures have been set up to provide and manage a public rented stock. In Italy, production and management of the social rented sector has an organisational structure, which is important in terms of institutions and practices involved, as well as in terms of employment. In the mid-1990s, more than one hundred *Istituti Autonomi per le Case Popolari*, special authorities operating on a sub-regional level responsible for the production and management of social housing, were managing 800 000 dwellings and employing 10 000 workers throughout Italy.

It is evident that southern European governments never developed a reasonably important social rented sector capable of meeting a variety of needs, either in the immediate post-war period when institutional structures in housing were re-framed, or in later periods. However, the size of the sector today does not reflect the scale of investment in it or the number of dwellings built in the past.

When the first significant public housing programmes were launched in Italy in the 1950s, it was intended that the whole stock would be sold to households with the right to occupy it. Public investment in housing during this period accounted for 17% of all housing investment. After sharp confrontations with the left-wing parties, a compromise was reached to sell only 50% of the dwellings, but in 1963, when a new agency (Gescal) replaced the agency which had built them (Ina Casa), there was a renewed political decision to sell the remaining 50% to sitting tenants at a very low price. In the late 1970s, when the development of a social rented sector began to be recognised as an important issue, a fragmented but numerically important privatisation of the stock went on. Then, in 1993, a new law dictated the sale of at least 50% of the remaining stock. Between 1951 and 1991, about 1.3 million social rented units were completed, through new house building or rehabilitation (about 33 000 units a year), yet this did not increase the size of the stock because sales over the whole period almost equalled the number of dwellings which were built.

Similarly, in Spain in the mid-1960s under the Franco regime, it was decided to stop the production of public housing for rent and most of this stock, mainly built during the 1950s and 1960s, was sold to tenants through a programme called *acceso a la propiedad*. Under this programme, tenants paid an additional sum over the normal rent and took ownership when the full payment was completed. When necessary, the buildings were refurbished by the local authority before being sold or, in the case of some older estates, buildings were demolished and rebuilt in another location to be sold to tenants under programmes such as the *Remodelación de barrios* in Madrid.

In Portugal, where a social rented stock does exist and the first laws introducing public housing date back to the early twentieth century, policies to develop this sector have been contradictory. The stock has constantly been sold to tenants willing to buy. After the April 1974 revolution, in a political climate that was more open to housing issues, some programmes to develop the social rented sector were implemented but, in the late 1980s, the building sector was liberalised and this form of public action in housing was reduced. Since the mid-1990s, public intervention in housing has regained some momentum, but the new policy focuses on eradicating shanty houses through a special re-housing program *(Programa Especial de Realojamento)*, which was launched in 1994.

There are many reasons why these countries never developed a large social rented sector but it is possible to identify two common factors:

(1) The southern countries share a strong political inclination in favour of home ownership because they consider it to be an effective way to achieve social stability. This was why Franco stopped building social rental housing in Spain in the mid-1960s and shifted public resources to promoting home ownership, and the centre-right governments and Christian Democratic party in Italy supported home ownership as a pillar of family welfare and social mobility. In Greece, home ownership was more popular and so promoting it over a social rented sector was considered politically more rewarding, and political demands for the development of social rented housing have been limited. Especially after the civil war in Greece, owner occupation helped to legitimise political power, and ownership was seen as both a means to and an expression of social mobility.

(2) The sale of the public rented housing stock is a product of the institutional difficulties of managing it. Traditionally, public administration in the southern countries has been oriented towards adopting and implementing rules to control private initiative, rather than developing 'entrepreneurial attitudes' within the public sector (Tosi 1994a). Civil servants have been trained to regulate and control private actors' plans and programmes, usually through complex bureaucratic systems which require advanced skills. They have not been trained to manage the effective delivery of public services, such as a housing stock, with sustainable economic results. The multi-faceted role assigned to public policies in housing did not put good management high on the agenda and the outcome was poor management of a badly maintained, small, social rented sector.

The combined effects of bad management and the laissez-faire attitude of the public bodies responsible for managing the social rented stock also produced negative effects. In both Italy and Spain, because of the lack of maintenance, tenants felt free not to pay their rent or to unilaterally reduce their payments. Some tenants genuinely could not pay, but others were opportunistically relying on the ineffectiveness of their landlord. Public bodies were not strict in collecting rents and reclaiming payments, and were unwilling to face the conflicts involved in evicting tenants. Thus, progressively, public agencies found themselves trapped in a difficult economic situation. Rent arrears and non-payment were becoming pervasive, and incomes from rents were very low, partly because they were fixed politically and not on the basis of costs. But, at the same time, the cost of maintaining and refurbishing an ageing, poorly built stock was growing. Selling the stock to tenants was seen not so much as a solution, but as a way out of the problem.

Finally, the coincidence of bad management, lack of maintenance, and the low quality of many of the post-war public housing estates which had been built very quickly under pressure to house a large number of families on low incomes, made them the ideal place for the social protest movements that developed throughout Europe in the late 1960s and 1970s. These groups were demanding improved housing conditions on public estates and a higher quality of urban life. For all these reasons, developing more social rented housing was seen as a hard task for the public sector and not very rewarding politically.

In the southern countries, demands for a right to housing have been weaker than in other countries with more robust welfare states. The demand has been reframed as a 'right to home ownership' and, within that frame, housing has been considered as a family issue rather than as an issue to be addressed by public policies and the welfare state.

Large role for the private rented sector in housing provision

The private rented sector has played a specific role in providing low-cost housing in the southern European countries. It has, in part, and perhaps paradoxically, performed a function that one would normally expect to be delivered by the public sector. Some explanation is required as to why and how the private rented sector has been able to perform this social function for middle- and low-income social groups since World War II, and what role the state has played in supporting the sector having this function.

Census data for 1950–51 show that at the end of World War II all four countries had a significant supply of private rented dwellings, nearly 50% of the occupied stock in Italy, Portugal and Spain, and 25% in Greece. The most recent figures show that it is now only 10% of the stock in Italy and Spain, and a quarter of the stock in Portugal, but in Greece there has been no decline in the proportion of the stock in the private rented sector (see Table 2.1).

In discussing the role played by the private rented sector, the first element to consider is the pattern of ownership of the private rented stock. The status of landlord has been much more socially diffused in southern Europe, particularly in Greece and Italy. Most landlords own only one or two dwellings. In very few cases do they own one or more multi-family buildings, and only a minor part of the stock is owned by public bodies or institutions such as banks, insurance companies, social security organisations or private enterprises. In Italy in the early 1980s and 1990s, 70 to 80% of the rented stock was owned by private individuals reflecting the high propensity of southern families to invest in housing, not only for their own direct occupation, but also for rent. Where a large number of dwellings are in multi-flat buildings, condominium forms of ownership have supported this fragmented pattern of landlordship. Housing investment is considered safe and, in the absence of alternative options for small investors, it is seen as a way of providing security for old age and for the family's future needs in the face of welfare states which provide only a limited range of services. This pattern of ownership was key to the feasibility of rent control in the decades following World War II.

The second element to consider is the social morphology of the private rental sector. With the social diffusion of access to home ownership, rented housing has not usually been the tenure of the poorest groups, especially where self-promotion and, particularly, illegal self-promotion has provided a substantial element in housing solutions for the growing urban populations. Moreover, renting, usually a transitory form of tenure in terms of its role in the household cycle, has been even more transitory in southern Europe. Most tenants develop a home ownership perspective at some point. Landlords are also transitory. Many small investors often invest in housing for rent with the idea of realising its use value in the future, particularly as a future home for younger members of families.

These factors, the profile of ownership, the transitory status of the private rental tenure both for landlords and tenants, and housing policies that were biased in favour of home ownership, create a tension between private renting and home ownership. Housing stock could shift from one tenure to the other, and rent control or rent freezes indirectly helped tenants to acquire the financial resources for home ownership. Private renting in southern Europe has increasingly become complementary to home ownership, both in terms of family housing strategies and in housing policies.

However, the private rented sector was and still is an important component of the housing stock, and so has been the object of regulation and control. Rent control policies have been recurrently used in emergency situations characterised by large discrepancies between supply and demand, as in the period immediately after World War II or in other circumstances. The chosen method was some sort of rent freeze, a blunt tool, but widely used in southern countries, particularly Italy and Spain, and which often lasted for many years. When control was introduced, there were political declarations about it being a temporary measure, but controlled dwellings were forgotten in this state for years. In the late 1970s, fair rent approaches were introduced with the aim of consolidating the private rented supply. But the unexpected result was a further reduction in supply and the reinforcement of home ownership as the dominant tenure.

In the four southern countries, the private rental sector has often been forced to offer low-cost housing to a variety of types of household and the variety of rent controls between the 1950s and 1980s is evidence of that. One could suggest that the rent control laws 'obliged' private landlords to provide housing for middle- to low-income groups as a substitute for a social rented sector and that it was the combination of the peculiar pattern of rented stock ownership, the absence of alternative investment options and the transitory status of this form of tenure in families' housing strategies that made this feasible.

However, rent controls can also produce unexpected and sometimes undesirable outcomes, with a strong impact on the pattern of housing tenure and the composition of housing supply. Ultimately, they led to reductions in the rented stock, a lack of maintenance and the progressive decay of the buildings. But in the post-war years, the policy seemed to work as families' incomes, housing prices and urban development grew. Increasing capital values counterbalanced low rental incomes. However, the policy was no longer viable in the economically stable or stagnant conditions in recent decades and, during this time, the supply of private rented housing declined sharply. In Spain, the proportion fell from 50% in 1950 to 13% in 2001, in Italy from about 40% throughout the 1950s and 1960s to 20% in 1991. The segment of the market which declined most sharply was the part owned by small landlords which had been providing mainly for middle- and low-income households and which had been the key to the success of the early rent control policies.

In Italy between the 1950s and mid-1960s, rent control laws helped to support the supply of rented low-cost housing in urban areas. The owners of flats in multi-storey, pre-1914 buildings in central and semi-central locations could accept rent controls, because housing and land prices were rising so fast that the profits produced by increases in capital values were higher than in any alternative form of investment (Secchi 1970). Under these circumstances, accepting low rents and failing to invest in maintenance was a reasonable and profitable strategy. At the first sign of a price recession, as in the mid-1960s, this strategy was abandoned and the owners tried to empty their buildings of tenants, refurbish or rebuild them and sell to promoters. However, the change was not straightforward. Tenants could not be quickly or easily evicted and local councils began to discourage new building in the historic centres in order to safeguard them from the mid-1970s onwards. Throughout this period, characterised by on-again, off-again rent control until the late 1970s, a part of the stock was rehabilitated or re-used as tenants were evicted, but other dwellings were forcibly kept in the rental sector.

In 1978, a new rent law was enacted with the aim of overcoming the segmentation of the rented market into two parts, one free and the other controlled, by regulating both rents and the length of leases. Rents were set through a procedure roughly simulating the market: 3.5% of the 'rental value' of the dwelling, based on the construction cost of public housing and modified to take location, age, maintenance, building type and so on, into account. The length of leases was established as four years, after which the landlord (or the tenant) was free not to renew the contract. The first unforeseen result of the 1978 Act was that, at the end of the first four-year period, many landlords did not renew the contracts. This started a long and complex judicial procedure to evict the tenants. But eviction was difficult and unpopular, and created a new demand for rented housing focused on the limited social rented stock. The political answer was to postpone implementing the eviction orders by establishing a limit on the number of evictions. It became politically very difficult for the government to implement the law and a large number of households were living, over long periods of time, under a Damoclean sword. In the early 1980s, there were 114 000 eviction orders a year, falling to 60 000 in the late 1990s. The number of evictions implemented remained at about 17 500 per year over this period (Censis 1995–2001). This state of affairs continued until new rent acts were passed in 1998 and 2002. Thus, the political management of the consequences of the 1978 fair rent law between 1978 and 1998 led to the progressive decline of the private rented stock: most units were sold to tenants and others were allocated to other uses. There are now two forms of private renting, one an unregulated free market and the other based on an agreement between landlords and tenants that may be renewed for a total of eight years.

The decline of the rented stock is today recognised as a major problem in Italy and policies to support it have been promoted. They have met with only partial success: only the supply of high-rent dwellings has increased. This trend is linked with the growth of ownership as the main form of tenure and the increased pressure on tenants brought about by the loss of private rented housing through its transfer into owner occupation since the 1980s. Until 1981, the size of the private rented sector was growing. Between 1981 and 1991, one million dwellings were lost.

A new segment of the private rented sector has been developing in the past decade. Some of the older private rented housing stock is being offered at high rents to immigrants from the Third World. While Italy has a high demand for foreign manpower, it has poor policies to supply housing for them. Thus, poor quality private rented stock is all that is on offer for them. This has led to parts of the stock becoming ghettoised, with no maintenance, high prices and very high densities. These trends contributed to the beginning of racist reactions towards new immigrants.

Similar trends may be found in Spain. In 1946, a rent freeze was enacted that lasted until 1964 when contracts were introduced that linked rent increases to rises in the cost of living. Rental contracts had no time limits, and the frozen contract could pass from parents to their heirs. Increases in the cost of living were far lower than increases in housing prices, which stabilised the sector in the same way as in Italy. In 1985 a new act, the *Ley Boyer*, liberalised the private rented sector. This was revised seven years later: rent contracts lasted five years and during this time rents could only be increased in line with the official rise in prices. The older 'timeless contracts' were also revised through a complex system that took account of the households' income. Only tenants below a certain level of income were allowed to keep these unlimited contracts. The inheritance of contracts was also eliminated.

In real terms, the 1946 rent freeze had a positive impact on all social groups. The middle class benefited because it could rent big, old houses in city centres, where house prices were increasing sharply. Working-class households benefited because they could rent public housing, mostly on the periphery of urban areas, at low rents, initially determined by building costs, not market prices, and which became even lower as rent controls also covered this sector. Ultimately, rents did not even cover the cost of maintenance on the public housing estates.

Thus, in Spain, rent controls forced the private rented sector to provide housing at moderate costs, particularly in the initial post-war period. But, in the long term, controls also produced some negative consequences. When the gap between frozen rents and increasing housing values became too high, owners found it more profitable to sell rather than rent their property. This trend was given further impetus by eviction procedures that could be delayed for several years, during which time tenants did not pay their rent. This discouraged landlords from renting their dwellings, who preferred to keep them vacant rather than put them on the rental market. Another solution, when rents were insufficient to cover maintenance costs, was to stop any maintenance work or to demolish the building and sell the land. In Spain many valuable buildings in historic centres were lost during the 1960s and 1970s. Selling rented dwellings to the tenants was another option for landowners. Paradoxically, rent control encouraged families to become home owners. The protection it offered only covered the existing tenants when the law was published. Households who tried to get a rented home afterwards found it difficult to access the sector and were, thus, under pressure to buy their home.

In Greece severe rent control regulation was imposed from 1945 until the early 1950s. Varvaresos (2002) reports that, in 1952, salaries increased by five to ten times more than rents and agricultural products, by eight to nine times more. This strict regulation progressively withered and was abandoned in 1962 (Economou 1987). In the late 1970s, a new period of rent control began that lasted until 1990 when it was progressively dismantled. Economou (1987) points out that the rental market at the time did not justify this kind of regulation, since the number of vacancies was much higher (about 20%) than the optimum (5–8%) and was constantly increasing from the early 1950s. The second period of rent regulation reflects the changing character of the middle social strata, from traditional self-employed to salaried workers, especially in the public sector. The late 1970s were a period of intense inflation and anti-inflationary salary controls. Public sector employment increased rapidly during the late 1970s and the 1980s, as did its social and political importance, but salaries were unable to keep up with rent increases. This provided the political imperative, within the statist spoils system in Greece, for the second period of rent regulation (Economou 1987). Rent control during that period ultimately created more problems than it solved, leading to the reduction of supply and to the growth of informal agreements and a black market. Control was progressively abandoned as the new salaried middle strata turned to home ownership which, reflecting their social status, they accessed through mortgages rather than self-building when affordable credit started to become available in the early 1990s.

Forms of rent control have repeatedly been enacted in Portugal. The first time was between World Wars I and II. It was reintroduced in 1948, but only for the cities of Lisbon and Porto, and again in 1974 immediately after the Revolution, when it covered all newly-let homes. The outcome was not very satisfactory, so other acts were adopted to allow rents to rise, especially to cover the costs of rehabilitating properties. However, the legislation did not control rents effectively because of a range of informal added costs, and they encouraged disinvestment from this form of tenure and led to less maintenance. Not only did the private rented stock halve during the 1980s, a large proportion also fell into serious disrepair.

In summary, at the end of World War II, the southern countries were characterised by a significant supply of private rented dwellings and the owners were mainly private individuals. What distinguished the sector was the hybrid character of housing investments for the southern family, who saw ownership as a multi-faceted strategy, providing for old age and future family needs, as well as a financial investment. It was this hybrid character of the investment, combined with loosely defined rights and responsibilities between tenants and landlords, which allowed this sector to provide low cost housing, under rent control, for as long as it did.

Several factors created this paradoxical situation. In the earlier period, there were few alternative investments available to small investors while rapid urbanisation ensured that land and housing prices were also rising rapidly, guaranteeing a speculative profit even if rents were relatively low. By the mid-1970s, a number of factors had changed. Land and housing prices were increasing much less rapidly and economic growth was beginning to present alternative investment opportunities, which explains why the new forms of rent control developed in the late 1970s were associated with the decline of the sector.

But the landlords' side is only half the picture. In the post-war period, the rented sector was a significant source of accommodation for middle-strata households. Rent control helped to ensure the political loyalties of this group. Low rents benefited them as much as lower strata and enabled them to save money to become owner-occupiers. By the mid-1970s, rent control and de-control affected lower- and middle-strata differently. In both Italy and Spain, it has been difficult to regulate the market in ways which satisfy both groups. Looser controls threaten lower income groups, who have no alternative way to finding housing, but tighter controls mean that it is more difficult for newcomers to access rented housing. As access to owner occupation through the market has become easier (including tenants purchasing their rented accommodation), the social profile of the sector changes.

Although there have been differences among the countries, the overall result has been the same: the decline of the private rented sector. This decline is perceived as an important problem for several reasons. The need for flexibility and territorial mobility for the labour force is constrained by the supply of rented housing. Young people are having increasing problems leaving their parental home and starting a life on their own. Immigrants from Third World countries are experiencing severe housing problems. Still, the decline of the private rented sector has never been on the agenda as a problem in Greece although, in Italy and Portugal, it has been the object of some new public programmes to promote the development of housing to rent at affordable prices. But in none of the southern countries has this issue reached a high position on the public agenda.

As the Greek example in the 1970s and the Italian experience in the 1980s and 1990s show especially clearly, rent control is a form of public action in housing. This can only be fully understood by analysing the social characteristics of both landlords and tenants within the context of the ways that the southern political systems resolve conflicts, given the configuration of their welfare systems. Because the welfare system generally provides little for those in the informal labour market, and provides very little social rented housing, the politics of rent control have as much to do with political loyalties and legitimation as with the economics of the market.

Role of land development policies and land use control systems in providing homes for the less affluent

As an arena of public action, this characteristic illustrates how administrative discretion to enforce or not enforce norms and regulations, set within southern political systems, links state and family in the provision of housing in southern welfare systems.

Land use control is a complex process that operates formally, in the design and implementation of local plans or negotiation on local issues, and informally, through clientelism, local networks and systems of reciprocal trust, and through representative power at the central government level. What seems to distinguish these systems of control is a generous attitude that allows land to be made available for residential development and a similarly generous attitude in not enforcing building regulations or contributions towards the infrastructure required to support development. This attitude is legitimised by the 'sense of necessity' which is ascribed to a person or a family who is trying to provide a primary good, such as a house. This is further reinforced if the family has the voice and capacity to approach local technical staff or policy makers and if it is acting directly in self-promotion or through the small demand oriented co-operatives which characterised southern Europe especially in the first post-war decades of rapid urbanisation.

The specific capabilities of the civil administration, set within a highly party-politicised political system and a non-Weberian bureaucratic system, shape land development practices. Three aspects are especially salient:

(1) There is a gap between approving 'advanced' norms of land use control and management, either town planning acts at central government level or master plans at local level, while implementation and monitoring are almost completely ignored. Political discussion centres on the big macro-level economic, social and cultural issues involved, but very little attention is given to implementation.
(2) Technical staff in the public administration perceive their role as guardians of agreed norms within strictly defined administrative boundaries rather than problem-solving civil servants (Bobbio 2002).

This greatly lengthens bureaucratic routines and increases the power of these staff. The outcome of a request is largely dependent on their willingness to put it on top of the waiting pile. It also makes them open and vulnerable to any form of clientelism or corruption, the choice depending on local circumstances.

(3) Elected members of local governments are more responsible and responsive to their parties than affected by the effectiveness of the local programmes they promote, so they are not deeply concerned with the future consequences of the present management of urban development. Sustainability, environmental and urban quality issues tend not to be priorities on their agendas.

In the southern countries, particularly during the periods of intense urbanisation, households were able to acquire and develop land for residential uses at less than market price and pay only a minimal contribution towards the costs of urban development. A variety of practices, formal and informal, legal and illegal, helped households to access homes through self-promotion and self-provision. Affordability was enhanced by reducing or postponing payment for the costs of land, urban infrastructure and land use control. Less technically formalised processes allowed families to organise flows of non-monetary resources and facilitated access to housing, especially for less privileged groups.

The nature of land development practices differs in each of the four countries, but two different models can be distinguished, lying at either end of a spectrum of practices. The first model is typified by informal, often illegal, developments and consists of a set of practices commonly found in southern Europe, but rarely in the other European countries. The second model is based on explicit formal policies to make low-cost land available for residential development.

Informal and/or illegal land development practices

These practices rely on weak control over land development and land use, which can come about because there are no plans or norms or because those that exist are not implemented. Poor planning was a widespread problem in the southern countries, especially during the 1950s and 1960s, while non-implementation and an inclination to adapt to local needs through small formal variants to land use plans remains a problem in Italy, Greece and Portugal. It is not a problem in Spain because a significant proportion of residential development is carried out by large construction companies who appreciate the control over speculative risk which a strong land use planning system gives them. In the other three countries, much of the uncontrolled development typically takes place on agricultural land which is not classified as development land in the local plan. Thus, it can be acquired at the lower prices associated with agricultural land or may already be owned as part of the family patrimony.

It is then developed for residential use in a variety of ways. Possible outcomes can include: small self-promoted single-family houses in low-density, non-urban areas or at the periphery of the urban area; secondary home developments on state-owned land along the coastlines; and large housing developments at the periphery of the urban areas. Large, informal or illegal developments have been an important component of low-cost housing provision in some periods in Italy, Greece and Portugal. A variety of examples can be observed.

In Italy, one example is the *Corea* model (the name derives from the Korean War) developed at the edge of the Milanese metropolitan area in the building boom years in the 1950s and 1960s. This low-rise illegal self-promoted housing was soon absorbed into the urban fabric as Milan expanded, and some of it now has a relatively high status (Crosta 1985). Another example of illegal self-promotion is the *Borgate* around the periphery of Rome. They were self-promoted illegal developments, composed by low-rise groups of dwellings constituting some sort of community. The first ones were built during the Fascist period, and the most recent in the early 1980s (Clementi *et al.* 1985). In the south of Italy, illegal developments have been built around major cities as in the case of Reggio Calabria, Naples and Palermo. Alongside informal housing development, a parallel, informal economic sector composed of technical expertise, building materials markets and building firms developed in cities such as Rome and Reggio Calabria (Clementi *et al.* 1985; Fera & Ginatempo 1985).

In most cases, successive *post-facto* arrangements have given legal status to these developments. The Roman *Borgate* had a long tradition: since the Fascist period of absorption in the legal town development, different public programmes have been successively implemented to legalise them in the course of the years. In other cases, as for instance in Reggio Calabria, the situation has been much more problematic since these developments were composed of high-rise buildings which have never been fully completed, with some floors totally empty while others are occupied by families (Fera & Ginatempo 1985).

Formal policies and low-cost land availability

This model of land development relies on policies that have been explicitly and specifically designed to make low-cost land available for private and public residential development. In Italy since the mid-1960s, local authorities have had the power to adopt special ten-year housing land use plans. Once such a plan has been formally adopted, it designates land which may be expropriated for a public purpose at significantly less than market prices and which can then be allocated to public institutions or private builders to implement a variety of housing schemes. Most of the land which is covered is vacant, but in some cases, built-up land is also designated. These plans could affect between 40 and 70% of the total land necessary to satisfy a ten-year estimate of the housing needs in the commune (Ave 1997).

A special fund was established at the *Cassa Depositi e Prestiti*, the autonomous public agency for deposits and loans, to provide 35-year interest-free loans to local authorities to acquire land under this scheme. This procedure was widely and successfully used, particularly during the 1970s and early 1980s, to provide land for the social rented sector and for partially subsidised forms of ownership, as well as to attract private investors into partnerships with the public sector under the *edilizia convenzionata* programme (a judicial decision early in the 1980s declared some of the expropriation measures to be illegal, so that implementing these programmes is now much more difficult and costly). In Spain, special agreements oblige developers to allocate a quota of land to local authorities for public purposes, based on the volume of new development. The impact of land costs on housing prices has always been a problem in Spain and has become worse recently. Currently, almost all the social housing, owner-occupied or rented, produced in and around large cities is built on land acquired at lower than market price, either from private developers or from the local authority's patrimony. Developers are also required to contribute to services, streets and green areas designated in urban plans.

Between these two broad models of land development processes lie a variety of other practices which can be classified as legal but which contribute to eroding land use controls and effective urban management. Of particular importance in Italy is the unbelievably large number of minor variants in land use plans. These have been used throughout the post-war period, but in recent decades the number of variants has increased sharply in response to attempts to control urban growth and change more tightly. These variants are supposed to include only minor changes in land use, consistent with the general scheme in the plan, but they all imply significant increases in urban development.

The weakness of public control over land development practices, whether informal and/or illegal or through more formal plans, has generated both positive and negative outcomes. On the positive side, households have been able to mobilise personal, family and local networks' resources to find a solution to their housing problems. In many cases, this was the only possibility open to low income groups. In other cases, it has helped other groups find housing solutions that meet their self-defined housing needs more closely. In some ways, these practices have offered freedom from the rigid straitjacket imposed by institutional controls and a bureaucratic inability to perceive differentiated needs (Tosi 1994a; Clapham 2002). On the negative side, there has been an uncontrolled spread of urbanisation at exceptionally low densities. The cost of *ex post* provision of urban infrastructure in the case of illegal developments is much higher than *ex ante* installation. Dispersed, low density settlement patterns increase the costs of providing other urban services and of managing the urban area. Furthermore, this pattern of development is now raising concerns about sustainability. In some areas, there is little land left for future use. For example, in some mountain tourism areas there is no land left to meet the housing needs of the local population or it has been priced out of their reach. A key issue is that the cost of infrastructure and improving the urban quality of areas is left to future generations.

Thus, in three of the southern European countries, Greece, Italy and Portugal, a substantial part of housing provision, especially in the periods of the most intense migration to urban areas, gave an enhanced role to non-state actors and self-promotion. Most of this provision occurred outside the formally structured housing market, using direct connections between families, small landowners and small builders (Maloutas 2000), and different methods, formal and informal, legal or illegal, of self-promotion. A model of self-provision, traditional in rural areas, was imported with some innovative features, to the outskirts of the cities which hosted migrant working- and middle-class families and which were characterised by intense processes of development. The rural background of most of the new urban inhabitants, their dependence for work and housing on immigrant *filieres*, the fact that their first jobs after arriving in urban areas tended to be in construction, combined with weak controls on land supply, planning and construction, favoured the creation of these informally structured, not fully marketised systems of housing provision.

The development of the construction industry has also been affected by the structure of housing provision. Until recently, it has been characterised by small, technologically backward, sometimes black market, firms. Profits have come more from small speculations on land development than from increases in productivity. Similarly, the housing finance system was not very developed. Family savings provided most of the finance for housing provision. In Italy between the 1950s and the 1980s, family savings made up between 50 and 71% of total housing investment. In 1986 in Athens, where family savings participation in housing investments must have been lower than in the rest of the country, such participation was more than 75% (Maloutas 1990).

It is difficult to quantify a phenomenon which does not follow routine rules, but self-promotion, in all its forms, has been widespread. In Athens in the 1960s and 1970s, the period of maximum growth, most new house-building was self-promoted, with a large incidence in the 1960s of illegal building practices. Between 1940 and 1970, some 140 000 illegal houses were built in the suburbs of Athens, housing 570 000 persons, equal to 35% of the city's population growth in this period (Maloutas, 2000; Leontidou 1990; Maloutas 2003c). In Italy, forms of self-provision covered a range of situations including: rehabilitation of newly acquired flats in inner city buildings; construction of free-standing houses in the diffused city of the 'Third Italy'; second homes in tourist areas; and, mainly in the south and parts of central Italy, fully fledged illegal building. This illegal building occurred mainly in the 1970s and early 1980s. Cresme (2003) estimates that illegal dwelling production increased from 65 000 per year in the 1950s, to more than 100 000 per year in the 1960s and 1970s, to 200 000 per year in the early 1980s. Since the mid-1980s, it has started to decline but has not disappeared completely. During the second half of the 1990s, it still accounted for 12 to 13% of new dwellings.

In Portugal in 1977, the Ministry of Housing and Public Works estimated the number of illegal houses as being 83 000 units, while other estimates put their number at 110 000 to 150 000 units. Portuguese census data gave the number of shanty dwellings in 1981 as nearly 800 000, or 24% of the housing stock. By 1991 the number had fallen to just over 600 000 units, or 15.6% of the stock. In Spain in the 1950s and 1960s, self-promotion was a normal way of housing low-income households arriving in cities from rural areas. Stronger controls on urban development and some programmes of social housing launched by the 1958 Housing Plan stopped this practice and it has since been restricted to small amounts of shanty town building which is addressed by specific local plans.

Policies to address the negative effects of illegal housing construction have followed two main directions. The first direction comprises *post facto* legalisation accompanied by declarations that severe restrictions would subsequently be the norm, a process known as the *condono edilizio* in Italy. The second direction, developed in the 1990s, relates to debates on the management of territorial transformation, environmental questions and increasing demands for better quality and more sustainability in housing and in urban areas. It reflects an increasing perception that environment and landscape are important resources, especially in low-density areas with high environmental quality. This new line of action, being developed in Italy and

Portugal, aims to prevent further illegal developments and set up more comprehensively-based approaches to absorbing these neighbourhoods and buildings into their surroundings. Innovative actions with this aim in Italy have been promoted through the 'integrated urban regeneration programmes' under the auspices of the Ministry of Public Works (Padovani 1998). In Portugal, it also aims to involve central government, local authorities and grass-root movements in a more participative way to improve living conditions in the *bairros clandestinos*.

Housing provision in Spain has shown a completely different pattern. Although there was some self-promotion in the early years after World War II, this soon stopped. The Franco regime formed a key political alliance with large promoters and construction firms, and implemented a land use planning system supporting their needs for large sites in urban areas. This configuration of large firms and strong planning also supported restructuring the mortgage lending system after the 1975 Revolution. Consequently, as we have shown in Chapter 4, the Spanish model of housing development differs from that found in the other three countries.

Overall, the southern approach to land use control and residential development has left room for, or pushed, the family to act 'alongside' the state and the market as an important actor in housing provision (Padovani 1998; Tosi 1984), thus enlarging its role in production and reproduction of household welfare. Public policies have indirectly supported their role, mostly through tax exemptions, not requiring the payment of urban costs, lenient implementation of land use control norms, as well as through a variety of clientelist behaviours.

The public action space associated with southern European models of development relies on the capacities of a variety of actors in the field of housing provision. In the context of the shift from government to governance, and the changes in the role of public administration from provider to enabler throughout Europe, some useful insights may be obtained from the southern European approach. On the precautionary side, the tight circle of relationships among the strongest actors can lead to clientelistic collusion and corruption. On the positive side, however, southern European approaches recognise the range of capacities available among non-state actors in civil society, and in particular, enable capacities for self-promotion.

Conclusions: public action versus state action

The purpose of this chapter has been to apply the concept of public action to housing in southern Europe. This concept is a useful tool for three reasons:

(1) It directs our attention to the constellation of institutional and non-institutional actors who operate together within a wider social context in order to produce public outcomes (Laino & Padovani 2000).
(2) It suggests that the appropriate criterion for assessing housing systems is the welfare effects produced for the population as a whole, rather than the reductive criteria associated with traditional state-centric models of housing systems.
(3) It emphasises the socially constructed nature of housing systems, so that identifying patterns of public action in different contexts, national or local, in different countries, at different points in time, supports robust comparative studies by putting housing systems and their social, economic and political contexts into a single frame.

Using the concept of public action builds on the arguments in earlier chapters which outlined the context of rapid urbanisation and economic change in the southern countries, identified key institutional processes within their welfare systems and focused on the strategies which families deploy to gain access to housing. This chapter looks at how the institutional relationships within housing systems bring state action, family strategies and market processes together.

This is an appropriate approach, given that state action in housing in southern Europe is indirect, rather than direct; diffusely targeted rather than focused on narrowly defined conceptions of housing need; and polymorphic, frequently seeing housing actions as a means to achieving other policy and political ends also.

Three fields of public action in housing in southern Europe are significant. First, there is the *avoidance* of creating a significant public rented sector and the commitment to the social diffusion of home ownership. While a predisposition to owner occupation seems reasonable in societies which were predominantly rural at the end of World War II, the avoidance of creating a public rented sector also reflects the political and institutional difficulties this tenure presented in each of the countries. In the context of limited state resources, it also makes sense of the decision to focus their welfare states on cash-based income-maintenance programmes, given the urgent need to establish the legitimacy of their governments in the immediate post-war era. While the detailed decisions, politics, circumstances and timing in each of the countries were different, all four countries exhibit this same broad pattern of public action: avoiding the creation of a public rented sector and supporting the social diffusion of owner occupation.

The second field of public action is the regulation of private renting. All four countries opted for rent freezes in the immediate post-war era. These primarily benefited the middle strata living in the sector, because lower strata were accessing housing largely through self-promotion and self-provision. For the first two or three decades after World War II, rent freezes were also reasonably acceptable to landlords. One the one hand, capital values of housing were increasing much more quickly than returns on the limited alternative investment opportunities open to them and, on the other hand, owning rental property was a hybrid strategy for most families because it satisfied both their financial and other broad welfare objectives. In the 1970s, the underlying economics of the private rented sector shifted and economic growth led to other outlets for investment. Rented housing was an illiquid investment which could only be realised either by evicting tenants or by selling it to them. After the mid-1970s, rent regulation became more unstable and created a set of difficult political problems, rather than a solution, as it had been in the immediate post-war period. The details vary from country to country, but public action in this field exhibits the same broad pattern in all four countries. Initially, regulation benefited the middle strata and ensured their political loyalty, while the hybrid nature of the investment meant that landlords could accept such regulation. Once the underlying economic situation and social morphology of the sector changed, regulation presented much more difficult political choices.

Third, land use controls in residential development have played an especially strong role in supporting the diffusion of home ownership. Here there are two models of public action, one in Spain and the second in the other three countries. In Spain, a strong land use planning system was part of a political alliance which the Franco regime forged with large promoters and developers of housing. In the other three countries, weak land use controls supported the social diffusion of home ownership, especially to lower strata, through self-promotion and self-building, both legal and illegal. The pattern of public action in these countries was characterised by detailed, often clientelistic, negotiations between a non-Weberian state bureaucracy supported by a political system in which party loyalty was more important to politicians than the effects of residential development on the urban living environment. The outcome was to support widespread access to home ownership at the price of storing up a set of problems about investing in urban infrastructure and environmental quality which are just now beginning to be addressed, at least in Italy and Portugal. In this field of public action, we can see how the same underlying structure of welfare and political systems can lead to substantially different patterns of public action.

Using a public action perspective to analyse housing in southern Europe highlights four features of their housing systems. First, it highlights *'whole system' achievements*. Over the last half century, housing conditions have improved dramatically in the four southern countries. There have been significant and rapid increases in the availability of housing to most of the population and in the quality and maintenance of this housing. In Spain and Italy, housing quality indicators now exceed the European Union average, while Portugal and Greece are still improving from a very low base. The widespread social diffusion of home ownership, in particular, has been effective in supporting the welfare, vertical social mobility and geographical mobility of families in the past. It has also contributed to political and social stability in all four countries, counterbalancing a welfare state which provides little for those outside the formal sector and little in the way of services. Second, the public action perspective highlights how a very wide range of social actors have been mobilised to contribute to achieving these objectives. In particular, self-promotion and self-provision are widespread in three of the countries, and the state has provided an important component of the resources available to families in aggressive strategies to access housing, even if those resources may be counted negatively in terms of relaxed controls over development and payment for urban infrastructure in many cases. Third, the public action perspective in housing allows us to identify a kind of strategy, even if not explicit, to mobilise significant resources for housing investment, monetary and non-monetary, from a wide range of actors in the unpromising circumstances of the early post-war period characterised by very low levels of per capita income, as well as the social and political turmoil which followed the wars in three of the countries. Fourth, the public action perspective shows how these outcomes have been achieved in the context of a non-Weberian state bureaucracy, attuned to regulating private actors but not to producing public goods effectively.

These are considerable achievements. A complex institutional system, at central and local government levels, has mobilised a wide range of actors, from families through to third sector organisations such as voluntary associations, co-operatives, trade unions, large charity organisations and political parties to meet a public need: the extension and improvement of housing in ways which have been sensitive to locally defined, sometimes highly differentiated needs. More recently, in Italy and Portugal, this complex system has also shown itself capable of reorientation to develop innovative transversal and participative initiatives bringing together a range of state and civil society organisations, designed to improve the quality of the urban living environment, and within which housing plays a role.

These achievements throw into question the relevance of state-centric concepts of housing action. Such concepts conflate public action in housing with state action, and tend to emphasise the development and management of a significant social rented sector. If southern housing systems are evaluated against these criteria, then the judgement can only be negative. None of the four countries has a significant social rented sector, and in Italy, certainly, its management looks incoherent, it is costly and it produces a financial deficit. The rents paid are unrelated to management and production costs. Most of the social rented stock which was produced in the post-war period was sold at prices significantly lower than the production costs. The important public resources used to produce this sector have effectively subsidised access to owner occupation for many of its tenants, either through sales programmes or by allowing them to save enough to buy elsewhere.

At the same time, it is inappropriate to categorise Italy, even though it has a very small social rented sector compared to northern European countries, as having a residualist model of social housing provision, in which minimum standard social rented housing is assigned to the most deprived groups (cf. Harloe 1995). During the years of the most intense urbanisation in Italy, between the 1950s and 1970s, public rented housing was designed to address the needs of all workers. The quality of the architectural design and layout of these estates was excellent. Designed by some of the best Italian architects, who had internalised the aim of inserting a rural population into an urban way of life, they proposed a new and modern model of residential development in the so-called public city. The quality of the buildings was the same as that being produced for private developers for middle-income households, and most of this stock has been privatised over the years and absorbed into the urban fabric on the outskirts of the cities. Serious problems of negative stigma affect only a minority of the publicly provided estates.

Nevertheless, the state-centric view, with its sharper focus on varieties of housing need, highlights emerging problems in the southern European countries. There is a growing and varied section of the population that faces serious problems of access to housing. In earlier chapters, we have highlighted the problems about the emancipation of young people in the face of a small private rented sector, and we have mentioned the problems raised by the expansion of higher education in Greece as well as the needs of a more geographically mobile and flexible labour force. In the past, both these problems were eased by the wider availability of private rented housing. We have not emphasised enough the growing and serious problems now facing Third World immigrants into the southern countries, who are forced into living in overcrowded conditions at very high rents in the worst parts of the private rented sector. And there has been no mention of what in northern European countries would be called people with special needs. Mentally and physically ill and handicapped people are still hidden within the welfare responsibilities of families, reflecting an inadequate recognition of their needs generally within the southern welfare states. What the state-centric view highlights is that there is little recognition in the southern housing systems of those who are outside family networks and working in the most irregular parts of the informal economy. In contrast, the public action perspective tends to explain the general patterns of the southern European housing systems. Using a public action concept to analyse housing in southern Europe, rather than a state-centric concept, does more justice to the broad nature of the housing systems in these countries and how they sit within a wider societal context, but less justice to the specific problems common to them all.

There are both practical and theoretical implications of shifting to a public action concept. The practical implications are the way in which lessons can be drawn from the southern experience for changes facing all European countries. These lessons are relevant to the increasing emphasis on local governance, as well as to mobilising and empowering local residents in urban policies which have broader aims than simply improving housing conditions. Public action in southern European housing certainly mobilised a wide range of actors, but in what sense did it empower them? Empowerment within clientelistic political relations is socially and politically selective. It reduces the legitimation of the state, but generates social adherence and has an important political impact. Empowerment of self-promotion and self-provision, legal or illegal, relieved the state from taking explicit responsibility, and the attendant financial burdens, for the housing conditions of the majority of the population during the period of intense urbanisation. It used the family as the basic social agent in organising housing provision and access and left relatively untouched, or even reinforced, traditional conservative and gender-divided family structures, especially among the lower social strata in the southern societies. Empowerment within a clientelistic political system is hardly the transparently democratic idea of empowerment which characterises emerging debates. However, the southern European system did mobilise a wide range of actors towards a public objective, and what might be learned from this is that the idea of mobilisation which underlies debates about local governance in northern Europe may require more particularism than the more universalistically oriented welfare states in these countries are used to.

At a theoretical level, applying the concept of public action to housing leads to looking at the role of the state in housing policies in a different way. There are a number of different theories and ideas about the role of the state in the housing literature, but these have not been developed in a way which can satisfactorily underpin comparative studies. Some of the examples see the state as: a neutral arbiter among conflicting interests; an actor working in the interests of society as a whole; subject to the development of advanced capitalism; as remediating the imperfections of markets; as the product of political ideologies and cultural norms (cf. Donnison 1967; Ball & Harloe 1992; Kemeny 1995; King 1996). These examples present an altogether unsatisfactory jumble of ideas, partly because they tend to reify the concept of state and market, while ignoring wider social structures and, especially, the structured configuration of the institutions which link state, market and society. The example of the southern European countries suggests that we cannot consign the family to a nebulous Habermasian life world. Rather than arguing for, or assuming, particular concepts of the state, as much of the comparative housing literature does, the public action concept suggests that it might be more fruitful to develop a typology of states in relationship to the other major providers of household welfare: market, family and civil society.

7

Conclusions

This is the first book to undertake a comparative analysis of southern Europe's housing systems. We have sought to explain how they are organised, answer questions about their distinctiveness and demonstrate how their distinctiveness arises out of a different socio-economic context. Analysis of national forms of housing provision has been the subject of considerable interest during the past two decades. We believe that the findings presented in this book build on and add to this literature. The paucity of available data means, however, that the analysis can only be seen as partial. Its strength is that the research has allowed us to identify areas for future work. Three areas in particular stand out:

(1) There is the precise nature of the cross-national variations in welfare systems both *within* southern Europe and *between* the north and the south. Of particular importance is identifying the way in which housing rights in the southern European countries are expressed within their welfare systems. The development of a welfare state is sometimes seen as a product of the modernisation processes at work in economies. Interventions to provide housing and ensure minimum standards are, to a greater or lesser extent, part of this. There is a need to find rigorous ways of characterising the approaches to welfare provision, and their attendant implications for housing rights, found in southern Europe, with their distinctive relationships among state, family and market.

(2) This book has not dealt with housing and welfare *outcomes* for families and individuals in southern Europe. This is a wider project that will require careful thought on how to characterise outcomes. It should be more than a simple, static cross-sectional comparison of the situation of different types of household. While European countries, north and south, may well be subject to 'universal' trends, such as labour market flexibilisation or supra-national European Union policies, the point of

departure varies considerably. The presence of a distinctive kind of welfare state, cash-rich and services-lean, coupled with extended family structures in southern Europe, can be expected to lead to rather different outcomes than in the northern countries. These are, therefore, likely to be more subtle than the way national statistics portray them.

(3) In developing our analysis, we have drawn on the ideas which researchers in southern Europe use to make sense of their own housing systems. These ideas are not in common usage in the north-centric literature and some thought needs to be given to how they could be applied to non-southern systems. In particular, the concepts of housing practices and family strategies point out that both household and family have been reduced to mere ciphers in the north-centric literature, perhaps reflecting the ways that families were stripped of their functions in the process of fordist industrialisation.

Data which would help to provide a richer analysis are also lacking in several key areas. Little is known, for example, of the *detail* of second home ownership. While some aggregate data are available, more research is needed on the residential practices of owners and, in particular, the linkages between second home ownership, household life-cycles and tourist development. Other areas where lack of data has posed problems for a complete understanding of southern housing systems relate to mortgage finance and the changes to mortgage supply, and to the scale of construction activity and its wider impact on housing market cycles. Even where data are available, there are problems of comparability in terms of time periods over which they are collected and underlying assumptions. Finally, the shortage of suitable data on Portugal, especially historical data sources, is evident from the scant treatment which we have been able to give it in our analysis. This is a particular problem because there is evidence that Portugal has taken a rather distinctive path, with later and more rapid urbanisation and the expansion of home ownership underpinned by a high level of residential debt.

What, then, are the main conclusions we can draw from our analysis? Our general argument is that the housing systems we have explored can only be understood within a specifically southern social, economic and historical context. This book has approached this question in the following way. Chapter 2 described the essential features of housing systems in the chosen countries: tenure, second home ownership, family structure and housing production. We also discussed the adequacy of different approaches in the general housing literature for interpreting observed differences between countries. Chapter 3 explored the links between urbanisation and economic change. In Chapter 4, we developed a theoretical framework for analysing southern Europe's welfare systems. This enabled us to suggest why they need to be seen as something more than a variant on a general European model and how they support a specific kind of housing system. Key issues include the relationship between familialism, the capacities of their civil administration, particularly the role of clientelism in some regions, and the operation of strongly segmented labour markets. Chapter 5 focused on the role of the family and its practices and strategies for accessing housing for its members. Chapter 6 discussed the role of public action in housing and how the pattern of state intervention is different from countries in northern Europe.

The principal theme that emerges is the interplay between extended family structures and what may be characterised as a southern European welfare system. Together with more contextual factors, such as demographic trends, and political systems arising from late democratisation and recent urbanisation, this interplay leads to particular forms of housing provision in each of the four countries.

We argue that comparative research must address more than housing matters: such a restricted approach explains policy outcomes but not processes. Unless housing systems are placed within their societal contexts, it is impossible to explain why different approaches to housing policy are taken and how their outcomes vary. This concluding chapter addresses this issue in more detail and then considers some of the trends that might shape southern Europe's housing systems in the future.

The distinctiveness of southern European housing systems

Our first concluding point addresses the question of whether there is a separate southern European housing system. Are the southern countries similar enough to form a grouping which is distinctive in relation to rest of the Europe Union in terms of housing provision? We believe that it is inappropriate to formulate the question in this way. A more legitimate question, and the basic argument in this book, is that the articulation between housing systems and societal context is different in southern Europe because the societal context is itself different. In particular, the different welfare systems and different set of social relations in the four southern countries both impact on how people are housed in a way that marks them out when compared with other European Union countries. The surface phenomena of housing systems, especially forms of housing tenure and promotion, are merely configured differently across Europe. How these interact with more basic societal features such as late urbanisation, family structures and the nature of the state creates a unique approach to housing provision. It is therefore not possible to talk of a 'separate' housing system in southern Europe if we are merely focusing on the basic features of housing systems. It is 'separate', however, if housing is considered in its wider societal context.

The wider societal context has been shaped by the historical trajectories of the southern countries since World War II. With the exception of northern Italy and northern Spain, the four countries only began to industrialise in the late-1950s. This process was stopped by the oil crisis of 1974. Most significantly, however, processes of late, rapid and massive urbanisation have primarily been associated with the disarticulation of the rural economy and coincided with the rapid growth of the tertiary sector in the cities. In contrast to the northern countries, rural to urban migration was not induced by industrialisation.

To rehearse briefly our empirical findings, we have suggested that four aspects of southern Europe's housing systems are distinctive:

- High rates of home ownership coupled with sparse social rented housing
- High level and significance of secondary housing
- Relationship between access to housing and family structures
- Role of self-promotion and self-provision in supplying housing.

The distinctive tenure pattern in the four countries, with owner occupation dominating all other forms, is confirmation, at one level, of the existence of a different kind of housing system. The main form of access to housing is almost entirely through home ownership. In these circumstances the extended family plays a strong role in supporting access to housing by developing strategies to secure housing for its members. Many of the elements of the social, financial and institutional frameworks which shape access to housing are similar to those in northern Europe, that is, there are builders, planning systems, mortgage lenders, private landlords, and so on. However, when combined with other formal and informal, financial and non-financial resources available to families, we can observe distinctively 'southern' strategies to support access to home ownership, especially by newly forming households.

A similar observation can be made about housing promotion as a way of organising the linkages between supply and demand. Again, the elements of housing promotion, for example developers and a land use planning system, are constant throughout Europe, but the way they are configured and their interaction with wider societal features is distinctively southern. There is little direct public or semi-public promotion in southern Europe, but high levels of self-promotion exist where the initiative for development is located within the family itself. While self-promotion is also widespread throughout northern Europe, in the south it is associated with a weak urban planning system, relatively easy access to small plots of land and a weak credit system for both building and purchase. The significance of these factors is highlighted by the insignificance of self-promotion in Spain, where housing development is dominated by large construction companies and there is a strong land use planning system.

Secondary home ownership is another phenomenon that on its own cannot be seen as characteristic of southern Europe alone, yet when we explore the reasons for its growth, its distinctiveness emerges. Across Europe, investment in secondary housing has been facilitated by the rise in real incomes from the 1960s onwards. However, in our four countries, the growth in secondary home ownership is a direct result of the combination of housing policies emphasising construction activity as a way to fight unemployment and to develop the economic base of peripheral regions, and the migration of households from rural to urban areas. Together, these have resulted in a supply of housing which is available for purchase for leisure reasons or which has remained within the ownership of extended families.

Our explanation therefore rests on the way family structure, welfare provision and housing systems interlock in the four southern countries. The southern European model is one which sees households as part of wider extended family relationships. The welfare state provides generously for those in core sector employment. Those without families and working in the informal sector receive little. This stands in contrast to the individualised welfare systems found in Scandinavia, where individuals are deemed to be entitled to state welfare support and there are few expectations of family support, or the United Kingdom, where welfare benefits and tax credits are designed to support family obligations within households. The north is different from the south in important ways. A further important difference is that family networks and solidarity are shaped by the specific pattern of welfare state provision found in southern Europe and facilitate the functioning of the large informal employment sector. This may be a fruitful area for further research.

Thus, the pattern of housing tenure, for example, does not simply reflect policies which have supported the growth of home ownership at the expense of public rented housing. It also reflects more complex inter-relationships formed by the nature of extended family relationships, their degree of solidarity, and the nature and scale of monetary and other resources which families can mobilise to access housing. And housing policies, themselves, are shaped by the state's expectations about these family strategies as well as by general conceptions about the relative roles of the state and the family in satisfying housing and other welfare needs. In this context, what is called housing policy also needs to be seen as a means to achieving other state objectives, such as full employment and economic growth. Housing policy can be shaped in this way because the state assumes that families will play a leading role in housing provision.

We do not wish to suggest that these inter-relationships are uniform throughout southern Europe. Similar welfare state, family and labour market systems are present in each country, but there are variants both between countries and within countries. But these structural factors also shape specific practices in specific places. For example, clientelism is very important in some regions and has almost disappeared in other regions. Another example is the way that housing is now embedded in transversal localised policies to regenerate urban areas in Italy, while such regeneration is only just beginning in the other countries.

Theorising housing provision: lessons from southern Europe

We noted earlier that there is a large literature on comparative housing research, part of which seeks to develop a better understanding of different housing systems in their broader context (Oxley 1991). Accompanying this literature has been a debate on methodologies for conducting such research (Boelhouwer *et al.* 2000). Oxley (1999) has suggested that much of the confusion about method arises from a failure to define the purpose of comparative research and to ensure that it is underpinned by an appropriate theoretical framework. According to Oxley, 'high-level' comparative research, which systematically investigates an issue across several countries using a common theoretical approach, is rare.

This book is concerned with such an investigation and leads us to draw conclusions on how to conduct comparative research. Our findings suggest that there are a number of important assumptions underlying comparative studies which do not apply to the southern European countries as fully as they do in the richer economies and longer established democracies. Two assumptions are especially important:

(1) The underlying way a democratic political system has become consolidated is important. In the four countries, unlike other states in Europe, the development of a democratic system occurred much later

and in tandem with the shift from a rural agricultural society to an urbanised service sector society. Furthermore, democratic consolidation began long after corporatist income-maintenance systems were institutionalised. This has two implications. One is that there is a specific pattern of capabilities in the civil administration in these countries, ranging from the persistence of clientelism in some regions through to highly developed skills in regulating private sector activities. The second is that political structures are dominated by vertical interest aggregation through political parties, which inhibits extending the range of welfare state services and creates difficulties in regulating informal labour markets. The entire system exhibits a kind of stasis, which means either that pressures must build up to the point of 'crisis' before significant changes can be implemented or that changes can only be made in a piecemeal, decentralised way.

(2) The structure of labour markets is also important. In the southern European countries, the presence of a large, irregular and informal segment within a dual labour market, unlike those associated with northern European corporatist welfare systems, has not been matched by welfare systems which provide appropriate compensation. This has required networks of family solidarity to provide support and facilitate the functioning of the informal employment sector. The pattern of extended family relationships has persisted, at least in part, as a result of the interplay between state capabilities, the dual labour market and familialism as a form of welfare provision. This increases pressures on the family at precisely the moment when the pattern and scale of resources available to them are changing.

Questioning these assumptions lends weight to the view that the comparative analysis of housing systems requires an approach that takes into account broader socio-economic structures and socio-economic change. We have argued that the weakness of the housing provision thesis is its inability to provide a theoretical explanation for the patterns of institutional relationships in a housing system. To begin to fill this gap, we have used and adapted the concept of welfare state regimes as a basis for analysing welfare systems. This has provided us with a systematic way of identifying differences in the role of the welfare state within the wider European context. It has also provided us with a way of identifying key institutional configurations which shape how the welfare system in southern Europe works and which allow us to link housing systems and welfare systems. In particular, it highlights the role played by the family, a role which is as strong as the state's, in the delivery of welfare, including access to housing. We needed to fashion this tool because there is no existing typology of welfare systems which would serve our purposes in understanding housing.

The research presented in this book also emphasises the importance of avoiding the mistake of assuming that key concepts do not vary in meaning across different housing systems. For example, one problem with generalised comparative arguments is the way tenure is treated in a naturalistic way, assuming that its meaning is fixed outside the wider social contexts within which housing is used and provided. As we have seen, 'owner occupation' as a way of regulating access to housing and as a category describing ownership relations between households and physical homes, has a different meaning in southern Europe, where extended families play a fundamental role in managing the acquisition of housing for their members. 'Self promotion', found throughout Europe, has a role within southern European housing systems that is far wider than simply being an alternative method of acquiring a new home, which is primarily the case in the north. We have already noted the much more robust meaning of 'family' in southern Europe. Of the four southern European concepts highlighted in Chapter 1, the concept of patrimony, the landed resources available to the southern family in forging its housing strategies, is never used in north-centric literature.

The future of southern housing systems

How will southern housing and welfare systems develop over time? How will economic development and political change influence these housing systems? To discuss these questions it is necessary to consider the possible implications of key political projects and the constraints imposed by market and other trends on housing and welfare systems.

At the broadest level, Chapter 4 points out that there are two competing meta-narratives of change in southern Europe. One sees future economic growth as eroding key differences between north and south. This is a modernisation meta-narrative, crudely based on a leaders-laggards model and on the processes of change which accompanied early industrialisation in the north. The second meta-narrative is post-modernist, crudely seeing all of Europe as becoming a favoured locus for a globalised tertiary sector. (This vision also lies at the heart of the European Union's political project.) Within this frame, the different trajectories towards post-modernity found in southern Europe, changing from a rural agricultural to an urban tertiary economy, and in the de-industrialising northern countries, are likely to have different consequences for change in their welfare and housing systems.

There has been considerable debate over the extent to which welfare systems will ultimately converge around some European Union norm (cf. Sykes

& Alcock 1998; Sykes *et al.* 2001). These competing meta-narratives provide a perspective on this debate but, as yet, neither fully incorporates the emergence of the European Union as a political project involving all the European countries, both the existing member states and the candidate countries. The term 'convergence' conveys the idea that the policies underpinning welfare systems are necessarily becoming more alike through some form of causal process. Convergence is felt by some to be more helpful than the concept of policy cycles, which emphasises the circulation and repetition of policies and fails to grasp notions of dynamic change (Kleinman 1996; Kemeny & Lowe 1998; Doling 1997). Convergence arguments tend to be rather untheorised, but the issues raised are nonetheless of importance for addressing the future direction of housing systems. It is by no means clear that there is an impetus towards a convergence of housing systems in the European Union but there are, nevertheless, three areas that need consideration:

(1) It can be argued that a supranational system of regulation will emerge, accompanied by the principle of subsidiarity in implementation. Housing policy is considered to be a matter of subsidiarity, and is likely to continue to be so given the scale of cross-national transfers required to harmonise elements of housing provision (Kleinman 1996; Priemus 2000). There is, however, already an element of regulation in those areas of social policy concerned with the harmonisation of working conditions. This is clearly of some relevance to the argument in this book because of the significance of informal labour markets in relation to southern European housing systems, although how different labour markets will respond is a matter of conjecture (Esping-Andersen 1999).

(2) The harmonisation of financial markets may impact on southern European housing systems. Currently, the European Union's mortgage finance systems are diverse, with a variety of institutions, products and prices. Some believe that the introduction of the euro will help to shift mortgage markets towards an intermediate position of financial integration (Stephens 2000). Here, the risk and option-adjusted prices of mortgages are similar, but institutions and mortgage products will continue to vary. This will be achieved through increased transparency in mortgage pricing and by making retail savings markets more competitive. However, Stephens believes that it is unlikely that there will be a fully integrated market with a standard pan-European mortgage product because of the continued privileged availability of cheap funds to some financial intermediaries and the presence of locally specific non-financial barriers, such as legal frameworks. Nevertheless, there is some very recent evidence that the introduction of the European Central Bank, with centralised control over interest rates, is filtering

through into country-specific mortgage and credit markets, and in Spain, particularly, is easing some problems of access to owner occupation.

(3) The welfare system as a whole in each of the four countries also needs to be considered. The argument here is about the extent to which peripheral countries are required to adjust their economic policy in order to join the common currency and the way that housing policy is closely linked to economic policy in the southern countries. Under this scenario, housing becomes even less important as an area for policy intervention.

Given the generally weakened perception of the importance of housing as a priority issue in northern Europe, as quantitative need is met and central governments attempt to reduce their shares of direct housing costs, it is arguable that in policy terms there will be a degree of convergence across Europe. Early indicators are that this will be linked with decentralised public action in housing and its role in transversal urban policies. In this case, convergence will be as much about change in the north as it is about change in the south.

To some extent, our perspective mirrors the arguments about path dependency as applied to the analysis of changing housing systems in eastern Europe. The durability of housing systems ensures that elements of existing approaches tend to endure, even in political contexts where governments are seeking to make radical changes. It is necessary, therefore, to allow for different trajectories of future development in housing and welfare systems throughout Europe while still acknowledging the significance of supranational factors in shaping those trajectories.

One important issue in discussions about the future trajectory of southern European countries is over the prospects for change in the way their political systems support clientelism. A modernist rationalisation of civil administration may indeed emerge. Some suggest that change may come through the development of meso-level organisations which build on existing primary solidarities (Hespanha *et al.* 1997) while others argue that it will come through the spread of innovations based in 'local citizenship systems' (Fargion 1996). A key question, however, which lies beyond the scope of this book, is the potential for developing institutions of horizontal interest aggregation to inhibit the effects of vertical aggregation through the political parties (Alexander 1998).

How will these broad trends make a difference in terms of people's access to housing in southern Europe? We have argued that their impact is mediated through the labour market and through family structures and that it is not sufficient to think that economic modernisation will automatically lead to a more universalistic welfare system. Chapter 4 suggests that the most likely course of change is for the boundaries between public and private to become blurred, as state provision attempts to capture the strengths of family and locality in responding to change. But our argument in Chapter 5 qualifies this view by reflecting on the extent to which such changes will have a negative impact on the capacities of the southern family. In any case, this path of change will represent a continuation of the distinctive southern European approach.

Can the longstanding trend towards home ownership survive under the emerging pattern of economic development and welfare provision? A key challenge is the changing nature of family and household structures and, in particular, the increase in the number of people without an immediate family or in a transitional position. Although the increase of single person and other forms of non-family households is slow, traditional gender roles are becoming less sustainable as younger women are beginning to participate more fully in the labour market. Family structures and practices are also being reshaped by the low birth rates in much of the region. These are resulting in an ageing population, with consequent implications for the demands placed on social security systems. Moreover, the increased numbers of elderly people will make it harder to maintain the extended family welfare model, as a mismatch begins to emerge between the growing need for, and scarcity of, domestic labour.

When these broad social and demographic shifts are combined with labour market restructuring, especially the growth in temporary work contracts and increased immigration, the prospects for a sustainable housing model, where access is largely dependent on ability to achieve owner occupation, seem bleak. Already, southern Europe is experiencing increased housing pressure in some cities and the emergence of new forms of social cleavage between young and old, between those in the formal and informal labour markets, and between immigrants and nationals.

Perhaps the most important conclusion of this book, however, can be posed as a question: How and why is the north different from the south? Throughout this book, we have noted the differences between north and south and how arguments implicitly embedded in northern processes of change fail to capture important elements in the southern experience. This book presents southern housing as seen through (largely) southern eyes. It would now be interesting to look at northern housing systems using the lenses we have developed. It is likely that this will turn up features of northern housing systems which have so far not been discussed and, so, would contribute to a truly pan-European discussion of housing.

References

Abellán, A. (1996) *Envejecer en España*. Fundación Caja Madrid, Madrid.

Abrahamson, P. (1992) Welfare pluralism: towards a new consensus for a European social policy? In: *The Mixed Economy of Welfare, Cross-National Research Papers* (L. Hantrais, M. O'Brien & S. Mangen, eds). Cross-National Research Group, Loughborough University, Loughborough.

Alberdi, I. (ed.) (1994) *Informe Sobre la Situación de la Familia en España*. Ministerio de Asuntos Sociales, Madrid.

Alexander, J. (1998) Introduction: Civil Society I, II, III: Constructing an empirical concept from normative controversies and historical transformations. *Real Civil Societies: Dilemmas of Institutionalization* (J. Alexander, ed.). Sage, London.

Alivisatos, N. (1983) *Political Institutions in Crisis 1922–1974. Aspects of the Greek Experience*. Themelio, Athens [in Greek].

Allen, J. (1996) Traveller's tales: validating work done in another country. *European Spatial Research and Policy* **3** (2), 79–93.

Ambrose, P. & Barlow, J. (1987) Housing provision and housebuilding in western Europe. Increasing expenditure, declining output? In: *Housing Markets and Policies in an Era of Fiscal Austerity* (W. van Vliet, ed.). Greenwood, Westport, CN.

Arbaci, S. (2002) Patterns of ethnic and socio-spatial segregation in European cities: Are welfare regimes making a difference? In: *Immigration and Place in Mediterranean Metropolises* (M. Fonseca, J. Malheiros, P. White, N. Ribas-Mateos & A. Esteves, eds). FLAD Luso-American Foundation, Lisbon, 83–115.

Arbonville, D. (1998) Ménages et modes d'habiter. In: *Logement et habitat: l'état des savoirs* (M. Segaud, C. Bonvalet, & J. Brun (dir.)). La Découverte, Paris.

Ave, G. (1997) *Urban Land and Property Markets in Italy*. UCL Press, London.

Balchin, P. (ed.) (1996) *Housing Policy in Europe*. Routledge, London.

Ball, M. & Harloe, M. (1992) Rhetorical barriers to understanding housing provision: what the 'Provision Thesis' is and is not. *Housing Studies*, **7** (1), 3–15.

Ball, M., Harloe, M., & Martens, M. (1988) *Housing and Social Change in Europe and the USA*. Routledge, London.

Barlow, J. (1995) *Public Participation in Urban Development: The European Experience*. Policy Studies Institute, London.

Barlow, J. & Duncan, S. (1988) The use and abuse of housing tenure. *Housing Studies*, **3** (4), 219–31.

Barlow, J. & Duncan, S. (1994) *Success and Failure in Housing Provision: European Systems Compared*. Pergamon, Oxford.

Barlow, J., Savage, M., Dickens, P., & Fielding, T. (1992) *Property, Bureaucracy and Culture: The Middle Classes in Contemporary Britain*. Routledge, London.

Barrett, M. & McIntosh, M. (1982) *The Anti-social Family*. Verso, London.

Benassi, B., Ghezzi, S., & Mingione, E. (1997) La restructuration économique et la pauvrete urbaine dans les pays européens. In: *La polarisation sociale des villes européennes* (A. Martens & M. Vervaeke, eds). Anthropos, Paris.

Bobbio, L. (2002) *I Governi locali nelle democrazie contemporanee*. Laterza, Rome.

Boelhouwer, P., Haffner, M., & Van Der Heijden, H. (2000) Putting comparative housing research into practice. *Journal of Housing and the Built Environment* **15** (1), 3–9.

Bonvalet, C., Gotman, A., & Grafmeyer, Y. (1999) *La famille et ses proches*. PUF, Paris.

Brandsen, T. (2001) Bringing actors back in: towards an institutional perspective. *Housing, Theory and Society* **18** (1–2), 2–14.

Castles, F. (1994) On religion and public policy: does Catholicism make a difference? *European Journal of Political Research* **25**, 19–40.

Castles, F. (1995) Welfare state development in southern Europe. *West European Politics* **18** (2), 291–313.

Castles, F. (1998) *Comparative Public Policy: Patterns of Post-war Transformation*. Edward Elgar, Cheltenham, UK.

Castles, F. (ed.) (1993) *Families of Nations: Patterns of Public Policy in Western Democracies*. Dartmouth, Aldershot.

Castles, F. & Ferrera, M. (1996) Home ownership and the welfare state: Is southern Europe different? *South European Society and Politics* **1** (2), 163–85.

Castles, F. & Mitchell, D. (1993) Worlds of welfare and families of nations. In: *Families of Nations: Patterns of Public Policy in Western Democracies* (F. Castles, ed.). Dartmouth, Aldershot.

Censis (1995–2001) *Rapporto sulla situazione sociale del paese*. Milano, F. Angeli. (Annual reports)

Cer Minstero LLPP (1996) *Rapporto sulla condizione abitativa in Italia*. Rapporto per Habitat II, Rome.

Clark, W. & Dilleman, F. (1996) *Households and Housing*. Center for Urban Policy Research, Rutgers NJ.

Clapham, D. (2002) *Housing Policy in a Risk Society*. Paper for the International Research Conference: Housing Cultures – Convergence and Diversity, ENHR 2002, 1–5 July 2002, Vienna.

Clementi, A., Perego, F., & Olivieri, M. (1985) Mezzo secolo di baracche e borgate abusive. In: *Abitazione e periferie urbane nei paesi in via di sviluppo: area Mediterranea e America Latina in una prospettiva comparata* (A. Clementi & L. Ramirez, eds). Angeli, Milan.

Cnel (1995) *La politica abitativa in Italia*, Documenti Cnel n. 79. Cnel, Rome.

Cortes, L. (1995) *La Cuestión Residencial: Bases Para una Sociología del Habitar*. Ed. Fundamentos, Madrid.

Cortes, L. (1998) *La solidaridad familiar en el acceso a la vivienda: El caso español*. Unpublished paper presented at the International Housing Conference, Housing in Southern Europe, A Separate Path? 2–4 December, Madrid.

Costa-Pinto, T. (1998) *Social Groups, Ways of Life, Forms of Habitation*. Unpublished paper presented at the International Housing Conference, Housing in Southern Europe, a separate path? 2–4 December, Madrid.

Cremaschi, M. (1998) *Family Strategies and Housing Practices in Italy*. Unpublished paper presented at the International Housing Conference, Housing in Southern Europe, A Separate Path? 2–4 December, Madrid.

Cresme (2003) <http://www.cresme.com> downloaded 16 January 2003.

Crosta, P. (1985) Forme anomale di urbanizzazion e la questione del governo del mutamento. In: *Abitazione e periferie urbane nei paesi in via di sviluppo: area Mediterranea e America Latina in una prospettiva comparata* (A. Clementi & L. Ramirez, eds). Angeli, Milan.

Cuturello, P. (1987) *Les nouveaux 'castors': des solidarités collectives aux solidarités familiales. Les pratiques d'auto-construction des ménages accédant à la propriété en maison individuelle.* GERM-CERCOM, Nice.

Cuturello, P. & Godard, F. (1980) *Families mobilisées. Accésion à la propriété du logement et notion d'effort des ménages.* GERM-CERCOM, Nice.

Delgado, M. (1997) La fertilidad de los jóvenes. In: *La Emancipación de los Jóvenes* (R. Vergés Escuin, ed.). Editorial Centro de cultura contemporánea de Barcelona, Barcelona.

Diamandouros, N. (1983) Greek political culture in transition: Historical origins, evolution, current trends. In: *Greece in the 1980s* (R. Clogg, ed.). Macmillan, London.

Diamandouros, N. (1991) PASOK and state-society relations in post-authoritarian Greece. In: *Greece on the Road to Democracy: From the Junta to PASOK 1974–1986* (S. Vryonis Jr, ed.). Caratzas Publishers, New Rochelle, NY.

Diamandouros, N. (1994) Cultural dualism and political change in post-authoritarian Greece. Estudio/Working paper 50, Centro de Estudios Avanzados en Ciencias Sociales, Instituto Juan March de Estudios e Investigaciones, Madrid. Greek edition (2000) Alexandria, Athens.

Diamandouros, P., Puhle, H-J., & Gunther, R. (1995) Conclusions. In: *The Politics of Democratic Consolidation: Southern Europe in Comparative Perspective* (R. Gunther, P. Diamandouros, & H-J. Puhle, eds.). The Johns Hopkins University Press, London.

Di Biagi, P. (ed.) (2001) *La grande ricostruzione: il piano INA-casa e l'Italia degli anni cinquanta.* Donzelli, Rome.

Doling, J. (1997) *Comparative Housing Policy.* Macmillan, London.

Donner, C. (2000) *Housing Policies in the European Union.* Christian Donner, Vienna.

Donnison, D. (1967) *The Government of Housing.* Penguin, Harmondsworth.

Economou, D. (1987) Housing policy in post-war Greece: basic interpretations, housing credit and policies for the rented sector. *The Greek Review of Social Research* **64**, 56–129 [in Greek].

Economou, D. (1988) Land and housing system. In: *Problems of Welfare State Development in Greece* (T. Maloutas & D. Economou, eds). Exandas, Athens [in Greek].

Economou, D. (1997) Planning system and rural land use control in Greece: A European perspective. *European Planning Studies* **5** (4), 461–76.

Economou, D. (2000) Urban policy in the '50s. In: *Second Congress of the Association for the History of the City and Urban Planning.* University of Thessaly Press, Volos.

Economou, D. & Maloutas, T. (2002) The large cities. In: *Man and the Environment in Greece* (H. Coccossis, ed.). Ministry for the Environment, Spatial Planning and Public Works – Kapon Editions, Athens.

EKPAA (2001) *Greece: The State of the Environment.* EKPAA (National Centre for the Environment), Athens.
Emmanuel, D. (1975) Anticapitalism and autonomy in the post-war illegal house building. *Bulletin of the Architects Association* **1**, 10–14 [in Greek].
Emmanuel, D. (2002) Social segregation, polarization and inequality in the geography of Athens: The role of housing market and development mechanisms (1980–2000). *Geographies* **3**, 46–70 [in Greek].
Emmanuel, D., Velidis, S., & Strousopoulou, E. (1996) *The Housing of Low Revenue Households in Greece.* DEPOS, Athens [in Greek].
Engels, F. (1872 [1974]) *Zur wohnungsfrage.* Leipzig. Translated into Spanish (1974) *El problema de la vivienda.* Gustavo Gili, Barcelona.
Esping-Andersen, G. (1990) *The Three Worlds of Welfare Capitalism.* Polity Press, Cambridge.
Esping-Andersen, G. (ed.) (1996) *Welfare States in Transition: National Adaptations in Global Economies.* Sage, London.
Esping-Andersen, G. (1999) *Social Foundations of Postindustrial Economies.* Oxford University Press, Oxford.
European Commission (1998) *Equal Opportunities for Women and Men in the European Union, Annual Report 1997.* Office for the Official Publications of the European Communities, Luxembourg.
Eurostat (1996) *Social Portrait of Europe.* Office for the Official Publications of the European Communities, Luxembourg.
Eurostat (1997a) *Statistiques en bref.* Office for the Official Publications of the European Communities, Luxembourg.
Eurostat (1997b) *Living Conditions in Europe. Selected Social Indicators.* Office for the Official Publications of the European Communities, Luxembourg.
Eurostat (1997c) *Eurostat Yearbook '97.* Office for the Official Publications of the European Communities, Luxembourg.
Eurostat (2002) *Housing Statistics in the European Union 2002.* http://mrw.wallonie.be/dgatlp/HousingStats, downloaded 5 May 03.
Eurostat (2003) *Growth Rate of GDP at Constant Prices.* http://europa.eu.int/comm/eurostat/Public/, downloaded 10 May 03.
Fargion, V. (1996) Social Assistance and the North-South Cleavage in Italy. *South European Society and Politics. Special issue on Southern European Welfare States* (M. Rhodes, ed.) **1** (3), winter, 135–54.
Fera, G. & Ginatempo, N. (1985) *L'autocostruzione spontanea nel Mezzogiorno.* Angeli, Milan.
Ferrera, M. (1996) The 'southern model' of welfare in social Europe. *Journal of European Social Policy* **6** (1), 17–37.
Ferrera, M. (1998) The four 'social Europes': between universalism and selectivity. In: *The Future of European Welfare: A New Social Contract* (M. Rhodes & Y. Mény, eds). Macmillan, London.
Forrest, R., Murie, A., & Williams, P. (1990) *Home Ownership: Differentiation and Fragmentation.* Unwin Hyman, London.
Freitas, M. (1998) Mobilising community resources in Portugal. In: *Social Exclusion in European Cities: Processes, Experiences and Responses* (A. Madanipour, G. Cars & J. Allen (eds). Jessica Kingsley, London.

Fribourg, A-M. (2002) *Le logement en Europe*. European Commission: Direction Generale de l'Urbanisme, de l'Habitat et de la Construction, Luxembourg.
Frisby, D. (2002) *Georg Simmel*. Routledge, London.
Gallent, N., Shucksmith, M., & Tewdwr-Jones, M. (eds) (2003) *Housing in the European Countryside: Rural Pressure and Policy in Western Europe*. Routledge, London.
Garrido, L. & Requena, M. (1996) *La Emancipación de los Jóvenes en España*. Ministerio de Trabajo. Dirección General de la Juventud, Madrid.
Ghékiere, L. (1992) *Les politiques du logement dans l'Europe du demain*. La Documentation Française, Paris.
Godard, F. & Bloss, T. (1988) La décohabitation des jeunes. In: *Transformation de la famille et habitat* (C. Bonvalet & P. Merlin, eds). PUF, Paris.
González, M., Jurado, T., & Naldini, M. (2000) Introduction: Interpreting the transformation of gender inequalities in Europe. In: *Gender Inequalities in Southern Europe: Women, Work and Welfare in the 1990s* (M. González, T. Jurado & M. Naldini, eds). Frank Cass, London.
Gortsos, K., Kamoutsi, P., Sayas, J., & Panayotatos, E. (2000) Second home and settlement space growth: the Greek experience. *Rivista Geografica Italiana* **CVII** (3/4), 17–56.
Grafmeyer, Y. (1993) *Héritage et production du statut residential: elements pour l'analyse de milieux locaux*. L'Harmattan, Paris.
Guerra, I. (1998) *The Dynamics of Housing Occupancy in Portugal*. Unpublished paper presented at the International Housing Conference, Housing in Southern Europe, a separate path? 2–4 December, Madrid.
Guerrero, J. & Naldini, M. (1996) Is the south so different? Italian and Spanish families in comparative perspective. In: *South European Society and Politics*. Special issue on *Southern European Welfare States* (M. Rhodes, ed.) **1** (3), winter, 43–66.
Guibentif, P. (1996) The transformation of the Portuguese social security system. In: *South European Society and Politics. Special issue on Southern European Welfare States* (M. Rhodes, ed.) **1** (3), winter, 217–39.
Guillen, A. & Alvarez, S. (2001) Globalization and the southern welfare states. In: *Globalization and European Welfare States* (R. Sykes, B. Palier & P. Prior). Palgrave, Basingstoke.
Gunther, R., Puhle, H-J., & Diamandouros, P. (1995) Introduction. In: *The Politics of Democratic Consolidation: Southern Europe in Comparative Perspective* (R. Gunther, P.N. Diamandouros & H. Puhle, eds). The Johns Hopkins University Press, London.
Haffner, M. (1998) *Housing Statistics in the European Union 1998*. European Commission, Brussels.
Halbwachs, M. (1970) *Morphologie sociale*. Armand Colin, Paris.
Harloe, M. (1995) *The People's Home? Social Rented Housing in Europe and America*. Blackwell, Oxford.
Harloe, M. (2001) Social justice and the city: The new 'liberal formulation'. *International Journal of Urban and regional Research* **25** (4), 889–97.
Hespanha, P., Ferreira, C., & Portugal, S. (1997) The welfare society and the welfare state. In: *European Citizenship and Social Exclusion* (M. Roche & R. van Berkel, eds). Ashgate, Aldershot.

Iacovou, M. (2000) Regional differences in the transition to adulthood. *Annals of the American Association of Political and Social Science*, no. 580, 40–69.
Indovina, F. (ed.) (1981) *Lo spreco edilizio*. Marsilio, Venice.
INE (National Statistics Institute of Spain) (1987, 1991, 1993, 1995) *Encuesta de Población Activa* (Spanish Labor Survey). INE, Madrid.
INE (National Statistics Institute of Spain) (1970, 1987, 1991, 2001) *Censo de Población y Vivienda* (Census of Population and Housing). INE, Madrid.
Jaffe, A. (1989) Concepts of property, theories of housing, and the choice of housing policy. *Netherlands Journal of Housing and Environmental Research* **4** (4), 311–20.
Katrougalos, G. (1996) The south European welfare model: the Greek welfare state, in search of an identity. *Journal of European Social Policy* **6** (1), 39–60.
Kemeny, J. (1981) *The Myth of Home Ownership*. Routledge and Kegan Paul, London.
Kemeny, J. (1995) *From Public Housing to the Social Market: Rental Policy Strategies in Comparative Perspective*. Routledge, London.
Kemeny, J. & Lowe, S. (1998) Schools of comparative housing research: From convergence to divergence. *Housing Studies* **13** (2), 161–78.
King, P. (1996) *The Limits of Housing Policy*. Middlesex University Press, London.
Kleinman, M. (1996) *Housing, Welfare and the State in Europe. A Comparative Analysis of Britain, France and Germany*. Edward Elgar, Cheltenham.
Kleinman, M., Matznetter, W. & Stephens, M. (1998) *European Integration and Housing Policy*. Routledge, London.
Knox, P. & Pinch, S. (2000) *Urban Social Geography. An Introduction*, 4th edn. Prentice Hall, Harlow.
Kolberg, J. & Uusitalo, H. (1992) The interface between the economy and the welfare state: A sociological account. In: *Social Policy in a Changing Europe* (Z. Ferge & J. Kolberg, eds). Westview Press, Boulder CO.
Laino, G. & Padovani, L. (2000) Le partenariat pour rénover l'action publique? L'expérience Italienne. *Pole Sud* **12** (May), 27–46.
Leal, J. (1987) El boom inmobiliario madrileño: Precios altos para rentas bajas. *Alfoz* **46**, 23–84.
Leal, J. (1992) *Informe Para una Nueva Política de Vivienda*. Ministerio de Obras Públicas y Transportes, Madrid.
Leal, J. (1995) La cuestión de la vivienda o la vivienda como problema social. In: *Pensar la Vivienda* (L. Cortés & J. Leal, eds). Talasa, Madrid, 17–30.
Leal, J. (1997) Emancipación y vivienda. In: *La Emancipación de los Jóvenes* (R. Vergés Escuín, ed.). Editorial Centro de Cultura Contemporánea de Barcelona, Barcelona.
Leal, J. (1999a) Construcción y vivienda en Madrid. In: *Estructura Económica de Madrid* (J.L. García Delgado, ed.). Ed. Civitas, Madrid.
Leal, J. (1999b) Crecimiento económico, empleo y desigualdad social en Madrid. *Papeles de Economía* **18**, 116–28.
Leal, J. (2002) Retraso de la emancipación juvenil y dificultad de acceso de los jóvenes a la vivienda. In: *La Sociedad: Teoría e Investigación Empírica. Homenaje a José Jiménez Blanco*. CIS, Madrid.
Leal, J. (2003) El sector de la construcción y la vivienda en Madrid. In: *Estructura Económica de Madrid* (J.L. Garcia Delgado). Ed. Civitas, Madrid.

Leontidou, L. (1990) *The Mediterranean City in Transition.* Cambridge University Press, Cambridge.

Leontidou, L. (1996) Alternatives to modernism in (southern) urban theory: Exploring in-between spaces. *International Journal of Urban and Regional Research* **20** (2), 178–95.

Lewis, J. (ed.) (1997) *Lone Mothers in European Welfare Regimes: Shifting Policy Logics.* Jessica Kingsley, London.

Liebfried, S. (1992) Towards a European welfare state? On integrating poverty regimes into the European Community. In: *Social Policy in a Changing Europe* (Z. Ferge & J. Kolberg, eds). Westview Press, Boulder CO.

Linz, J. & Stepan, A. (1996) *Problems of Democratic Transition and Consolidation: Southern Europe, South America, and Post-Communist Europe.* The Johns Hopkins University Press, London.

Lles, C. & Tobio, C. (1990) Pobreza y desigualdad en la Communidad de Madrid. *Alfoz* **4**, 89–105.

Lyrintzis, C. (1987) The power of populism: The Greek case. *European Journal of Political Research* **15** (6), 667–86.

Malefakis, E. (1995) The political and socioeconomic contours of southern European history. In: *The Politics of Democratic Consolidation: Southern Europe in Comparative Perspective* (R. Gunther, P.N. Diamandouros & H. Puhle, eds). The Johns Hopkins University Press, London.

Maloutas, T. (1990) *Housing and Family in Athens: An Analysis of Post-war Housing Practices.* Exantas, Athens [in Greek].

Maloutas, T. (1995) Ségrégation urbaine et relation familiales dans deux villes grecques: Athènes et Volos. *Sociétés Contemporaines* **22/23**, 89–106.

Maloutas, T. (2000) Housing tenure. In: *Social and Economic Atlas of Greece. Vol. 1: The Cities* (T. Maloutas, ed.). University of Thessaly Press, Athens and Volos: National Centre for Social Research (EKKE), 66-7 [in Greek].

Maloutas, T. (2003a) Les habitations vacantes. In: *Atlas de la Grèce* (M. Sivignon, O. Deslondes & T. Maloutas, eds). CNRS-Libergéo, La Documentation Française, Paris, 70–71.

Maloutas, T. (2003b) Promoting social sustainability: The case of Athens. *CITY* **7** (2), 167–81.

Maloutas, T. (2003c) La vivienda autopromovida: soluciones de postguerra en Atenas. *Ciudad y Territorio* **xxxv** (136–7), 335–45.

Maloutas, T. (2004) Segregation and residential mobility: spatially entrapped social mobility and its impact on segregation in Athens. *European Urban and Regional Studies* **11** (2), 171–86.

Maloutas, T. & Deffner, A. (2002) Urbanisation et patrimoine culturel: Athènes face aux jeux olympiques de 2004. *GEOCARREFOUR Revue Géographique de Lyon* **77** (4), 353–8.

Maloutas, T. & Economou, D. (eds) (1992) *Social Structure and Urban Organization: The Geography of Collective Consumption in Athens.* Paratiritis, Salonica [in Greek].

Maloutas, T. & Karadimitriou, N. (2001) Vertical social differentiation in Athens: Alternative or complement to community segregation? *International Journal of Urban and Regional Research* **25** (4), 698–716.

Maloutas, T. & Pantelidou-Malouta, M. (Forthcoming) The glass menagerie of urban governance and social cohesion. *International Journal of Urban and Regional Research.*

Maloutas, T., Emmanuel, D., & Pantelidou-Malouta, M. (2002) *Social parameters for promoting sustainable development in Athens-Attika.* Final research report, Laboratory of Spatial Analysis and Thematic Mapping, University of Thessaly, Volos [in Greek].

Maratou-Alipranti, L., & Fakiolas, R. (2000) Foreign female immigrants in Greece. Papers. *Revista de Sociologia,* Universitat Autonoma de Barcelona **60**, 101–17.

Martin, C. (1996) Social welfare and the family in southern Europe. *South European Society and Politics. Special issue on Southern European Welfare States* (M. Rhodes, ed.) **1** (3), winter, 23–41.

Mény, Y. & Rhodes, M. (1997) Illicit governance: Corruption, scandal and fraud. In: *Developments in West European Politics* (M. Rhodes, P. Heywood & V. Wright, eds). Macmillan, London.

Mingione, E. (1993) New forms of urban poverty and the crisis in the citizenship/ welfare system: The Italian experience. *Antipode* **25** (3), 206–22.

Mingione, E. & Morlicchio, E. (1993) New forms of urban poverty in Italy: Risk path models in the north and south. *International Journal of Urban and Regional Research* **17** (3), 413–28.

Módenes Cabrerizo, J. (1998) *Flujos espaciales e intinerairos biográficos: la movilidad residencial en el area de Barcelona.* Doctoral Thesis, Universidad Autónoma de Barcelona, Departamento de Geografía, Barcelona.

Moreno, L. (2000) *Ciudadanos precarios.* Ariel, Barcelona.

Morvonnais, P. (1998) Comparaisons internationals. In: *Logement et habitat, l'état des savoirs* (M. Segaud, C. Bonvalet & J. Brun, eds). Editions La Decouverte, Paris.

Mouzelis, N. (1987) Continuities and discontinuities in Greek politics: From Elefterios Venizelos to Andreas Papandreou. In: *Political Change in Greece: Before and After the Colonels* (K. Featherstone & D. Katsoudas, eds). Croom Helm, London.

Neves, V. (1998) *Owner Occupied Housing Finance in Portugal.* Unpublished paper presented at the International Housing Conference, Housing in Southern Europe, A Separate Path? 2–4 December, Madrid.

Nicolacopoulos, I. (2001) *The Weak Democracy. Parties and Elections 1946–1967.* Patakis, Athens [in Greek].

NSSG [National Statistical Service of Greece] (1975) *Statistical Yearbook of Greece 1974.* NSSG, Athens.

NSSG [National Statistical Service of Greece] (2000) *Labour Force Statistics.* NSSG, Athens.

NSSG [National Statistical Service of Greece] (2001) *Statistical Yearbook of Greece.* NSSG, Athens.

NTUA–NCSR (1996 and 1998) *Second Homes and Settlement Development: The Greek Experience.* Research Reports. National Technical University of Athens – National Centre for Social Research, Athens [in Greek].

Oxley, M. (1991) The aims and methods of comparative housing research. *Scandinavian Housing and Planning Research* **8**, 67–77.

Oxley, M. (1999) *Meaning, science and confusion in comparative housing research.* Paper presented to the workshop on 'Approaching the Cross-national Comparison of Urban, Housing and Planning Phenomena', 16–17 December, Amsterdam.

Oxley, M. & Smith, J. (1996) *Housing Policy and Rented Housing in Europe.* E and FN Spon, London.

Padovani, L. (1984) Housing in Italy. In: *Housing in Europe* (M. Wynn, ed.). Croom Helm, London.

Padovani, L. (1988) Housing provision in Italy: the family as emerging promoter. Difficult relationships with public policies. Quaderni del Dipartimento di Ingegneria, Università degli Studi di Trento, Trento.

Padovani, L. (1991) Qualità dell'abitare nella città di fine secolo. In: *La costruzione della città Europea negli anni '80,* Vol. 1 (L. Bellicini, ed.). Saggi, Credito Fondiario, Rome, pp. 203–22.

Padovani, L. (ed.) (1995) *Urban Change and Housing Policies: Evidence from Four European Countries.* Collana Daest, Venice.

Padovani, L. (1998a) Public intervention in housing in Italy. Unpublished paper presented at the International Housing Conference, Housing in Southern Europe, A Separate Path? 2–4 December, Madrid.

Padovani, L. (1998b) Public and private partnerships in urban regeneration programs. In: *Housing in Transition* (B. Cernic, K. Dimitrovska, & B. Turner, eds). Conference Proceedings, Urban Planning Institute, Ljubljana.

Padovani, L. & Vettoretto, L. (2003) Italy. In: *Housing and the European Countryside* (N. Gallent, M. Shucksmith & M. Tewdwr-Jones, eds). Routledge, London.

Pahl, R. (1988) Some remarks on informal work, social polarisation and the social structure. *International Journal of Urban and Regional Research* **12** (2), 247–67.

Pantelidou-Malouta, M. (1988) Women and the welfare state. In: *Problems of Welfare State Development in Greece* (T. Maloutas & D. Economou, eds). Exandas, Athens, 183–220 [in Greek].

Pantelidou-Malouta, M. (2000) Women's employment. In: *Social and Economic Atlas of Greece. Vol. 1: The Cities* (T. Maloutas, ed.). University of Thessaly Press, Athens and Voles: National Centre for Social Research (EKKE), 62–3 [in Greek].

Park, R. (1925 [1957]) Community organisation and juvenile delinquency. In: *The City: Chicago* (R. Park, E.W. Burgess, & R.D. McKenzie). University of Chicago Press, Chicago. Reprinted in R. Park (1957) *Human Communities.* The Free Press, Glencoe, IL.

Park, R. (1929 [1957]) The city as a social laboratory. In: *Chicago: An Experiment in Social Science Research* (T.V. Smith & L. White). University of Chicago Press, Chicago. Reprinted in R. Park (1957) *Human Communities.* The Free Press, Glencoe, IL.

Pedro Bueno, A. & Sanchís Cuesta, J. (eds) (2000) *Problemas de acceso al mercado de la vivienda en la Unión Europea.* Ed. Tirant lo Blanch, Valencia.

Pereirinha, J. (1996) Welfare states and anti-poverty regimes: The case of Portugal. In: *South European Society and Politics. Special issue on Southern European Welfare States* (M. Rhodes, ed.) **1** (3), 199–218.

Pérez-Diaz, V. (1998) The public sphere and a European civil society. In: *Real Civil Societies: Dilemmas of Institutionalization* (J. Alexander, ed.). Sage, London.

Petmesidou, M. (1991) Statism, social policy and the middle classes in Greece. *Journal of European Social Policy* **1** (1), 31–48.

Petmesidou, M. & Tsoulovis, L. (1994) Aspects of the changing political economy of Europe: Welfare state, class segmentation and planning in the postmodern era. *Sociology* **28** (2), May, 499–519.

Pfau-Effinger, B. (1998) Gender cultures and gender arrangement – A theoretical framework for cross-national gender research. *Innovation* **11**, 147–66.

Power, A. (1993) *Hovels to High Rise: State Housing in Europe since 1850*. Routledge, London.

Prevelakis, G. (2000) *Athènes: urbanisation, culture et politique*. L'Harmattan, Paris.

Priemus, H. (2000) Hacia una politica de vivienda en Europa. In: *Problemas de Accesso al Mercado de la Vivienda en la Union Europea* (A. Pedro Bueno & J.A. Sanchís Cuesta, eds). Ed Tirant lo Blanch, Valencia.

Pugliese, E. (2000) Immigration policies and the new refugees in Europe. International Conference: *Towards a Radical Cultural Agenda for European Cities and Regions* (Paros, September 1999). Kyriakidis, Athens and Thessaloniki.

Rafols, J. (1997) *Politica d'habitage en l'Estat de les autonomies*. Institut d'Estudis Autonòmics, Generalitat de Catalunya, Barcelona.

Reher, D. (1996) *La Familia en España, Pasado y Presente*. Alianza Editorial, Madrid.

Reis, E. (1998) Banfield's amoral familism revisited: Implications of high inequality structures for civil society. In: *Real Civil Societies: Dilemmas of Institutionalisation* (J. Alexander, ed.). Sage, London.

Rex, J. & Moore, R. (1967) *Race, Community and Conflict*. Oxford University Press, Oxford.

Rhodes, M. (1996) Southern European welfare states: Identity, problems and prospects for reform. In: *South European Society and Politics. Special issue on Southern European Welfare States* (M. Rhodes, ed.) **1** (3), 1–22.

Rodriguez, J. (1990) La política de vivienda en España: una aproximación a los principales instrumentos. *Revista Española de Financiación a la Vivienda*, 12, 11–24.

Roniger, L. (1998) Civil society, patronage, and democracy. In: *Real Civil Societies: Dilemmas of Institutionalization* (J. Alexander, ed.). Sage, London.

Rose, G. (1996) Locality, politics and culture: Poplar in the 1920s. In: *Social Geography: A Reader* (C. Hamnett, ed.). Edward Arnold, London.

Rugg, J. (1999) *Young People, Housing and Social Policy*. Routledge, London.

Ruspini, E. (2000) Social rights of women with children: Lone mothers and poverty in Italy, Germany and Great Britain. In: *Gender Inequalities in Southern Europe: Women, Work and Welfare in the 1990s* (M. González, T. Jurado & M. Naldini, eds). Frank Cass, London.

Santillana del Barrio, A. (1972) *Análisis Económico del Problema de la Vivienda*. Ediciones Ariel, Barcelona.

Saunders, P. (1984) Beyond housing classes: The sociological significance of private property rights in the means of consumption. *International Journal of Urban and Regional Research* **8** (2), 202–22.

Secchi, B. (1970) Va tutto bene quando l'edilizia va bene? *Archivio di Studi Urbani e Regionali* **2** (7–8), 112–29.

Stephens, M. (2000) Convergence in European mortgage systems before and after EMU. *Journal of Housing and the Built Environment* **15** (1), 29–52.

Sykes, R. & Alcock, P. (eds) (1998) *Developments in European Social Policy: Convergence and diversity*. The Policy Press, Bristol.

Sykes, R., Palier, B., & Prior, P. (eds) (2001) *Globalization and European Welfare States*. Palgrave, Basingstoke.

Symeonidou, H. (1996) Social protection in contemporary Greece. In: *South European Society and Politics. Special issue on Southern European Welfare States* (M. Rhodes, ed.) **1** (3), winter, 67–86.

Symeonidou, H. (2002) *Fertility and family surveys in countries of the ECE region. Standard Country Report, Greece*. United Nations, New York and Geneva.

Taltavull, P. (2000) La situación de la vivienda en España. In: *Vivienda y Familia* (P. Taltavull, ed.). Argentaria, Visor, Madrid.

Therborn, G. (1993) Beyond the lonely nation state. In: *Families of Nations: Patterns of Public Policy in Western Democracies* (F.G. Castles, ed.). Dartmouth, Aldershot.

Tosi, A. (1984) Bisogni e pratiche abitative, alcuni problemi di ricerca. *Sociologia urbana e rurale* **14–15**, 97–115.

Tosi, A. (1994a) *Abitanti: le nuove strategie dell'azione abitativa*. Il Mulino, Bologna.

Tosi, A. (ed.) (1994b) *La casa: il rischio e l'esclusione: rapporto IRS sul disagio abitativo in Italia*, for Caritas italiana. Angeli, Milan.

Tosi, A. (1995) Shifting paradigms: the sociology of housing, the sociology of the family, and the crisis of modernity. In: *Housing and Family Wealth in a Comparative Perspective* (R. Forrest & A. Murie, eds). London, Routledge.

Trilla, C. (2001) *La Politica de Vivienda en una Perspectiva Europea Comparada*. Fundación la Caixa, Barcelona.

Tsoukalas, K. (1987) *State, Society, Work in Post-war Greece*. Themelio, Athens [in Greek].

United Nations (2002) *World Urbanization Prospects: The 2001 Revision*. United Nations Department of Economic and Social Affairs, Population Division, New York.

Urbanistica (1994) n. 102, special issue 'La casa. I nuovi termini della questione' edited by A. Tosi. See articles by M. Coppo, 'Mercato, politiche ed evoluzione del sistema abitativo', 10–15; G. Roma, 'Domanda marginale di abitazione e politiche urbane', 16–17; L. Seassaro, 'Continuità e discontinuità nelle politiche della casa – Un'interpretazione', 17–22; M. Cremaschi, 'La denazionalizzazione del problema abitativo', 23–8; A. Tosi, 'Un problema di povertà', 29–37.

van Vliet, W. (2000) Vivienda accesible y desarollo urbano: busqueda de modelos. In: *Problemas de Acceso al Mercado de la Vivienda en la Union Europea* (A. Pedro Bueno & J.A. Sanchís Cuesta). Ed Tirant lo Blanch, Valencia.

Varvaresos, K. (2002) *Report on the Economic Problem of Greece*. Savalas, Athens [in Greek].

Venieris, D. (1996) Dimensions of social policy in Greece. In: *South European Society and Politics. Special issue on Southern European Welfare States* (M. Rhodes, ed.) **1** (3), winter, 261–9.

Vergés Escuin, R. (ed.) (1997) *La emancipación de los jóvenes*. Editorial Centro de Cultura Contemporánea de Barcelona, Barcelona.

Vrychrea, A. & Golemis, C. (1998) Spatial segregation and social exclusion in a peripheral Greek neighbourhood. In: *Social Exclusion in European Cities: Processes, Experiences and Responses* (A. Madanipour, G. Cars & J. Allen, eds). The Stationery Office, London.

Wirth, L. (1938 [1964]) Urbanism as a way of life. *American Journal of Sociology* **XLIV** (1–24). Reprinted in A.J. Reiss Jr (ed.) (1964) *Louis Wirth on Cities and Social Life*. The University of Chicago Press, Chicago.

Index